AF593870

THE PROSECUTOR

By the same author

THE MAD MOTORISTS

THE SPLENDID PAUPER

THE PROSECUTOR

The Life of M. P. Pugh
Prosecuting Solicitor and Agent
for the Director of Public Prosecutions

by

ALLEN ANDREWS

With a Foreword by
SIR NORMAN J. SKELHORN, K.B.E., Q.C.
Director of Public Prosecutions

GEORGE G. HARRAP & CO. LTD
London · Toronto · Wellington · Sydney

TO THE LADY
who always opts for
Nolle prosequi

First published in Great Britain 1968
by GEORGE G. HARRAP & CO. LTD
182 High Holborn, London, W.C.1

SBN 245 59259 8

Composed in Linotype Caledonia type and printed at the St Ann's Press, Park Road, Altrincham. Made in Great Britain

FOREWORD

By SIR NORMAN J. SKELHORN, K.B.E., Q.C.
Director of Public Prosecutions

I am pleased to have this opportunity of paying a tribute to Mervyn Pugh, who once served in the department of which I am now head. He joined in 1921 and left just over three years later on his appointment as Prosecuting Solicitor, Birmingham. However, during his long tenure of that post he was in constant touch with the department, acting as the Director's agent in most of the major prosecutions which arose in that city and retaining personal relationships with many of the staff here. On his visits to London he was always a welcome visitor to the office, and he never failed to show great kindness to members of the department who found themselves in Birmingham.

He was held in high esteem by all his old colleagues in the Director of Public Prosecutions Department, where his name continues to be revered for the high standards which he consistently set both for himself and others.

CONTENTS

		page
1.	*"I will not be browbeaten"*	11
2.	*Into Battle*	31
3.	*He danced with the Maid*	55
4.	*Craftsmanship*	63
5.	*The Smile on the Face of the Jury*	76
6.	*The Carnal Cases*	101
7.	*The War Crimes*	148
8.	*"The Great Mr. Pugh"*	158
9.	*The Lion draws Blood*	178
	Epilogue	226
	Acknowledgments	227
	Index	229

ILLUSTRATIONS

	page
M. P. Pugh sketched in Court at the Height of his Career	48
"Unlike many former officers, he never obtruded his rank or his decorations"	49
"Fat supers, all sticking out as much before as behind"	49
Lord Ilkeston	64
"The shrewdest dandy in Birmingham"	64
The Victoria Law Courts, Birmingham	65
No. 1 Court, the Victoria Law Courts	65
"I shouldn't have noticed £100,000"	104
"The Prof"	104
Principal Solicitor-advocates of Birmingham at Pugh's Farewell Party	104
M. P. Pugh's Lecture Notes on Evidence given by Doctors	104, 105
M. P. Pugh, back in Private Practice	105

CHAPTER

1

"I will not be browbeaten"

IN Birmingham in the summer of 1927 every man wore a waistcoat and almost everyone a hat or a wide-peaked flat cap with a press-stud buttoning the front, even in the July heat-wave that baked the city. The tramcars hissed and moaned on rails that shone like slate in the sun. The hot, dry wind span shreds of desiccated horse-dung into the dust eddies. In the streets and public vehicles no-one talked or thought or read of international crises. Except for the widows, they had largely forgotten the World War, and did not dream of another. Men talked incessantly of sport, and women of Jack Payne's Band on the wireless, and the only foreigner who excited the interest of both sexes was young Lindbergh, who had just completed the first solo flight across the Atlantic and made the Air Pageant by three light biplanes in Himley Park so much more topical. Warwickshire were doing well in the County Cricket Championship.

On the morning of the 4th of July a man caught a tram at the Five Ways, and sat on the top as it bucked down Broad Street. He wore a hard bowler hat, which suited his status as an official who was going to work half an hour later than business-office staff. A pipe was firmly held between thin lips above an extremely strong and prominent jaw. And, if he was scowling, the expression could perhaps be attributed to the fact that Worcestershire, whom he passionately supported against the Brummagem barbarians, were not doing so well at the cricket; or to the depressing impact of Monday morning on a vigorous bachelor of thirty-three; or to the natural fall of his down-drooping mouth in repose. What did *not* cause it was the big splash of local news in his paper. For the account was of murder, and not a simple intra-family murder, either; it promised activity, which he welcomed. M. P. Pugh, D.S.O., M.C., Prosecuting Solicitor to the City of Birmingham and Agent for the Director of Public Prosecutions, was on the way to his office in the Victoria Law Courts.

He paused at his chemist's for his regular morning throat-spray, and passed into the court building, a figure of medium height and generous build, wearing the well-tailored black jacket and striped trousers over the cost of which he pugnaciously fought the Income Tax, year by year, in a claim for indispensable uniform. As he came upstairs the word had already gone round: "The Guv'nor's arrived", and half a dozen detectives and uniformed police, some waiting with their witnesses and some solitary, straightened themselves in the corridor. "I don't want to see *you*; I'll see you in court," he said, pointing in turn to three of them as he passed. He went into his office, and thirty seconds later a bell rang sharply in the outer office in the code for his clerk, A. E. Field, who put his head round the door into the corridor and told the first policeman, "Mr Pugh will see you now."

The Prosecuting Solicitor began to go over the evidence in one of the morning's cases with the police-officer involved. But he had hardly heard three answers from the officer when he said suspiciously, "Have you got a cold?" "Just a summer one, sir," said the policeman. "Then don't bloody talk to me here; stand over there," said Pugh, pointing to the other side of the room. He finished the interview, dismissed the officer, and, crossing to a medicine cabinet on the mantelpiece, selected a bottle of throat lozenges before again ringing the bell on his desk.

At twenty past ten Pugh's junior clerk made the first of his journeys downstairs to Number One Court to carry the tools and impedimenta which the prosecutor would need: *Stone's Justices' Manual, Archbold,* relative volumes of the *Justice Of The Peace* or the King's Bench Law Reports, two foolscap notebooks, a bundle of coloured pencils, and the great office diary, about which the work of the department revolved.

At about the same time the two other figures who formed with Pugh the vertices of the main triangle of forces in Number One Court were also approaching the arena. Balthazar Stephen,

Lord Ilkeston, aged sixty but with twenty-three years more to serve, was the Stipendiary Magistrate—a title he abominated, since he considered it the height of bad taste to emphasize that he was paid for his services. He had already left Snow Hill Station, where he had arrived from his home in the old High Street of Warwick, and saluted the Great Western Railway. From an early stage in his career—he had been Stipendiary since 1910—he had had his season ticket sewn inside his bowler hat. When he came to the barrier he raised his hat. In this fashion he could, with one motion, pay a courtesy to the staff, display his ticket, and save himself the ripple of discomposure occasioned by taking off his glove to fumble in his pocket. From Snow Hill he made his stately way the very short distance down Steelhouse Lane to the block enclosed by that street, Corporation Street, and Newton Street, which contained the Magistrates' Courts, the Assize Courts, all the ancillary offices and apparatus from the Fines Receipt Book to the Lock-up, and in addition the offices of the Chief Constable and his staff and the Prosecuting Solicitor and his; the Criminal Investigation Department, the Coroner's Office, and even the Mortuary were all conveniently adjacent.

No sooner had the Stipendiary passed a solicitor's office at the top end of Steelhouse Lane than an extraordinary procession emerged from this door. It was headed by the shrewdest dandy in Birmingham, and tailed off into a selection of some of the city's most unfortunate women and most habitual criminals, who with few exceptions had had to pay in advance for the privilege of joining the parade. Herbert Willison, known as the most melodramatic criminal-defence advocate in the summary courts, was leading his clients into the fray. He was in his early sixties, but as vigorous as his contemporary Lord Ilkeston was composed, strident where the magistrate was quiet, and in appearance altogether flamboyant. He was tall, thin, angular, and ugly. On his jug-handle ears rested an immaculate grey top-hat. He wore a grey tailed morning coat with a high collar and stock, and he carried a cane and lavender gloves. In his buttonhole was an elaborately mounted orchid. The buttonhole was constant, though it changed through the seasons from orchid to hothouse roses and so on; the morning coat also depended on the season: it was grey from the 1st of May through the summer, and went back to black on the 1st of October.

Herbert Willison, attended by his clerk, Mr Daniels, led his flock down Steelhouse Lane, into Newton Street, and straight into the Law Courts by way of the short cut through the Chief Constable's entrance, spurning the long way round by the main door. Under the silent but not inexpressive gaze of the policeman guarding the porch, his clients followed him through the corridors to the mosaic-floored assembly hall for the courts. There they would meet the friends who had come to support them or, not seeing them, would go straight to join them on the public benches of Number One Court, where the spectators sat, not in a strict gallery, but on a stepped daïs at the back.

By now Pugh's procession would have formed and be entering the court. The junior clerk would have arranged the last pencils, notebooks, and rubbers in the prosecutor's sacrosanct place, facing the witness-box across the head of Willison, now arranging his papers opposite: when the defence advocate addressed the witness he had to turn round—always a disadvantage to Willison because he was volatile, moved his feet constantly, and threw his arms around. Next in the prosecutor's retinue came his secretary, Miss Selwyn, who sat at the desk behind Pugh's. Next, for all important cases where a point of law might be argued, came the clerk, Mr Field. And finally, with exquisite timing, on the tick of the clock as the punctual Lord Ilkeston came in from his private room at the side of the Bench and everyone rose in court, the Prosecuting Solicitor entered from the far door and the two men bowed together.

The first case was called, the defendant put in the dock, the charge read, and the plea made. Pugh rattled off his prepared opening statement summarizing the prosecution at a speed which would have baffled the Press had Pugh not found a moment beforehand to indicate to them which were the headline cases and give them an outline of the allegations. Soon Willison and Pugh were entangled in noisy in-fighting as they clashed, protested, and interrupted over examination and cross-examination. Larceny, loitering, common assault, and indecent exposure were all fought by Willison in the same boisterous fashion. He gave his clients a show for their money and formidably shook any indecisive witness, not excluding inexperienced policemen. In what seemed perpetual anger, Willison asseverated his points in a ripe Birmingham accent which was at first quite incongruous with his dandified dress. Pugh, much more rarely passionate, continued his prosecution in a clipped, level, but rather strident voice with intonations, particularly in the vowel sounds, of a Berkshire accent—he had been born in Reading when Berkshire was a province rather than a London suburb. When Willison interrupted, Pugh would habitually not yield, but merely increase the pressure of his voice and go on with his delivery, crisply ordering "Sit down!" between the sentences. In cross-examination he tended to press his points with a controlled remorselessness that sometimes allowed the defendant no opportunity to affirm or deny what was being alleged. "Let him answer, Mr Pugh," roared Willison. "Sit down," reprimanded Pugh, and continued on his course. "Let him answer, Mr Pugh," repeated Willison, waving his arms, and finally thumping the desk. "You're not cross-examining, you're making a speech." Apparently unaware of the commotion, Lord Ilkeston gazed abstractedly down until he ventured a mild protest, in the cultivated accent of the Bar: "Really, Mr Willison, you should be addressing these remarks to me." The atmosphere seemed chaotic, but somehow the process worked, for Ilkeston was a good magistrate with a remarkable record of unreversed decisions. Pugh, still fairly new to Birmingham, had come to the city as a strong man in a turbulent court to be a pillar of support for the police, but only as an officer of the court, not as a partisan, and always concerned solely with the furtherance of justice as he saw it. "I am not going to be browbeaten by professional showmanship," he told Willison, and it was now an admitted fact that, in the three years he had been in Birmingham, defence advocates were finding it much harder to secure an acquittal.

But because he was an officer of the court Pugh declined to transmute his relationship with Willison or any other defence advocate to the level of a feud. If in his opinion the interests of justice could be served by mercy he would direct his powerful weight to convincing the magistrate that this was the right course. He said to Willison before the hearing of a receiving charge in which Willison was defending, "I've been looking into it. There's a case for this lad. He knows now that the goods were stolen, and he knew soon after he got them, but he may not have known at the time. I'll do what I can"—and when Pugh spoke in mitigation he was influential. At the same time, because Willison was a brother-advocate, Pugh could appreciate his skill and occasionally pay him a goading tribute in court. On a charge of indecent exposure where it was alleged that the defendant had been stationed at the sunken window of a semi-basement waiting for women to pass by, Willison's virtuous defence was that his client was only adjusting his fly-buttons and had in any case by no means gone to the length of exposing himself. "I am going to show you," he told the girl complainant in the witness-box, "exactly what he was doing. I am going to unbutton my own trousers, and I want you to tell me to stop as soon as I get to the point which you say the defendant had reached." The girl, already highly embarrassed, gazed at the advocate with horrified fascination. He undid the top button. "Now?" he asked. "No," said the girl. He undid the second. "Now?" The girl shook her head with choking tension. He undid the third. "Now?" he asked again. "Yes!" gasped the girl, and, of course, she had stopped him well within the limits of decency. "Herbert," said M. P. Pugh across the court with admiring menace, "I shall be prosecuting you next for indecent exposure."

Rarely—for he worked extremely well with Lord Ilkeston—Pugh's sense of scalping humour propelled him towards making a butt of the Stipendiary, particularly when a decision had gone against him. A long prosecution over obscene photographs had resolved itself into a bitter battle between Willison and Pugh on whether a particular set of nude pictures showed the pubic hairs—in which case they would be classed as pornographic. Finally all the photographs were passed up to Lord Ilkeston. The Stipendiary, who wore large round spectacles, reinforced them with a six-inch magnifying-glass. The atmosphere was tense as he studied the exhibits. Finally he pronounced that what Pugh had claimed was pubic hair was in reality shadow. Pugh hated losing, and in his pique made an aside about the magistrate's age. "He didn't remember what to look for, really," he muttered to a newspaper man on his left.

On the morning of Monday the 4th of July, 1927, M. P. Pugh finished the morning court session with his usual organizational perfectionism. He had a somewhat despotic relationship with his staff, who all sat behind him. Pugh started with his files of individual cases, and when one was finished passed it over his shoulder without turning his head, and an aide took it. When he wanted a particular note made of a defending witness's statement he would snap "Get this," again without turning his head, and if he held up his hand he would expect a pencil of the right colour to be placed into it. Now he passed the last file over his shoulder and walked out of the court clean-handed. The Stipendiary walked, as he did every working day of his life, to Snow Hill Station and the reserved table in the restaurant on platform 7, where he ate his lunch—constant over forty years—without ever removing his bowler hat. His ticket was still inside it. Willison went to his club. Pugh, in the corridor upstairs, ran into the burly figure of his great friend Chief Detective Superintendent James Burnett, head of the C.I.D., and had a pint with him.

Burnett was the first focus of Pugh's intense affection for the Birmingham City Police. "Listen, boy," he told his brother Maurice at this time—Maurice was a solicitor in private practice—"I've got one job in life. That is to protect the police. They can't get up and answer back." This was one of the mainsprings of his zeal in the lower courts, where allegations against the police handling of investigations and arrests were and are in common currency. Organizationally he was doing his best to improve police morale by advancing their efficiency in giving evidence—which obtained more successful prosecutions. He supported them strongly in court. "He's a fighter" was his reputation in the ranks, though it was equally well known that any policeman who attended a conference before a case might find himself being individually leathered harder than any prospective witness. In addition, by shrewd advice, Pugh was coaching the detective force. He was open to consultation, so that a detective could bring him an incomplete file and establish how much more evidence he needed to secure for a safe conviction. But, in his earlier days, Pugh was not ultra-cautious. "Have a go," he would say. "Pull him in. Something is bound to follow. You'll never be any good as a detective if you don't sometimes take a chance." This relationship could never have been established but for the personal friendship between Pugh and Burnett.

"Well, Jimmy," said Pugh that lunch-time, "you've given the newspapers a hell of a lot of detail about this murder. You've cut any space I shall get for my opening statement."

"No, M. P.," said Burnett, "not all the details by any means. But I must get corroborative information quickly about what went on by that canal bank on Saturday night. There were courting couples, and I must get them to come forward now."

He recounted the case as it stood at the moment, part of which Pugh had already seen in the morning paper:

At 3.40 on the Sunday morning two police constables were patrolling the old cut of the Birmingham Canal between Rosebery Street and Winson Green Road where they saw two young men coming towards them. They stopped them and asked what they were doing there at that time of morning. One of them tried to answer, but he stuttered so much that his companion took over the story from him. He said that they were looking for the other man's young lady, who had been taken away from him on the canal bank that night.

The stuttering man, Charles Broomhead, aged twenty-two, had taken his young lady, Olive Turner, aged eighteen, to the Winson Green Picture Palace on Saturday night. He said they came out at twenty to ten and went for a walk along the canal bank from Winson Green Road towards Clissold Street. This, though technically a private path, was a recognized retreat for courting couples. As they walked they were passed by a man. After a while the girl stopped to pull her stocking up. Broomhead waited for her, and they resumed their walk. When they were near the bridge crossing the canal arm and leading to Lodge Road the man who had previously passed them came up to them and stopped them, saying that he was a police officer. He said they were trespassing and asked for their names and addresses. He took a newspaper from his pocket, apparently to write down their particulars, but did not in fact write them down. "Can you prove that these are your real names and addresses?" he asked. They said they could not. "Then you will have to come along with me," he said, and they turned and walked back the way they had come towards Winson Green Road. "I shall have to take you to the police station," he said. "Well, take me," said Broomhead, and lit a cigarette. "You must not smoke while you are in custody," said the man, and Broomhead squeezed out the cigarette. As they came up to the wall of the City Mental Hospital Broomhead, who in spite of his stutter seemed, by his account, to have had considerable spirit, pointed out two more courting couples and said, "Why don't you move those? They're standing." "No," said the man, "I've got two and that's enough for me." At this point, Broomhead afterwards said, he became convinced that the man was not a police officer.

"Let *her* go home," the young man said of his girl. Olive

Turner said, "If you had a heart you would let me go home. I have no mother or father, and my grandmother is waiting for me." "No, I'll take you," said the man, but after walking a few paces he said to Broomhead, "You can square it, but it is up to yourself." Broomhead pulled some coppers from his pocket and offered the man fourpence for a drink. "That's no good to me," he said. The girl said, "I have some money in my bag, Charlie," but the young man made no move to take it. Instead he said with sudden urgency to the girl, "All right, Olive, you can go home *now*." Quickly the girl turned and ran off the way they had come—the third and last course she took along that towpath. The man swung round and ran after her, and Broomhead ran after him. But within a few yards the man turned once more, gripped Broomhead's waistcoat with his right hand, and struck him a heavy blow on the face with his left fist. Broomhead was temporarily knocked out, and lay in a daze for perhaps two minutes. When he recovered he ran in the direction the pursuit had taken, but though he reached the bridge he could not see or hear anything, and he ran back along the canal-side to the Winson Green Road. There he met a man and told him what had happened. The man said, "I have got to go to Smethwick." He pulled his watch out of his waistcoat and added, "It's half past eleven. Still, I'll come with you." Two other men came up, and the story was passed to them. All four of them agreed to look for the girl, and they ran up the canal, again as far as the bridge. Then Broomhead went to Olive Turner's home. She had not come back, but her sister sent James Rooke, the man who was courting her, back with Broomhead to search again. Previously they had ignored an arm of the canal leading off to the left under the bridge which had been the boundary of their search, and going towards Lodge Road. Now they went down this cut, and near the end, by Lodge Road, they found Olive Turner's hat, handbag, and fur. And this is what they showed to the police officers at four o'clock on Sunday morning.

Very soon the police had brought a boat and grappling irons to the spot and the canal was being dragged. Soon after six the girl's body was brought up at the spot where the clothing had been found. A wrist-watch had stopped at 11.40 on her wrist. Her left shoe was missing, and her right suspender broken. Before seven o'clock Detective Sergeant G. A. Edwards was interviewing Charles Broomhead on the canal-side while the early-morning sun glinted over the dirty roofs on to the limp body of his sweetheart, and rivulets oozed back to the canal.

A cut inside his mouth from the blow that dazed him was all the corroboration Broomhead could offer for his story, and the impediment in his speech made any understanding slow. But, having heard it vaguely once, Edwards asked the two young men to go to Kenyon Street Police Station for statements to be made in writing, and in the meantime scribbled down his comprehension of the description Broomhead had given of his attacker: dressed respectably like an ordinary working-man, in a dark grey suit and cap, the cap rather old. A dirty white collar, and an old tie which was dark and twisted. The man was aged thirty-eight to forty, and he had something round in his buttonhole. He was a tall man and spoke with some authority, which caused Broomhead to accept that he was a policeman.

Within half an hour of assimilating the description Detective Sergeant Edwards had called on his first suspect, an ex-policeman with a criminal record who had recently served two months' hard labour for assaulting a young man who had been courting on the canal near the same spot. This man gave an account of all his movements on the Saturday night which, after Edwards had confirmed it with his wife and neighbours, satisfied him that the man was not connected with the incident.

Edwards returned to Kenyon Street, where Chief Superintendent Burnett, with the Coroner's Officer, Chief Inspector Hawkins, and Superintendent Penrice, was interviewing Broomhead. The questioning was interrupted while the four officers accompanied the young man to the canal-side and got him to point out various spots where different incidents in the night had happened. Back at the station the officers tried to get a written statement from Broomhead's account, but because of his severe shock overlaying his stutter it was difficult to get a clear notion of the time of various incidents between 9.40 and 11.30 P.M. But there was no doubt that Broomhead was saying that there were two other courting couples on the canal-side, whom he pointed out to the supposed policeman; and it was in the urgent hope of getting these couples or any other witnesses to come forward that Chief Superintendent Burnett gave to the Press the extremely full version of Broomhead's account that they printed alongside their own personal interviews with the witness (which would not now be tolerated).

As a result of this decision, even while Burnett and Pugh were discussing it over a lunch-time drink, witnesses were coming forward with accounts that corroborated Broomhead's story; and later, while Pugh, in conference in his office, was painstakingly running over with the officer concerned the evidence in a brothel-keeping charge for the morrow, two people came to the police with a description of the wanted man which even confirmed the flower in his buttonhole. They were a courting couple who said that a girl had run up to them in a terrified condition while they were standing by the canal-side that night. "Quick," she gasped, "a policeman is chasing me, and he will have you, too." All three of them ran together for a distance of over 600 yards along the towpath. But at Western Road Bridge a man overtook them. He said, "I want that girl." The girl was then leaning, very ill, against the body of the young man she had warned. The young man said, "What do you want with her?" The other answered, "I am a police officer. I want that girl." He put his arm round her waist. The girl whimpered, "Oh, no!" and was led away. The man took her towards the Lodge Road arm of the canal, but he had to support her because she was fainting.

The C.I.D. team working on the case believed, from the attitude and certain turns of phrase of the unknown man that had been reported, that he had some experience of police matters. They concentrated their inquiries on the movements of ex-policemen and men who were known to have impersonated policemen. At the end of the next working day, Tuesday, Sergeant Edwards took Charles Broomhead to the gate of a Smethwick factory and told him to watch the men leaving while Edwards stood fifty yards away. Broomhead did consider one man very carefully; he said he walked like the man he was seeking, but it was not his attacker. (This man was in fact one of Edwards's suspects.) There was still time for Edwards to drive Broomhead back into town and station him opposite the factory exit of Canning and Company, Drysalters, of Kenyon Street and Great Hampton Street. Edwards told Broomhead to watch the workers leave and, if he saw his man, to step forward into the road. Only in this way could he see or attract the attention of Edwards, who, reinforced by Detective Constable Hewins, went round the corner, fifteen yards away, into Livery Street. This particular trap was laid almost within spitting distance of Kenyon Street Police Station.

After three-quarters of an hour Broomhead had made no move, though two hundred men and women had left the factory. During much of this time, it was later learned, one employee was trying to coax a timekeeper to let him have a key to a back exit to the factory. Finally this man emerged and walked towards Great Hampton Street on the other side of the road. Broomhead stepped into the road and pointed, and somehow said, "That's him. Go after him," at which point he seemed so overcome with excitement that he was about to collapse, and Detective Constable Hewins rushed to support him.

Edwards hurried after the man, and Broomhead, who was stronger than he looked, bustled after them. Edwards knew the man's name, for he was on the list of suspects, and he called, "Just a minute, I want to speak to you, Power." Before any reaction could be made Broomhead faced the man and said resolutely without a stutter, "Hallo. Do you want that fourpence now that you asked me for on Saturday?" The man said, "I don't know what you're talking about."

Edwards said, "You know me, don't you?" The man answered, "I don't think so." Edwards continued, "Are you James Joseph Power of 28 Heath Green Road, Winson Green?" The man said, "What if I am?" Edwards said, "I am Detective Sergeant Edwards, and this is Detective Hewins. This man states that you are the man who assaulted him on the canal-side on Saturday night last. Before you answer, I must caution you. You are not obliged to say anything, but anything you say will be taken down in writing and may be used in evidence against you.[1] Do you care to say where you were between ten and eleven thirty on Saturday night last?" The man answered, "I was with a pal." Edwards said, "Do you care to say who the pal was?" Power said, "A man named Jack Davis." Edwards said, "You will have to accompany us to Kenyon Street Police Station." Power went on, "I was never near the cut on Saturday night."

Chief Superintendent Burnett was at Kenyon Street. Edwards told him in front of Power that Broomhead had identified him as his assailant. Power said, "I was with Jack Davis all night. I went to the cricket match at Cape Hill and did not leave there until the finish. We then went to a pub opposite the Brewery and stopped there until ten o'clock. I left him on the corner of

[1] The last two words of this caution were then constantly used, and Pugh and others had to campaign persuasively to get them omitted.

Heath Green Road at about 10.45, went home, had a bit of supper with the wife, and we went to bed together at half-past eleven." He was then cautioned and charged with causing the death of Olive Turner (since there was as yet no sanction from the Director of Public Prosecutions for a charge of murder) and with impersonating a police officer. Power said, "Well, as I said before, I was never near the place. I am not guilty."

As Power was brought into Kenyon Street station another courting couple were in the C.I.D. office reporting that a man who said he was a policeman had accosted them on the canal-side on a night in February. They saw Power pass the door, and both immediately identified him.

Immediately after the charge Burnett sent Edwards with Detective Inspector Richardson to Power's home. They told Mrs Power that her husband was in custody on a serious charge, and asked her if she would tell them his movements after he left work on the Saturday. She said, "He went to the cricket match and came home at about eight o'clock. He went out shortly afterwards, and when I went to bed at half-past ten he had not come home. I did not hear him come in, although I lay awake with a bad back for a long time. He did not sleep with me that night. He slept with the children."

John Davis later said that they had been to the cricket match together, and afterwards to the Beehive public house, where each had bought a red rose for his buttonhole. They met again after supper, but said goodnight at 10.20 P.M. Meanwhile, on the same night, Tuesday the 5th of July, two more witnesses came forward to say that they had seen a man talking to couples on the canal-side on Saturday, and could identify him. Consequently, early next morning an identification parade was held. The first witness, a girl, could not identify anybody among the ten men. Before the next witness came in Power changed his position. The next witness was a tough old boatman who had confidently claimed to Edwards, "I could tell him in a hundred." The man came in and looked around. "I ain't got to go far," he said. "This is the man." As his hard fingers fell on Power's shoulder like a lobster claw the man went deathly white in his first sign of the strain. Of the three following witnesses, two identified Power and one could not decide between him and one other.

Power's age was thirty-two, and physically he was a magnificent specimen: he had been heavyweight boxing champion of the

Birmingham Police. On the morning of the identification he was brought before the Stipendiary. A queue right round the vast lobby wanted to enter the court. Power had engaged Herbert Willison as his advocate. Pugh leant neither on oratory nor on argument to overcome him that morning, but merely relied on the police evidence. As many litigants have ruefully discovered when their advocate has expressed full confidence after an unthorough briefing, Willison had got his facts wrong. In his righteous indignation in the courtroom he went almost berserk with fury over the identification parade. He was cross-examining Superintendent Penrice. "The identification parade was an outrageous farce," he shouted. "Only one out of six definitely identified him. Is it suggested that anyone else picked him out?"

"Last night," said Penrice curtly.

"By whom?"

"By Broomhead."

"Where?"

"In the street."

It was the quickest deflation Willison had known, for the identification out of a choice of two hundred workers hurrying home was justifiably considered definitive. But what Pugh expressed himself particularly proud of (when a remand had been ordered) was the quick rebuttal of Power's alibi by the account given by his wife, which was not, of course, put in.[1] "Albert," said Pugh—Edwards was called "Albert" by his superiors and "Tricky" by his colleagues, and his son, Detective Sergeant Harry Edwards, has inherited the nickname—"that is a classical example of a negative statement." And Pugh used the instance constantly afterwards in his lectures to the police on evidence. "But," he reminded Edwards after the hearing, "I don't have to tell you that you've still got some homework to do."

"On Broomhead's time sequence," said Edwards. "Yes, he's coming to Kenyon Street tonight."

That evening Edwards explained to the young man the inconsistency in his story. Too long a space of time seemed to have elapsed between leaving the cinema at 9.40, being accosted soon afterwards (Broomhead had said it must have been at 9.50, when Power was still at the Beehive), on to the time when Broomhead asked a passer-by to help him, and the man looked

[1] It never was put in. It was a voluntary verbal statement, and the wife was never called against her husband.

at his watch and made it 11.30. "You must see the importance of filling that gap," said Edwards, "and I feel you have not told us everything." In some confusion Broomhead then said he had taken his young lady down the canal arm and had stood by the wall there with her for a considerable time, during which Power first passed them and afterwards came back and spoke to them. He said he had held this back because he did not want Olive's sister and grandmother to know that she would stop down the canal arm with him.

Edwards went on with his inquiries and got a fresh lead from a paid informant. It was that a war widow had been taken by a married man on to the canal-side in May, and a man who said he was a policeman had told them they were trespassing, asked them what they would do about it, and suggested that he should have the woman. When the man protested he was hit so violently that he was knocked out for two hours, and while he was unconscious on the towpath the 'policeman' raped the woman. Edwards found it extremely difficult to get an admission of this from the couple concerned, for the man said it would ruin his life and break up his home. But the widow finally made a statement and an identification, and on the third remand—when the murder charge had been already preferred —a charge of rape was added.

Power was now represented by a barrister, Mr P. W. Williams, who made a most vigorous protest at the rape charge being considered at this stage. "The prosecution," he said in the Stipendiary's Court, "want to bolster up the murder charge by the second charge. They want to prove my client was in the habit of frequenting the canal-side and molesting people. The whole defence in the murder charge lies in the matter of identity. The Press is present in court, and the proceedings this day will be read by a population of one million people who will learn that this man has been frequenting the canal-side. That is bound to have some effect on their minds, and will not ensure a fair trial. The prosecution can come to no harm by a postponement of the second charge. The point is so vital to the defence. The whole defence to the case is 'I was not there'. Hence I ask for an adjournment *sine die.*"

Pugh refused to be moved. "I strongly oppose any such course," he said, and he sprang, as he always did, to defend the public reporting of proceedings before examining justices. "With regard to the presence of the Press, the reporters have a right to come into any court. Power is charged with the offence of rape, and it is only right that he should be committed on that charge to the next Assize."

The Clerk, Mr W. H. S. Walker, presented the point of law: "The question is whether it is the Stipendiary's duty to hear the evidence and either commit the prisoner or dismiss the charge. The witnesses are here and he is charged."

Lord Ilkeston looked towards M. P. Pugh, from whom he tended to take his law.

"I suggest it is your duty, sir," said Pugh.

"I don't see any grounds for postponing the charge," said the magistrate. He remanded the case for the last time.

On the 11th of August the court was prepared for a full hearing. After summarizing the facts of the case, and mentioning that Olive Turner had not been raped, Pugh turned to the legal exposition of what constitutes murder. "It has been laid down," he said, "that if, owing to violence or threats, a person jumped through a window or into a river, the one using the threats or violence was responsible for the consequences. On the other hand, it is held that if a person who suffered from a weak heart died as a result of threats, that would be manslaughter.

"I attach considerable importance to the evidence of the doctors, which revealed the fact that there was no water in the stomach. In that case the screaming must have taken place [a courting couple had heard terrifying screams from the canal-side at 11.35 P.M.] before the girl entered the water. I suggest that at that time the girl was incapable of shouting in the water, being in a collapsed and exhausted state and unable to save herself. The doctors who made the post-mortem examination found a bluish discoloration on the left side of the girl's forehead, and it was clear that this mark was not there before she was dragged along the canal-side by the man who is alleged to be the prisoner. There was no swelling from the bruise, and it is evident that the blow that produced it must have been struck within a minute of the girl's death, and probably before she entered the water. It might be that the screams were the consequence of the girl being struck."

A witness was called who said he had seen Olive Turner talking to two men, and that he recognized the taller of the men.

"Who was he?" asked Pugh.

"That man there."

"You mean that man who is laughing in the dock?"

"Yes."

Mr Williams rose to protest at Pugh's venom. "He does not seem to realize that this is a murder trial. This is not the occasion for a remark of that sort." But the attitude of the prisoner was doing the defence no good. He had been sneering and making loud remarks at the witnesses through the trial. "You liar!" he called to one who said he had identified him. "What will they give you for this?" As he went down the steps to the cells, committed to take his trial at the Assize, he gibed, "This is British justice!"

Detective Sergeant Edwards had not finished his investigations. He received an anonymous letter from Hockley: "You've got the right man. Now dig in his garden for the other body." He went to Power's house and was warned by his wife, "He does nothing but talk of what he'll do to you." Edwards thanked Mrs Power and went to dig in the garden. He unearthed the skeleton of a dog with a rope round its neck in a hangman's noose. But he did not forget Mrs Power's warning, and he became quizzically on his guard when he was ordered by Chief Superintendent Burnett to go to Winson Green Prison and deliver to Power additional evidence which had not been presented in the Stipendiary's Court, regarding further identifications of Power at other times masquerading as a police officer on the canal-side.

Consequently, when Edwards was shown into the waiting-room in the gaol to which Power would be conducted he chose a position by the fire on the farther side of a table from the door, and noted the position of a poker. Power had been committed in August, and it was now November, but he had to await the December Assize. Edwards had Detective Thomas Hewins to support him, and the prisoner was escorted by two officers. As soon as Power saw Edwards he burst away from his guards and rushed at Edwards with a torrent of obscene observations. Edwards picked up the poker and said, "Half a minute, Jimmie. Don't come any further, or I'll part your hair, and I'll do it properly." The guards caught Power, and Edwards gave him the papers of additional evidence, which the prisoner immediately tore up amid oaths, retiring with further abuse. Later Edwards mentioned this incident to Pugh. "Well, there was a letter from the Home Office enclosing one from the Governor, saying we ought to have you followed because of the threats Power had been making against you. He told his wife that if he got out of this lot he'd be back for murder, and if he got life he would still do the swine. That was *you*," Pugh added unnecessarily.

"You might have told me," grumbled Edwards.

"We didn't want to have you upset," laughed Pugh.

But Edwards was still glad that he had gone to dig up the dead dog. The warning he had had then had been sufficient for him to look for the poker. And, in his opinion, Power could have held him long enough to choke him to death.

For the trial Pugh had retained Norman Birkett, in his fourth year as a K.C., leading Mr Bousfield. For the defence Sir Reginald Coventry, K.C., led Mr P. W. Williams. The case was heard by Mr Justice Rigby Swift. Birkett arrived at 4.30 on the afternoon before the trial and explained to Pugh (now controlling the case as Agent for the Director of Public Prosecutions) that he had been able to look at the evidence only on his train journey from London. Without a note in front of him, Pugh answered all Birkett's detailed questions. The trial began on the 7th of December. Birkett followed Pugh's exposition of murder. "The swallowing apparatus of the girl was out of order before she entered the water," he told the jury, "and her lungs were in such a state that when the girl entered the water she was incapable of making any resistance, perhaps due to exhaustion caused by running, terror, or mental fright."

When technical evidence of the recovery of the body was being given, Sir Reginald Coventry, for Power, rose to ask that the drag which had been used should be produced.

"Does anything turn on this?" asked Mr Justice Rigby Swift.

"I should like the jury to see the business end, my Lord."

Birkett explained to the judge, "It may be in connection with the injury to the forehead."

"What exactly is there about this?" persisted the judge.

"My Lord," said Sir Reginald, "it is only on the question of the discoloration of the forehead."

"We have heard that there was a discoloration on her forehead," said the judge. "But what does that matter? I understand from your cross-examination"—he was speaking to Sir Reginald —"that your defence is that you were not there at all."

"Not there at all!" said Sir Reginald.

"What does it matter what happened to the unfortunate girl if your client was not there at all?"

"Your Lordship knows," said Sir Reginald, "that I have to meet other suggestions."

The defence called no witness except the prisoner. He gave an account of his movements on the fatal night. "Did you murder this girl, Olive Turner, on the night of July the 2nd last?" gravely concluded Sir Reginald.

"Certainly not, sir," said Power. "I know nothing about it."

"Were you on the canal-side that evening at all?"

"No, sir."

Birkett rose to cross-examine, and, as his clerk, A. E. Bowker, recounted, began with a 'Marshall Hall' gesture which was rare in this undemonstrative advocate. There had been suggestions that Power had been wrongly identified, because all the witnesses said the man on the canal-bank had worn his cap over his eyes to hide his face, whereas Power was said to wear his cap flat. Birkett's first question was:

"Do you look very different in a cap, Power?"

"No."

"Is this cap yours?" Birkett had an exhibit.

"Yes."

"Were you wearing it that night?"

"I may have been."

"Put the cap on, Power." Birkett passed it to the prison officer guarding Power.

Power put the cap almost comically flat on top of his head.

"Put it on, sir," Birkett snapped, "and pull it down over your eyes."

Power made feeble efforts to lower the brim. "I can't pull it down without hurting myself," he said. "It's too tight."

"Warder!" said Birkett. "Pull the cap down over the prisoner's eyes."

The guard swiftly pulled open the press-stud in the peak and pulled down the cap. The transformation was theatrical. Not only was it clear that Power could have used the simple disguise alleged, but to the jury he had suddenly been made to look indescribably villainous. Pugh remembered the sharp change of mood that headgear can make in the box, and on another occasion (which will be recounted) brilliantly recaptured credence for the prosecution by a double camouflage.

The jury brought in a verdict of Guilty, but Power was insolent and threatening to the last. Edwards had been told to keep out of court when Power was sentenced because a violent scene was expected. "Damn that for a tale," said Edwards, "he's my man and I've watched him all through." But Edwards agreed at least to keep out of sight, and he stood at the back of the dock.

The Clerk of Assize said, "Prisoner at the Bar, you stand convicted of murder. Have you anything to say why judgment of death should not be pronounced upon you according to the law?"

Power, quite calm, said, "Yes, my Lord. I still maintain that the jury and the witnesses have made an honest mistake, and if it was not for the prejudice of a certain detective sergeant"—his eye went to Edwards's place and, not finding him, roved round the court. "Well, he is not here," he continued, and spoke for some minutes about Edwards. Then Power turned to the jury. "You have found an innocent man Guilty," he told them.

The judge addressed the prisoner. "James Joseph Power, for the crime of which the jury have found you Guilty our law knows but one punishment, and that punishment is death."

"I quite understand that," Power coolly told the judge. "I don't want any sympathy from you."

Mr Justice Swift then pronounced the sentence.

"I will appeal against that sentence, you know," observed the prisoner, and went down to the cells.

Power did appeal, unsuccessfully. He was hanged in Winson Green Prison on the 31st of December, 1927. Baxter performed the execution and, looking at his handiwork afterwards, said he had never seen a man with a finer physique.

Edwards told this to Pugh. "You could still have got me choked, sir," he said.

And Pugh said, "But I should always have had your magnificent negative statement."

CHAPTER 2

Into Battle

MERVYN Phippen Pugh was born on the 15th of September, 1893, at Reading, Berkshire, the third child of Henry Thomas (Tom) Pugh and his wife, Elizabeth Hannah. His father was the son of a Hereford boot-maker who had married just over the Welsh border, beyond Hay-on-Wye. Young Henry Thomas was sent to a dame school when he was two, and began his studies from a hornbook. He was not sent to a regular school until he was ten, but once there he became a monitor within two years, and earned twopence a week for teaching sixteen smaller boys. At thirteen he became a pupil teacher, and he then went to the great Cheltenham Training College. As a trained schoolmaster he came to Reading to work at the Kendrick School for Boys, then the town's best secondary school. When he was second master there he shyly courted—he had to propose in writing—Elizabeth, the elder daughter of George Phippen, founder of the business of nurserymen and florists in Broad Street, Reading. They were married in 1885, and within three years they jointly opened the Reading Collegiate School, themselves progressively providing five of its pupils in their sons Maurice, Douglas, Owen, Mervyn, and Gwynne. The Phippens and the Pughs between them mustered, with all their families and fosterlings, a bustling, jolly, boisterously social, but incredibly hard-working group: Tom Pugh continued evening tutoring at the Kendrick School, and Elizabeth catered and house-kept for resident masters, boarders, and day-boys at the Reading Collegiate School, besides mothering her large family. When

Mervyn was eight his father additionally sought and won election to the Reading Town Council. He resigned this position in 1903, when he was appointed Chief Education Officer to the Corporation, and consequently relinquished the Collegiate School. He took a temporary house while he built a home at Hillowen, Shinfield Road, and at this house Mervyn's brothers, Owen and Gwynne, both died tragically of attacks of appendicitis within a year. The address was 13 Addington Road, and Mervyn, always superstitious in later life, had a special abhorrence of the number thirteen.

Tom Pugh continued as Director of Education in Reading until he retired after twenty-five years. He had sent his eldest son Maurice to the Moravian School at Neuwied, on the Rhine, and later Mervyn followed. Apart from appreciating his acquaintance with the German language, Mervyn was not later impressed with his formal education. He decided to follow the example of his brother Maurice and make the law his career. The family agreed that, particularly for the younger boy, it was a natural choice. Mervyn was an intellectually truculent youth who spent much of his time arguing with his father, an exercise which Tom Pugh generally relished. As a boy Mervyn was known as Tiny Talker Tinribs, and the reference to his garrulity (but not to his slimness) was valid throughout his life. At the age of seventeen, in February 1911, Mervyn Phippen Pugh was articled as clerk for five years to Frederick James Ratcliffe, a solicitor in practice at 1 Blagrave Street, Reading, in consideration of the sum of one hundred guineas paid in three instalments. On the first day of his service Pugh was taken by his principal to the office of the cashier. Ratcliffe said, "This is the most important man in the office. Unless fees are charged and collected we cannot live." The lesson was not lost on young Pugh, who always had to match his tastes as an enthusiastic spender against a basic caution regarding security.

When war broke out in 1914 Pugh joined a public-school battalion as a private, and was commissioned in the Royal Berkshire Regiment in February 1915. After further training he joined the fighting First Battalion of his regiment in France. He was taken on the strength at Béthune and posted to A Company amid replacements after half the battalion had been lost in an abortive moonlight attack on a nameless quarry slag-heap between Hulluch and Fosse 8. Seven officers had been wounded and six killed, including one, Second Lieutenant A. B. Turner, who gained a posthumous V.C. From this date, the 14th of October, 1915, with the single exception of a period spent recovering from wounds, Pugh fought in France until the end of the War, becoming over the three years one of the stalwarts who kept the battalion going when casualties altered the composition and spirit of it from one day to the next. General Sir Miles Dempsey,[1] then serving with the Royal Berkshires as an officer slightly junior to Pugh, remembered him after fifty years as "a tough determined officer, and a very courageous leader of men in battle".

Pugh was wounded during heavy German bombardment near Gouy on the night of the 1st of June, 1916. He wrote to his mother: "Got it last night. Buried three times and bits of shell in face, left leg and hand . . . . I thought I was going to be finished off but as usual have scraped out lightly." When he returned his battalion was in the back areas, but almost immediately came up to the line. On the 10th of March they were ordered to attack and take the Grevillers trench, a tactical objective fronting them for half a mile. Zero hour was 5.15 A.M. The weather had been icy, but during the night it thawed, and the dark stretch ahead of the troops was further obscured by thick fog. At zero hour the British artillery directed every gun available in a concentrated bombardment of the German lines. The barrage lasted only six minutes, and as it lifted the Royal Berkshires charged, their own hoarse shouts as they scrambled over the top blanketing the screams of the German wounded. The British leaped down into the enemy trenches, but the fog which had masked them in their approach now aided the Germans, as desperate pocket resistance followed in the knots of the defending trench system. Pugh rapidly organized and led parties to seize and consolidate all objectives, and as a result of what his citation later referred to as conspicuous gallantry, the culmination of fine work done on many previous occasions, he was awarded the Military Cross.

News of the awards to Lieutenant M. P. Pugh and Captain W. J. Green came to the battalion at the front on Good Friday. Before the decorations could be officially gazetted the Berkshires were ordered to attack Oppy Wood. Only fifteen officers and 250 other ranks had survived as combatants for this operation, and

[1] Colonel, The Royal Berkshire Regiment, 1947–56.

they had to take and hold 500 yards of trenches protected by wire which the British had not been able to cut well in one sector. The Berkshires had to lie all night in extremely shallow jumping-off trenches which afforded minimum protection from enemy fire. Greener troops would have been emotionally shattered by the night-long cries of their own men, comrades whom they knew by name, who lay between the lines, wounded in the last attack, and unable to be rescued. But at four in the morning the battle-hardened remnant went forward, loaded down like furniture-removers, as a friend of Pugh's described it, with weapons, tools, food and ammunition, but as casually "as though going over the top were a daily occurrence". The German machine-guns were firing high, and the Berkshires captured and consolidated the trench within an hour and pushed snipers forward into the wood, taking three enemy machine-guns on the way. Then, from five in the morning until nine-thirty, the battalion endured five heavy counter-attacks. They held the line until their ammunition was exhausted, and their bombs ran out. Lance-Corporal J. Welch, who had begun the morning by taking a trench at the head of his section, killing the last occupant with his bare hands, and chasing four Germans over open ground at the rear and capturing them at the point of an empty revolver, settled down to work an enemy machine-gun against the counter-attacks. When his ammunition failed he went over the top to find and bring in further boxes, and when his gun jammed he went out again for spare parts, with which he repaired the weapon. After five hours he was wounded by a shell-burst. Lieutenant Pugh was now commanding only thirty men, the active remnant of two companies; the rest of the battalion, from whom he was now separated, numbered only forty combatants. At noon the Berkshires retired to the point from which they had started. With 65 killed and 93 wounded, their strength had been halved again in both officers and men. Four days later they mustered eight officers and 210 men in a further attack on Oppy from which only two officers and 94 men came back. The wounded Lance-Corporal Welch was awarded the Victoria Cross for the first action.

Pugh, as a survivor, was immediately promoted Acting Captain, and he led A company through Givenchy and the epic Battle of Bourlon Wood, the crowning achievement of the 1st Battalion, Royal Berkshires, in the War. They came up from Beaumetz-le-

Cambrai in a continuous rainstorm which irretrievably soaked them, and on the night of the 28th/29th of November, 1917, took over the left flank of the newly acquired Cambrai salient. They were ordered to hold this at all costs to prevent the flanks' being driven in and the cutting off of the troops at the apex. Pugh's company held the centre, manning the trenches and putting outposts in adjacent shell-craters. After heavy bombardment from both sides during two counter-attacks the main strength of the German forces came over a ridge, advancing thousands strong in full marching order, for they had been told they could walk over the British at that point. At 9 A.M. SOS signals for immediate artillery support were flying from twenty-seven different positions in the ragged British line, which was based largely on parties in shell-craters. In continuous German attacks supported by low-flying aircraft almost all the posts of the Berkshires were overrun, the soldiers dying to the last man. But the advance was repulsed, and two German divisions were smashed. When the line was restored, on the 2nd of December, it was impossible to find the bodies of the British beneath the universal carnage.

The Royal Berkshires regrouped to endure the last desperate German push of the War. In March 1918 they were heavily hit in a mustard-gas bombardment which took twelve officers (including Captain M. C. Dempsey, M.C.) and 257 other ranks out of the battle. On the 21st of March the battalion, in corps reserve at Manancourt, was ordered to stand by for the opening of the enemy offensive on the Somme. On the 23rd, amid an atmosphere of great uneasiness in the face of obvious signs of disintegration, Pugh with A Company and Lieutenant Valentine with B Company were sent forward to reinforce the line at Equancourt. They found no line, for beyond the deserted wagon-parks there were only Germans, the British having retreated northward. The big breakthrough had come. Pugh and Valentine were back to Napoleonic open warfare, and like other reserve troops on their flanks, they halted in open green fields and dug a light cover of earth. They could watch the main German forces group in front of them, with skirmishers deploying ahead, and heavy guns and mortars actually being set up between the skirmishers and the main German divisions. Then, as the guns fired, the aircraft came in, and after the holocaust the German infantry moved forward. Pugh had no support at all. One British field-gun battery fired until its shells were finished, then limbered up and galloped off. Pugh consulted a colonel in the London Division on his left, and they decided to retire to higher ground and try to form a line. Under heavy fire the infantry retreated up a hill and formed behind the ridge. But once there the Berkshires were alone, for the other troops had gone farther back to improvise a line.

Throughout the day Pugh conducted a fighting retreat. When he made contact with C and D Companies he learned that the battalion's commanding officer, Lieutenant-Colonel G. P. S. Hunt, had been killed while rallying all available troops in a rearguard action. Pugh, as senior surviving officer, took over command of the battalion. He had no provisions beyond what his men carried, for Brigade had sent his transport far to the rear. Early next morning he conducted a calculated battle of endurance, a slow fighting retreat by Headquarters and C and D Companies, who allowed themselves to be pushed inch by inch through Gueudecourt under attacks down the road and from both flanks. Then, when he had taken the strain, Pugh moved up A and B Companies to hold Gueudecourt with the 23rd Royal Fusiliers. At 4 P.M. they were relieved, and the remnants of the four companies joined and held a front of 600 yards through a night of extreme cold. Under heavy attack at dawn they fell back to higher ground, but the companies were disorganized and Pugh had to regroup them around Headquarters. Next day, recreated as a fighting unit, the 1st Royal Berkshires turned and went back to hold the line at Auchonvillers. Then, on the fourth day of the breakthrough, they were moved back again, but to the womb-like comfort of a real trench system, the old neglected British line near Beaumont Hamel. Behind these defences the British artillery was being set up once more, and the infantry responded to the booming reassurance of guns behind them, without which they had felt so naked after years of trench warfare. The Berkshires held Beaumont Hamel all day against heavy bombardment and rifle and machine-gun attack. Late at night the New Zealanders came up to relieve them, and, long past midnight, Pugh and his men stretched out on the frosty earth outside Mailly Maillet, their exhaustion making them impervious to the cold as they took their first trusting sleep for six days. Pugh commanded the remnant of the battalion until replacements could be brought from England; the strength of the

Berkshires was too depleted for normal company organization. While the spirit of the 1st Battalion was being instilled into the new men the award was announced of the Distinguished Service Order to Temporary Lieutenant, Acting Captain M. P. Pugh, M.C.:

> For most conspicuous gallantry, able leadership, and resource at MANANCOURT on March 23rd, 1918, at ROCQUIGNY on the same day, at GUEUDECOURT on March 24th, and at AUCHONVILLERS on the 26th. His Commanding Officer was killed on the 23rd and he at once assumed command of the Battalion, without any previous experience of handling large bodies of troops. By his own personal bravery and an altogether remarkable appreciation of very difficult and intricate situations, he withdrew the Regiment from position to position, always keeping it intact and ready for further fighting. On the night of the 26th/27th March, when the Battalion was relieved, he re-organized personally the four Companies, nearly all the officers having become casualties. The determination and qualitics of leadership shown by this officer were beyond praise, and undoubtedly saved the Battalion on four separate and distinct occasions.

Pugh was promoted Major on the 19th of October, 1918, and a Mention in Despatches came through on the 8th of November, by which time the 1st Battalion, Royal Berkshires, was at last marching irresistibly to the Rhine. When the Armistice was signed on the 11th of November Pugh, Dempsey, and three other officers acquired transport and rode across the unregarded frontier into Belgium—the little country whose invasion had decided Britain's entry into the War, and which these soldiers had never yet penetrated. They went to Brussels and passed a night which, says General Dempsey in reminiscence, "would be in keeping with the times!"

Pugh came out of the War a slim, tough, decorated major of twenty-five, with his articles of clerkship still uncompleted. He passed his examinations, and was admitted a solicitor on the 16th of June, 1920. He could not, under the terms of his clerkship, practise in Reading, even if he wanted to, and he went to London. The criminal side of the law had always interested him, and he took a position as assistant to Philip Conway, a well-known solicitor who ran a busy practice from an office opposite Marlborough Street Police Court. Pugh narrated of Conway that no client could see him until he had paid the clerk an initial fee of five guineas. He was then shown up to Conway and allowed to relate his circumstances, which most often demanded a somewhat desperate defence on a criminal charge. Conway would listen and then say, "Yes. I'll undertake your defence. It will cost you twenty-five guineas, but you have already paid five." Repeatedly at this stage the client would falter, protesting that he could not possibly afford such a fee. "I quite understand," Conway would reply. "Come!"—and he would lead him to the window. "You see that brass plate over there? Now there's a man who will take your case for five guineas. Good-bye"—and the client would feel his hand being shaken—"and do look me up when you come out of prison."

M. P. Pugh (unlike many former officers, he never obtruded his rank or his decorations) thus found himself in private practice as a defence advocate largely specializing in the seamy, if diverting, type of case which the Marlborough Street Magistrate was accustomed to deal with. He was not an immediate success. After listening to a three-hour defence put up by Pugh for a man charged with receiving, the magistrate declared, "Despite your efforts, Mr Pugh, I find the prisoner Not Guilty." Experience would come, but Pugh was persuaded that he would never get very far if he stayed long as a satellite to Philip Conway. Edwin Clayton, then a legal assistant in the Office of the Director of Public Prosecutions, appeared opposite Pugh at the Westminster Police Court on one occasion, and, in conversation with him afterwards, suggested that he should come into "The Department". Pugh considered it, but instead answered an advertisement notifying a post on the staff of the Solicitor to the Post Office. He was interviewed by Harold Pearce, the Assistant Solicitor, who had previously served under the Director of Public Prosecutions, and whose brother, Seward Pearce, was then Senior Assistant Director. Pugh was told that "The Department" was the place for him. He was sent along for approval by Seward Pearce and Sir Archibald Bodkin, the Director, and he was taken on.

Though created by Act of Parliament in 1879, the Office of the Director of Public Prosecutions was in 1921 comparatively new, having been redefined in 1908 after the Treasury Solicitor had discharged the duties of the Director (by an Act of 1884) for twenty-four years. In England and Wales, unlike Scotland and the states of Europe and America, there is no Public Prosecutor who automatically represents the Crown when wrong is thought to have been done, and straightway prosecutes the offender. In England the prosecution of most offences is left to private persons, or to police officers who act as private citizens paid by their community to undertake the increasingly technical task of securing the conviction of the guilty. Towards the end of the nineteenth century it was becoming evident that the police themselves could be dubious about the presentation and conduct of cases of exceptional difficulty, and also that a *consistent* administration of law and order throughout the country demanded the application of more fixed rules or attitudes to the prosecution of certain crimes. As a result, all cases occurring in England and Wales involving treason, murder, incest, bribery and corruption, coining, and an increasing number of offences created by new legislation were reserved for the attention of the Director of Public Prosecutions, who had either to undertake the prosecution of the offence alleged, or at least consent to the prosecution by the police of local communities after he had considered the evidence obtained. He could also intervene in other criminal cases which appeared to present exceptional difficulty, or be of rare importance.[1] Alongside this obligation to sanction prosecutions, the Director of Public Prosecutions achieved increasing status as a consultant from whom senior police officers and local prosecutors could seek advice if, for example, they were uncertain whether they had sufficient evidence to go forward on a charge of fraud or of murder.

The day-to-day prosecuting activity of the Director was carried out by his legal assistants, or, in rare cases, by a provincial agent. The qualities required were an exhaustive knowledge of criminal law, the ability to analyse and marshal evidence, and a talent for advocacy; and it was decided that Pugh had these gifts. He was assigned a 'circuit' in the North London courts, and for three years after 1921 worked assiduously on prosecutions of

[1] The offences in which the Director of Public Prosecutions was interested vary slightly according to the date, and the inclination of the Director: the date, because an Act of Parliament can specify a new offence which comes within the Director's province, and because the Department's regulations were recodified in 1946; the Director's inclinations, as when Sir Theobald Mathew (Director 1944–64) had indecency added to 'his' list, on the ground that, as with the treatment of obscene publications, there should be a common official attitude throughout the country.

major cases in the police courts, and on controlling the cases in their later stages.

In 1924 the position of Prosecuting Solicitor for the City of Birmingham fell vacant, and the Corporation consulted the Director of Public Prosecutions, in whose gift the appointment then virtually lay. Sir Archibald Bodkin recommended Pugh, Travers Humphreys and Bernard Spilsbury wrote references, and he was sent up for a week to conduct cases under the eye of the Chief Constable and the Chairman of the Watch Committee. After being formally short-listed he was offered the post, and in July 1924 he took up his appointment. He took over a small office, not greatly overworked, for police officers themselves at that time undertook most of the prosecutions. But Bodkin also appointed Pugh Agent for the Director of Public Prosecutions within the City of Birmingham, and after the files of all the relevant cases had been submitted to the Department in London Pugh was always assigned the responsibility of conducting the cases in the lower court and superintending the conduct of the prosecution at the Assizes through counsel. It was a rare appointment at the beginning of his career, and it became unique. The Director's responsibility for these important cases was decreasingly delegated until, after some years, Pugh was the only prosecuting solicitor in the country who retained the agency for handling the D.P.P.'s cases. It was a distinction of which Pugh was always very proud. Without it, of course—to mention only one type of crime—he would have had no connection with the prosecution of the hundred murder cases which he handled. Pugh was the last ex officio Agent for the Public Prosecutor: when he left, the Director resumed the practice of sending his representative from London to conduct the preliminary hearing of most Department cases in Birmingham.

While he served with the Department in London, Pugh had the reputation of being "a rough type, but a good sort". He was, perhaps, a little rough for Richmond Terrace, for he did not have a London accent, used soldier's oaths, and was not secretive about the fact that he drank beer and backed horses. He followed cricket, which was all right—he supported Kent at that time—but this was outweighed by the undisguised admission that he had patronized the Holborn Sporting Club, where heavily backed terriers chased rats round three sides of a large room. Pugh was not, in fact, a compulsive gambler, but conformed more to the bookmakers' propaganda myth of the 'shrewd investor'. He placed bets to make money, and keenly studied form. He used his winnings for pocket-money and further betting, and did not dip into his reserves. Late at night during one Ascot meeting he plunged into the room where his friend Philip Williams was sleeping, urging, "Come along. Up you get. Help me count the money." He emptied his pockets on to the bed, and they counted nearly £50. But this lasted to support his indulgences for six months.

In Birmingham nobody noticed that he was a rough type at all, but they agreed that he was a good sort. In the office he could be testy and caustic, but outside his wit became rounder. He was a natural focus among men gathering socially, a talkative raconteur but telling tales with reliable point, a leg-puller and tease in the slightly offensive English provincial tradition: naturally, he could not support Birmingham's county cricket team Warwickshire, and plumped for Worcestershire in joshing arguments which could arouse extraordinary heat.

He was a man's man and a policeman's man, and the soundest recommendation of Pugh to the Birmingham Police Force that could be made occurred on his first entry into the Victoria Law Courts, when their discreet scouts noted that the 'new man', in his black coat and hard hat, was escorted on terms of great friendliness by Jimmy Burnett of the C.I.D. Herbert Willison, waiting in splendour in the great hall, grudgingly conceded, "I'd better go and see what the new man is like," and doffed his top-hat to follow the pair into No. 1 Court. It was not long before they were in conflict. Willison's voice was deep and loud, and between his thunder and his furious gestures the delicate orchid trembled in his buttonhole amid the coarse protestations: "You don't imagine anyone is going to believe that rubbish! You're talking nonsense. You must know better than to say that . . ."; or, when Pugh's voice finally topped his, the patronizing "Calm down, sonny!" Against Willison's bass Pugh spoke in a strident tenor, but it cut like a whiplash, dominating the defence advocate; and Pugh could be patronizing, too, in his humour. When Willison asked for a remand for one of his clients Pugh would ask in mock surprise, "Hasn't he paid you?" For it was a standing fiction that during the remand the defendant would attempt another break-in in order to get the money to pay his solicitor.

From the beginning Pugh organized the fixed routine that set the stage for his impressive appearance in court, displaying something of the solemnity of the Speaker's Procession into the House of Commons. One morning he knew that Sir Edward Marshall Hall, the great defence advocate who was then nearing the end of his career, was to appear opposite him in the Birmingham Police Court—a decision which was surprising in itself. When Pugh made his entrance he found that all Marshall Hall's papers and accoutrements lay on the desk, facing the witness-box and almost at the ear of the magistrate, where Pugh always sat. He picked them up and put them on the other side. Marshall Hall came in and demanded to know who had moved his belongings. "I did," said Pugh. "I have never met such cheek from a young man," said Marshall Hall. Pugh replied, unabashed, "If you consider that cheek, you obviously can't be very experienced." After the uproar had subsided Pugh conceded to the visiting advocate the end of his own bench, but the far end. Pugh had no great esteem for Marshall Hall, though this may have been an allergy of affinity. Pugh was not a theatrical advocate, but he demanded a staged set-up. And the manner in which Marshall Hall's clerk bore in his chief's properties—multicoloured pencils, shagreen instrument-case with compasses, rulers, and magnifying-glass, throat-spray, air-cushion, and adjustable footstool—and completed his arrangement of them as The Chief strode in on the dot of time, all this bore a remarkable resemblance to Pugh's own ritual.

Pugh's fellow-advocates among the Birmingham solicitors—all of whom tended to be retained against him—were wary at first of the newcomer who was changing the atmosphere of No. 1 Court and, from the point of view of their personal prestige, making it more difficult to secure an acquittal. But one of them, Mr Arthur Hall-Wright, looking back judicially on those early days, has summed up Pugh's achievement: "He virtually created the Prosecuting Department. By painstaking preparation of the work, which previously had been done somewhat slap-happily by the police, he made prosecution effective. He organized his department and fought for its prestige, even against the Council House, and, as he saw it, in this way he was furthering the fight against crime. He was prepared to discuss with defence solicitors the presentation of his case, and in this way he saved much of the Court's time. We could not but admire the way in which he stood up for himself and for what he thought was right, even against the Stipendiary, on points of procedure and law. He certainly taught young officers the art of giving evidence and influenced detectives to prepare a proper case, and since he had the co-operation of Burnett of the C.I.D. he positively affected and improved the running of the Police Department. Really, he set up something which was entirely lacking in the city." Mr Howard Baker, also a brother advocate, said: "He moulded the Birmingham Police Force into an efficient evidence-giving machine, and as a consequence it became more difficult to get people off. Moreover, he fought like a tiger for the police, and the men knew it, however much they resented his martinet behaviour. His strength lay in his tremendous knowledge of the criminal law and also of human nature, and finally in the powerful police force that emerged in Birmingham."

"Never exaggerate. Never deviate. Just tell the bare, plain, simple truth." That was the motto which Pugh impressed first on every police witness in the conference he conducted before a case. Soon he was expanding the theme in lectures he gave to the Midlands police, and which had their final impact on a much wider area; for policemen were promoted out of the region—twenty future Chief Constables were strongly influenced by Pugh—and senior police officers came from abroad to take further training. Much of Pugh's advice was technical, but he did not scorn the simple, homely principles of police work, and always linked them to the one ideal which this worldly man always kept untarnished, the goddess-conception of Justice:

"When you give evidence of conversations with prisoners, give the exact words and not some other version. You often hear in the court: 'I told the prisoner I should arrest him for burglary.' The probability is that the police officer put his head through the broken shop window and said, 'Come out of it, I have got you now.' Don't be afraid. Nobody thinks you are saints, and they don't believe all those polite things you say you say. If you told a man you would arrest him for burglary his attitude after that remark would have a very different bearing on the case than if you said, 'You will have to come with me to Kenyon Street.' A police officer might be going along the street and he sees a man and says to him, 'I shall arrest you for loitering with intent to commit a felony.' He might have said that, and also he might have said something else, but remember the prisoner's attitude after he said that. If he did not protest it would go badly against him. But if you said, 'You will have to come to the C.I.D. with me,' and then at the C.I.D. you charged him with loitering at 10.45 P.M. and said you saw him go into several doorways, it would be a different matter. It is only right in the interests of justice and in the interests of prisoners that you should repeat the exact words of the conversation and not give some other version of it which, while it may be accurate, has not the degree of accuracy which the administration of justice demands.

"Never express an opinion while giving evidence unless you are asked. If in cross-examination counsel asks you for your opinion it is another matter, but in giving evidence for yourself never express an opinion at all. It slips out, and it is not fair to the prisoner, and it makes the officer look as if he is very keen on getting a conviction and therefore damages his own case. A policeman sees a man doing something he ought not to do. He goes towards him, the man looks round and runs away. The police officer goes into the box and says, "The prisoner saw me and tried to escape.' He does not know whether the prisoner saw him or not, and whether the prisoner tried to escape is purely a matter of opinion. The officer could not possibly swear to the fact, because the prisoner's own eyes are the only possible things that know whether he saw him, and the prisoner's brain is the only thing which can know whether it was his intention to escape. The only proper way of giving evidence of such a thing is to say, 'The prisoner looked in my direction and hurried off in the opposite direction.' This leaves it open to the court to conclude whether the prisoner was trying to escape or not. Merely state the facts, and the court can come to what conclusion it likes.

"When you come to present your case in open court the most important thing is: Never get excited. Stand up well, speak out loudly, slowly and distinctly, and do not try to supply the missing link. The officer who tries to supply the missing link will find that link will break one day, and the person who will suffer most will be himself. Don't show yourself too keen about getting a conviction. Police officers are not supposed to care a rap whether they get a conviction, but of course if they take any interest in their work they naturally desire that justice should be done and the guilty be convicted. But you are there in the course of your duty as a police officer to say exactly what you saw, what you heard, or what you know about the case, and a great number of police officers do considerable harm to themselves and to their cases by showing themselves too keen to give evidence, or too anxious to add something to what they have been asked, or, on the other hand, by not saying enough, and showing some feeling for or against the prisoner which they have no right to express. You ought to go into the witness-box and, no matter what you feel, if the prisoner has knocked you about or abused you, you ought not to show it. It is contrary to your case to do so. In a recent case which I conducted it is my opinion that the Stipendiary convicted on the evidence of one policeman only against a number of persons who also gave evidence, simply because the policeman showed absolute indifference as to the result. I told him to give his evidence very quietly and not show any feeling whatever. He went into the box, showed no feeling against the prisoner, but just told quietly how he had been assaulted, and when he was cross-examined he was very willing to give a good name to the prisoner. In the end, after the prisoner had gone into the box and shown great venom towards the police, the Stipendiary Magistrate believed this one witness, the young officer, and gave a decision in his favour. By giving your evidence fairly and speaking the truth, the court will get a good opinion of your fairness, and it is bound to help you in future cases, because it is by an officer's reputation that he is judged when he comes before the magistrates."

When Pugh made this incentive appeal to self-advancement he was not offering empty gestures. He had the ear of the Chief Constable, and it was his practice to recommend policemen for promotion merely on the basis of the way they presented their evidence. His practical hints to police witnesses, furthering the fair administration of justice as they did, were also extremely effective means to cut the time taken on hearing a case and to spike the guns of Herbert Willison. Willison was the man who gave a fireworks display on behalf of his client if the police officer said, "The prisoner saw me and tried to escape." By getting the fairer version the court was spared five minutes' pyrotechnics. Willison would attack in depth any evidence that seemed to fit too slickly, to raise the implication that it was concocted. When Mr W. J. Richards (now Chief Constable of Manchester) was a young detective in Birmingham he chased by car a suspect on a stolen motor-cycle through a network of streets that he knew by heart, with the suspect always taking first right and second left like a knight moving criss-cross over a chessboard. When he gave evidence of this Willison cross-examined him: "You've got a wonderful memory, haven't you? You stand up here and recite every road my client is supposed to have taken"—Willison had moved right in front of Richards by this time and was waving his hand in the policeman's face—"HOW CAN YOU DO IT?" Willison, perhaps over-zealous for his client's future interests, was always curious to know if the prisoner had been 'shopped' by an informer, and if so, who the informer was. Detective Richards had this treatment once, but he had been coached by Pugh always to reply in the minimum. The cross-examination went:

"You came upon this in the course of your inquiries?"

"No."

"You received certain information?"

"No."

"A passer-by came up to you and told you. . . ?"

"No."

"Can't you say anything but No?"

"Yes."

"ALL RIGHT"—and Willison crashed his law book down on the desk and ended the cross-examination.

Pugh had been using this tactic since he first came, and Willison showed his rage at it surprisingly often. Detective Constable Champkin (later Inspector) had been working with his colleague Constable Muscroft and, having completed the investigation, they were told by Pugh, "Just give your evidence. Say the least you possibly can. If there is anything I want to know I shall ask you." They did this, and in turn faced Willison. Muscroft yielded no other answer but "Yes, sir" and "No, sir," but when Champkin went into the box he had only produced two Yesses and one No when Willison snarled, "Ah, you're like your friend Muscroft, are you?" and threw down his brief. In other courts than Number One, in those presided over by lay magistrates before whom Pugh rarely appeared, Willison sometimes fared better, especially against young policemen who did not always get the protection they deserved. "And how long have you been a police officer? How many cases have you taken? Can

I see your notebook? Ah, so this is really the first time!"—and Willison would be set for a peroration on the fallibility of novice police officers.

It cannot be said that every policeman enjoyed the way Pugh trained him. At the conferences which he called—either of senior police officers to assess the weight of evidence in an investigation, or of all officers concerned in a case to outline its presentation and estimate the strength of the witnesses—anger and humiliation were often in the air as the sharp reprimands rang out:

"Why haven't you been to see Jones?"

"Do Smith and Brown work at the same place?"

"But it's your job to know!"

"So you've got a theory? Pearls of wisdom! Come on, let's have it!"

"Go and inquire into it."

"Get a statement."

"Don't come near me with that bloody sniffle."

"Why haven't you brought your witness?"

"I don't care if she does hate the sight of her husband. Get corroborative evidence. She can always refuse to go into the box at the last moment, and then you're scuppered."

"You detectives are always relying too much on voluntary statements by the prisoner. It's not the best evidence. Go for the best evidence. Who saw him do it? Who missed the money? Where was it found? There was a case in Warwick only the other day, and I should have had your guts for garters if it had happened here. A man was indicted for false pretences and the false pretence alleged was that he had said he was working for the B.T.H. Company. The only evidence of the false pretence was that he had made an admission to the police officer. They didn't call any evidence from the firm to show whether he had been working for them or not, and at the end of the case for the prosecution the Chairman of the Sessions asked the presenting counsel if he wasn't going to call any evidence from the firm. He said No, he relied on the admissions made by the prisoner. So the Chairman of the Sessions directed the jury to bring in a verdict of Not Guilty. Voluntary admissions are good corroborative evidence, but for Christ's sake bring me some good red meat."

It was all very informative, and an invaluable insight into the law, but the police found meeting Pugh a strenuous exercise.

With the detective force he was generally milder, for there was a propaganda battle to be won, and toes had to be trodden on more gently if he was to withdraw the conduct of even routine cases from court handling by the police. "All cases that go for trial need the attention of the prosecuting solicitor," he told Burnett. "You even need help to present a loitering with intent." Pugh would always make himself available to discuss with detectives the burden of proof they required on a particular case, and from his experience he could draw on examples that would illustrate the choice of the moment of arrest, for example, to get a receiver. Pugh was always keen to convict receivers, quoting the old saying that without them there would be no thieves:

"I remember there were three men broke into a warehouse and they stole a load of rolls of Viyella. The detectives were on to it, but they wanted to find the receiver. They found the lorry in the street at six in the morning and broke open the back to check that the stuff was still there. They waited, and followed this lorry and saw it drive into the receiver's garage. The three thieves took the bale off the lorry, and the receiver was there, but they started some sort of argument—a quarrel about the price or the division of the loot or something. The detectives pounced, and they arrested the three for breaking in and the other man for receiving. But the receiver got off, because they hadn't completed the bargain and he had not taken possession of the goods. Now we lost that case for a little bit of thought and perhaps a minute or two of patience."

A senior police officer said of Pugh, "A man like him can make a police force. Especially a detective force. You read these laws, but you need a man to tell you how to apply them."

Pugh applied his own perfectionism to the meticulous manner in which he presented his case. After an exhaustive opening statement—during which he was somewhat inclined to present every offence as "the worst case of this nature I have ever come across"—he would call his witnesses, clinch any cross-examination with a short re-examination, and, as the witness was signing the deposition, have the next witness in the box ready to be sworn. He drilled the court officers into effecting this smooth presentation, and was particularly concerned to avoid any noisy pause interrupting the build-up of his case: indeed, if there was any shuffling in the court while he was speaking he would savagely rap out, "SHUT UP!" without altering the flow of his remarks

M. P. Pugh sketched in Court at the Height of his Career

Drawing by Stanley Parker ("Sunday Mercury", 1946)

"Unlike many former officers, he never obtruded his rank or his decorations"

Pugh caricatured at a rare military reunion

"Fat supers, all sticking out as much before as behind"

The wedding of Mervyn and Dr Vera, Wolverhampton, 1930

or looking towards the offender. His understanding of human nature gave him a speedy skill in following the old detection maxim: "If you want to catch a thief you must live and think like a thief." He could almost intuitively see through a false alibi; and it was useless for a defendant to say that he had come by his cash gains through a betting coup, for Pugh would swiftly ask, "What meeting? What race? What horse?"—and Pugh would know the answers. But his ability to size people up, which many commented on, worked fairly. It is common for the man in the dock to interrupt the liar who is testifying against him with denial, protestation, and abuse; but occasionally Pugh, listening to the prisoner's outburst, would exclaim to the Clerk of the Court, "He's right, you know. He's telling the truth." On the other hand, when the deceptive flight of his cross-examination questions had culminated in a straight ball which the witness was incapable of blocking, Pugh would turn in his stance and murmur, "Middle stump!" with a certain air of self-congratulation.

With child witnesses he would completely alter his manner, never hectoring them and often standing quietly by their side in the witness-box. When cross-examining hostile adults he often seemed to lose his temper, and the speed of his questions sometimes prompted Lord Ilkeston to protest that the witness should be given time to answer. But in some prosecutions, often for motoring offences, he would cross-examine almost with a grin on his face: "But, Mr Jones" (said ingratiatingly), "surely we all do that sometimes? We all take our eyes off the road for a moment?" And his gaze would sweep round the court searching for someone who did not. But Pugh still wanted the verdict. A lost case was almost a personal insult to him. "Diabolical!" was his favourite cry; and, as he stumped out of the court: "That bloody witness let me down."

The most obtrusive file which Pugh found in his office when he took over as Prosecuting Solicitor in 1924 was an enormous bundle of documents referring to a long firm fraud which became notorious in Birmingham as the case of the Forty Thieves: thirty-nine men were in fact eventually charged. "I will be satisfied if we can get twenty convicted," said Pugh, long before the charges, as after a three-months personal struggle he handed over the files to Mr Arnold Churchill, the barrister, to weld the links between each suspect and each offence; but the prosecution did better than that, finally getting thirty thieves convicted.

A simple long firm fraud is the obtaining by a man, posing as a company, of goods on credit by giving false references and making other false pretences. For a successful operation it is advisable to pay the account the first time it is presented and afterwards to order much more heavily, and, when further accounts are presented, to order heavily again. The goods are sold, sometimes at receiver's prices, as they come in, and the cash goes to the organizer of the fraud, which continues as long as the faith of the supplying company in its customer can be sustained. The fraud becomes compound when the same man is carrying it on with a number of companies. It becomes complex when more than one fraudulent firm is dealing with a permutation of the companies. And it becomes an almost irreducible knot of tangled network when forty fraudulent firms in Birmingham conspire to defraud many scores of companies ranging geographically from London to Leeds and from Hereford to Leicester. The forty thieves worked the trick by forging false references to get six of their number appointments as agents or travellers representing the companies they had decided to defraud—firms which mainly supplied hotels, clubs, and institutions. These travellers put forward the other thieves as bona-fide customers, and soothed the supplying firms for as long as possible when they became uneasy over unpaid accounts.

To prosecute this conspiracy, which went on for over two years, involved tracing every representative transaction and linking a number of the thieves in prior knowledge and intent of it, to prove conspiracy. Every transaction involved at least an order form, an invoice, waybills (goods were then generally sent by rail, being collected by cart, dispatched by train, and delivered by cart), a signed delivery note, and at least two distant copies of demands for payment if it was to be shown that the customer did not intend to settle the bill. All these documents had to be gathered and correlated for every fraud the prosecution intended to cite. Pugh's clerk, A. E. Field, spent six months working over hours until midnight before the case could be presented. Though the goods obtained were mainly easily disposable wines and spirits and provision groceries, they also included motor oils, grease, cleaning powder, cattle beans, dusters, soap, belting, postcards, dyes, corn, rick sheets, and paint. When the case came before the Stipendiary, Pugh had to master six bound copies of documents, letters, invoices, and cheques. The preliminary hearing, with inevitable adjournments, took months. Pugh, in his opening statement, had no need for his usual superlatives. When he called it "a case of gigantic proportions" his description was not challenged. But Willison, in an ingenuous defence, claimed, "I venture to say if you take the first shop on the other side of Corporation Street, and go down the whole length of the street, you would not find a single shop where they have paid for everything in it. I don't say they are not going to pay. My clients had the goods, but there is no proof that they are not going to pay for them."

Pugh, however, was able to put up *prima facie* proof. The trial, with forty men on benches in and around the Crown Court dock like a class in an adult Sunday school, took, with continuous hearing, nearly three weeks. It was notable for the conspicuous absence of robed counsel in the body of the court. For the prisoners were now in penury and could retain no counsel; but for a fee of £1 3*s*. 6*d*. they could snatch any robed counsel in sight, pressing on him a 'dock brief' which the tradition of the Bar forbade a barrister to refuse. Since it was rumoured in the robing room that the case might extend into the Long Vacation of 1925, the Midland Circuit confined its professional interest in the defence to standing unrobed in the doorway of the court. It was not through inhumanity so much as self-preservation. Mr George Bancroft, Clerk of Assize on the Midland Circuit, who nobly volunteered to leave the Red Judge—the Judge at Assizes who takes the criminal, not the civil cases—and sit below the Commissioner of Assize, Sir Francis Taylor, K.C. (who had been especially appointed to take the trial), said it was "the dullest and most intricate case I can remember. It had 1750 exhibits and it took thirteen days to try without a moment being wasted. It was nothing but figures and billheads without a spark of human nature or a grain of humour in it."

The declaration of the General Strike in May 1926 armed the Birmingham Police, and all other local forces, with drastic emergency powers which Pugh did not hesitate to use. Ironically, he used them most effectively against criticism of, or propaganda about, these very emergency powers. He prosecuted Percy Shurmer, then a thirty-seven-year-old Birmingham City Councillor working as a Post Office engineer, for making speeches calculated to cause disaffection among the civilian population. What gave Pugh added fire in his blistering condemnation was the subject of Councillor Shurmer's speeches. High Tory as he was, Pugh had no sympathy for the Left in the strike struggle. But this man had actually attacked Pugh's Police! "From various platforms at Calthorpe Park," declared the prosecutor, "he made vile insinuations against the police. He said the police had bludgeoned and batoned men, women, and children in Broad Street for no cause at all, and that the superior officers of the police had kicked people and used sticks on them. He told his hearers that the powers that be were itching to get at them, and he told them, 'You are the power, and we look to you for the power when the time comes. We are not ready yet. But I have been in the front lines in France and Flanders, and I will be in the front line again, to lead you, and die for you, if necessary.'"

No efforts by the versatile Willison could fend off a fine of £10 or fifty-one days' imprisonment. Percy Shurmer reckoned it a battle honour. When he became M.P. for Sparkbrook in 1945, and so got into *Who's Who,* he listed "Arrested during General Strike 1926" with his subsequent dismissal from the Post Office among his principal inter-war achievements.

Pugh further proceeded, predictably, against the printers, publishers, and a selection of the many volunteer distributors of the strike news-sheet *Birmingham Worker,* alleging, under Regulation 21, Section 1, of the Emergency Regulations Act of 1926 that they had committed an act likely to cause disaffection among the civilian population by publishing the paper. He then advised the police to raid the offices in Corporation Street of the Birmingham Trades Union Emergency Committee. The committee's *Birmingham Strike Bulletin* had carried the following article:

> GOVERNMENT DEFEATED IN PARLIAMENT
>
> Tom Johnston, M.P. for Dundee, in the House of Commons moved the deletion of the regulations providing for the arrest without warrant for certain acts. The motion was carried by 316 to 75. Government defeat. Keep strong now and we shall win through. The general trend of public opinion is certainly with the miners and is growing.

When Chief Superintendent Burnett read this report, which affected his own powers, he got in touch with the Home Office and with Scotland Yard and heard that it was unfounded. The raid on the offices scored twenty arrests. Pugh prosecuted the principals under the Emergency Powers for printing and publishing the *Strike Bulletin,* and the others (who included City Councillors James Crump and Arkworth Edgar Ager and four magistrates with Labour sympathies) for doing an act calculated or likely to cause disaffection by authorizing the publication. The principals were John Strachey, journalist, aged twenty-four, who had already stood as Parliamentary Labour candidate for Aston in 1924 and was to win it in 1929, and Leslie Plummer, aged twenty-four, already a newspaper manager but not yet in his dominating position on the *Daily Express,* not yet a knight or a Labour M.P.

On any other issue but the political it was uncharacteristic of M. P. Pugh to attack the Press. He relished personal publicity, manipulated the Press where possible as a weapon of justice, and was its particular champion in emphasizing its right (censored only by its own standards of responsibility) to report the public administration of the law. His openness and friendliness towards journalists was never feigned, and they on their side appreciated this warmth, coming as it did from a quarter from which they more often received, from police or magistrates, a surly tolerance or unmasked repugnance. Birmingham newspapermen in their relation with the Law still glowed with the pride of the backlash by Mr Editor Gray in the *Birmingham Gazette* after a homily by Mr Justice Darling at Birmingham Assizes, forbidding the Press to publish details of a sordid case he was about to try. This leading article, perhaps the hardiest stand for responsible freedom of the Press against judicial muzzling in peace-time that has been made in this century, combines the independent *hauteur* which Birmingham has often maintained against all other cities, including London, with a statement of real nobility and a touch of common scurrility which is the spice of the best invective. The reference in the first paragraph quoted is to the fact that Mr Justice Darling was of small physical stature:

A DEFENDER OF DECENCY

If anyone can imagine Little Tich upon a point of honour in a public house, he has a very fair conception of what Mr Justice Darling looked like in warning the Press against the printing of indecent evidence.

His diminutive Lordship positively glowed with judicial self-consciousness. He felt himself bearing on his shoulders the whole fabric of public decency. Under the evident delusion that newspapers are always on the prowl for unseemliness, he warned their representatives against giving a full report of what was about to transpire in their hearing. He hoped his words would be sufficient, but, if not, he warned them of the penalties which he would make it his business to enforce in the event of disobedience.

The terrors of Mr Justice Darling will not trouble the Birmingham reporters very much. No newspaper can exist except upon its merits, a condition from which the Bench—happily for Mr Justice Darling—is exempt. There is not a journalist in Birmingham who has anything to learn from the impudent little man in horsehair, a microcosm of conceit and empty-headedness, who admonished the Press yesterday. It is not the credit of journalism but the English Bench that is imperilled by a speech like Mr Justice Darling's. . . .

One of Mr Justice Darling's biographers states that "an eccentric relative left him some money". That misguided testator spoilt a successful bus conductor. Mr Justice Darling would do well to master the duties of his own profession before undertaking the regulation of another.

Such a calculated attack could not be officially ignored, and Mr Editor Gray was arraigned for contempt of court. After making a full apology he was fined £1, a sum whose derisory significance was perhaps the best vindication of his bold stand.

M. P. Pugh, Prosecuting Solicitor, had no judicial horror of the Press. He relied on and assisted its reporting to emphasize to the public that justice was seen to be done. If the police were making a drive he would manipulate the prosecutions, whether against shoplifters or homosexuals, so that they were taken in a batch, and achieve the greatest deterrent publicity. Only one concession he would not make: he would never reduce the head of steam which projected his powerful opening statements at a minimum speed of 250 words a minute, sometimes accelerating to a rate that the most expert shorthand writers could not catch; but on these occasions he would rescue the Press later. Once Eddie Daniel, a veteran court reporter, seething with the tension of trying to keep up with Pugh, finally dropped his pencil in despair. Pugh heard the clatter, and this time did not hiss, "Shut up!" Instead he smiled. "All right, Eddie," he promised across the court, "I'll let you have a copy of that statement afterwards."

CHAPTER

3

He danced with the Maid

DOMESTICALLY, M. P. Pugh had installed himself comfortably enough in a private hotel in the Hagley Road called Hagley Grove, a long, white Georgian-style house kept by the Misses Crease, two ancient ladies with beautifully dressed white hair who maintained undisputed *tone* in their establishment. Hagley Grove developed as a sort of clearing-house for the brighter municipal officers—bachelors, betrothed, and newly wed. Among its thirty-odd residents were Tom Elias, the Clerk to the Justices, J. Percy Eames, later to become City Treasurer, and others who moved to the top of the Town Clerk's, Public Health, and other departments. Percy Eames, a newly-wed, and Kenneth Milliken Smith, a city stockbroker, became the special cronies of "Pug", as Pugh was almost universally known outside the Law Courts. Resident also were a handful of somewhat eccentric old ladies. They emphasized the formality of what was basically a most select institution, but they also tended occasionally to polarize the guests into the magnetic opposites of old against young, or starchy against gay, forcing the young into conspiracy against the old which could only be demonstrated by elaborate practical jokes, high jinks in the corridors, or merely wild attacks of the giggles at private jokes in the dining-room. Life at Hagley Grove seemed often to be adapting a lark from *Just William* to the age-group of the readers of *The Humorist,* and a bedroom coffee-party, with socks stuffed into the gramophone to mute it, had all the thrill—and the innocence—of a dormitory feast.

The house was generously staffed and well equipped. There

was a billiards-room, which was Pug's especial haunt, and he could also take refuge in the smoking-room, which was naturally reserved for men. Breakfast was a silent affair. Pugh sat alone at his own table, arguing with no-one, but devouring his newspapers. Afterwards he would liven as he walked down the Hagley Road with Percy Eames. Once, on the way to the office, Eames asked Pugh what was the difference between assault and battery. Pugh stopped in his tracks and raised his fist in towering menace, shaking it in his companion's face. A policeman sprang into alertness and moved towards them. "That is assault," said Pugh, not touching Eames. "And that is battery," he added, giving him a jolting clump. The policeman moved in for his kill, but at the last moment recognized Pugh and weakly saluted him.

Both inside and outside Hagley Grove, Pugh had a busy evening social life. He assiduously attended Freemason meetings and dinners: he was a member of Leigh Lodge, of which he became Master, and of the Royal Arch Chapter attached to Leigh Lodge, and had the reputation of being a good ritualist and a most witty after-dinner speaker. On quiet nights he strolled with Ken Milliken Smith for half-pints in the back room of the Plough and Harrow, or took him off to "see a bit of leg" at the Aston Hippodrome. Like many of his circle, he was a regular diner-out at the Grand Hotel, the Midland, and the old Queen's. He had his own table at these hotels, and his own bottle of brandy—the wine-waiter brought his labelled bottle of Otard at the end of a meal and took it back to the pantry afterwards. He welcomed formal dances, not so much for the foxtrotting as to indulge his easy skill as a raconteur and his somewhat pronounced nose for gossip; he was always curious as to who was partnering whom, and liked to maintain the fiction that he was the public moralist. "Who's that dancing with the girl in green?" Percy Eames once asked him under the balcony at the Grand Hotel. Pugh's eyes shot across the floor, and his mouth narrowed to a crescent slit. "I don't know, but we'll get him," said the Prosecuting Solicitor.

His jokes were often of brash, musical-hall unsubtlety. "It's a great day for the race" was one of his constant catchwords, long after most people had learned not to ask "What race?" and be told "The human race". But there was always a new generation to be taken in. Later than his stay at Hagley Grove—but how he wished he had thought of it then—he prepared a book boldly labelled SEX FOR THE OVER-SIXTIES, which he would leave about for maiden ladies to pick up. He shook with laughter in his hiding-place as he watched them cautiously open it and find all the pages blank. At Hagley Grove there was a tiresome old lady called Miss Bushell. She declared that she was extremely sensitive to draughts, and was always rearranging the curtains in the dining-room. When the guests took coffee after dinner she abstained, and went up to her room on the top floor, from which she stealthily emerged to force wedges into the windows of the other bedrooms on that landing (occupied by Ken Milliken Smith and Mr and Mrs Eames) to ensure that there would be no through draught that night. Ken Milliken Smith called a conference to deal with the nuisance. It was decided that he should put the key in the outside of his door and await his opportunity. At coffee time Miss Bushell left the room, and Milliken Smith unobtrusively followed. While Miss Bushell was adjusting the wedge in his room he turned the key, slipped downstairs, and quietly resumed his seat in the coffee-room. Soon a muffled thunder was booming from upstairs, but the young set drew no attention to it. Finally the uproar penetrated the consciousness of the queenly Misses Crease as they presided over the gathering. Their black skirts riffled as they stalked upstairs, supported by the residents. They flung open the shaking door. "I demand," said Miss Bushell, "that Mr Milliken Smith be dismissed from this hotel." "*We demand*," said the Misses Crease, "to know what you are doing in Mr Milliken Smith's bedroom."

The great annual event at Hagley Grove was the grand dinner-dance held in the New Year. Some eighty guests attended; there was excellent food; and the sophistication of cocktails was momentarily permitted. Percy Eames, who had already shown himself a dab hand at constructing a home-made wireless, fixed up temporary electric lighting to supplant the normal gaslight, getting the corporation's electric supply department to run a cable to the cellar from the nearest main, and persuading them to leave the rest to him. He borrowed stage spotlights from the Crescent Theatre and all the ladies stitched like mad to make counterfeit trailing mimosa fringes to hide the battens he had fixed in the dining-room. Percy was so busy technically that he could not provide the music for the dance: he was adept at playing the reedy kazoo inside a papier-mâché trumpet, with

Miss Thompson on the piano and Milliken Smith on the drums. Instead the Misses Crease engaged a semi-professional band. The guests arrived—dinner jackets and black waistcoats for the men, and beady surplices and bangles for the ladies. They tucked in, then the band played bright blaring quicksteps. Percy's big moment approached: the change of mood to soft romance. He had a set of seven-pound jam-jars filled with water for dimmers, and when the band-leader nodded he darted to his alcove, switched out the whites, and slowly brought up his reds and greens. There were murmurs of rapture as the dancers cuddled into a waltz. Waltzes, slow fox, blues—and over to gaiety again. The top lights went up, the band beat fast, a clarinet shrieked, and M. P. Pugh, who was about to take a sandwich from a pretty uniformed maid, swung her tray to the table and took her in his arms and whirled in quickstep chassés with her all round the floor, while her white apron billowed against him and all her ribbons flew out behind.

"He danced with the maid!" The effect on the *haut monde* of suburban Birmingham would have provided a score of models for the shocked spectators in an H. M. Bateman cartoon: but none for the central figure, for the grin on the face of the tough and agile, though incipiently portly, Pugh who finished the dance had none of the feckless anticipation of doom that characterized The Guardsman Who Dropped It. The fact that he had had this public gambol began to become the most important thing about Pugh in the estimation of Edgbaston, and the Misses Crease fervently thanked goodness that they had been preserved from the canard that they were keeping a disorderly Bohemian house by the saving clause that Mr Pugh was a solicitor. It was not a thing that Pugh's friends either mentioned to him or chaffed him with, for however eagerly Pugh would provoke an argument on abstract or public themes he could become dangerously offensive when the flames of criticism licked at his privacy. But people talked about it, just the same. And "He danced with the maid" was the one thing that Dr Vera Cullwick knew about M. P. Pugh before she met him. She came to take up residence at Hagley Grove, and as she parked her Austin Seven in the drive behind his open Ford two-seater she finally met the man who had done it. She had, in fact, chosen a dangerous position for the encounter, for she had boxed in Pugh, who, strangely, never shone as a driver, and in a motoring career of thirty-five years was never remembered to have reversed either accurately or good-temperedly. Driving backward on alternate full lock with one's chin over one's shoulder was one of the irritations, like going to the bank, answering the telephone, and buying postage stamps, that were best left to others.

Vera Cullwick, six years younger than Pugh but with almost as long experience in a civilian career, was the youngest daughter of Herbert Ernest Cullwick, a Wolverhampton dentist and prominent Freemason, and his wife, Edith Ada. She qualified in medicine at Birmingham University. She completed a term as resident in the Birmingham Children's Hospital, and then served two years at the Royal Hospital, Wolverhampton, as house surgeon and house physician. She began to specialize in anæsthetics, and took an appointment as anæsthetist at the Birmingham General Hospital. It was then that she came to live at Hagley Grove.

She had become engaged to a hospital doctor, but once they took up separate appointments found that they had increasingly less in common with each other. One day in April 1929 they met and, facing the facts, broke off the engagement. Vera Cullwick drove back late at night to Hagley Grove in natural distress, and by chance encountered Pugh in the dark drive. As he escorted her into the house he could see that she was upset, and, responding to his sympathy, she sat for a long time telling him the story. A few days afterwards he came to her at breakfast and suggested dinner that night. They had his reserved corner table at the Midland, he ordered the best wine—with his German education he always favoured hock—and he christened her Cully and she called him Pug. Soon he was waiting every evening for her in the drive as she came home. The immediate impact of their friendship on Pugh's staff and police contacts was that he bullied more work out of them; for he now took a lift in Miss Cullwick's car to the General Hospital by Steelhouse Lane, and Miss Cullwick was in the operating theatre before nine in the morning. In August Mervyn Pugh took Vera Cullwick to his parents—to whom he was exceptionally devoted—at their new home at Highcliffe, Hampshire. Tom Pugh had retired the previous year from his post as Education Officer at Reading. Cully saw the real Pug, who had been so solitarily quiet over his newspapers at Hagley Grove, in action in passionate intellectual argument with his father every breakfast-time. The parents were delighted to meet Vera, for they had given up hope of Mervyn's ever settling down into marriage. The engagement was announced, and Pugh set about organizing their dual life. He strongly believed that a wife should be independent, but his principles did not take him so far as approving a hospital appointment which could place Dr Cullwick on emergency call. She took up a post as Assistant Medical Officer of Health to the Worcestershire County Council, working in welfare clinics, mainly with children. They set about making a home. Pug wanted a flat at the Five Ways, but Cully's mother thought that flats were only places where kept women were maintained. In November Pugh went to an auction and bought a semi-detached house which neither of them had been inside. It was at 5 York Road, one block from the Hagley Road, and for a ten-year lease he paid £1200. After this onslaught on his capital, Pugh borrowed £500 from his father-in-law-to-be to start his married life. Pugh's father furnished the dining-room in oak, Pugh bought the rest of the furniture, and Dr Cullwick provided the curtains. They were married on the 29th of January, 1930, and as they came out of St Peter's Collegiate Church, the thick-set groom looking monumental in his superbly tailored tailcoat and trousers rising from white spats, six prize beefy men in blue with the froggings of rank across their tunics raised their staves in an arch of honour. The police force had turned out to see their man off: Burnett and three other Birmingham superintendents—Pinkerton, Harrison, and Cook—were there, with the Chief Constable and his assistant from Wolverhampton. But at the reception the fat supers, all sticking out as much before as behind, and with the rolls on their red necks creased white with the effort, sang, "Why was he born so beautiful, why was he born at all?"

After a ten-day honeymoon at Cannes Mr and Mrs M. P. Pugh came back to York Road. They had a resident maid, paid twelve shillings a week, and a part-time gardener at six shillings the half-day. When their only son, John Mervyn Cullwick Pugh, was born on the 18th of May, 1933, they added a nanny to the establishment, and when later on they sought a third maid and found she wanted £1 a week they realized that the cost of living was rising. Pugh was extremely proud of his house and family, and reacted warmly to the intimate social criss-cross of suburban Birmingham in days when the wireless was no longer a novelty and people liked talk, cards, and an elaborate hospitality. Besides their frequent informal entertainment for coffee and drinks the Pugh's gave a formal dinner once a week—black bows and evening dress, tremendous hustle in the kitchen beforehand, and panic fuss as Pugh repolished the glasses, heated the mist out of the decanter, and practised furtively on a new cocktail with which he meant to galvanize his guests: it was a time when cocktails were taken seriously. After slow cigars and the best brandy they would play auction bridge, or something far more speedily cut-throat like gin-rummy or vingt-et, for Pugh liked the pace of gambling, and if there was not much money in it at least there would be a chance for an argument. He was one of the few authentic characters who would bet half a crown on which fly flew off a window first, and in a conversational gap among men he would pull a half-crown from his pocket and toss it heads or tails.

On summer weekends there were country jaunts in the Ford: Dr Pugh had sold her Austin Seven for £90, only losing £30 on its price new. They had croquet in the garden, the culture of which Pugh directed with great interest and authority, but only directed: he never bent down. His wife had given up riding and golf on her marriage, for Pug declined to "chase a silly little ball". But he was good at tennis, and remarkably crafty at table tennis. Still the best outing he could suggest, however, was a race meeting, and he would go to any neighbouring course except Birmingham itself. He thought that was too near his own manor: he did not want to be bothered by seeing all the pickpockets he had personally prosecuted. He had the strongest antipathy against letting official business or contacts encroach on his off-duty hours. He never brought work home except, before an especially difficult case, to allot it half an hour in a solitary session in the dining-room.

Immediately after the wedding H. T. Pugh had written to H. E. Cullwick: "Dear Bro. Cullwick, Thank you sincerely for your loving kindness to me and mine. You are truly inspired with the Masonic spirit which is shared in abundant measure by your dear wife. . . . Although naturally we are prejudiced judges yet we believe that Mervyn & Vera are divinely chosen the one for the other and that Our Lord & Master blessed their union. . . . Yours fraternally." Mr Cullwick himself had given his son-in-law one piece of advice about women: "Never let 'em know when you're coming home." But Pugh rarely had need to apply it, and only quoted it as a masculine gibe: he changed, indeed, with extraordinary speed to a man of almost rigidly regular habit, and his staff noticed a diminution in the morning choler which they had previously ascribed to a hangover. The 1930's, however, were an age when husband and wife had more mutual independence than thirty years later, and women did not feel deprived or outraged by the frequent evening functions for men only which have now been largely shifted to lunch-time. Pugh would never miss his Lodge Night three times a month, and gradually there were more Masonic obligations. He attended Toc H, and liked his regimental reunion, though he never ordinarily cared to discuss the War.

He contributed enormous warmth and jollity to the family which he had made his centre, but he could frighten them, too, with his strong whims, his savage sensitivity, and a meticulous old-maidishness about his wardrobe. Soon after they were married Pugh—as he was being carefully brushed before he went to the courts—asked his wife to be sure to send a pair of trousers to the cleaners that day. When she went up to fetch them she found two pairs of trousers in his dressing-room. Neither seemed to her to need cleaning, but she dare not wait to put this point to him in the evening, and she knew he was in court all day. She therefore took both pairs of trousers to his office and asked his secretary for help. Miss Selwyn walked into court with the trousers over her arm and interrupted the prosecutor while he selected which of his breeks should be cleaned. Dr Pugh said of her husband, "He was a man who needed a lot of loving." It is a certainty that he got it.

CHAPTER

4

Craftsmanship

SIR Malcolm Hilbery, Mr Justice Hilbery of the King's Bench Division from 1935 to 1962, observed in *Duty and Art in Advocacy*: "Never do you hear an account of the adroit and impeccable examination-in-chief. Yet nothing is more important and nothing better displays the craftsmanship of the master. The establishment of the facts depends upon the witnesses relating them. They will only relate them if questions are put which give them the opportunity to say what is required."

In this craft M. P. Pugh approached mastery. It was his opening statements that the newspapers printed, for nothing could suit the reporters better than a clear outline of all that the prosecution alleged, put together with logic and dramatic skill, and both phrased and delivered in a reaction of shocked horror and condemnation; a statement, above all, which was complete before the case really started, and allowed a busy journalist time to file it without the necessity of hearing the proof slowly substantiated by question and answer at dictation speed. A newspaper report could be complete, from a sub-editor's point of view, by half-past eleven in the morning, for in a major case any refutation of the charges could be ignored, since the defence was reserved for a higher court. Yet a purist in advocacy could deprecate Pugh's openings as being too contrived for a magistrate's court, where there was no jury to arrest with verbal headlines, and condemn some of his cross-examinations as too torrid. It was difficult, however, to fault his examinations-in-chief. Here he displayed the trained quickness of mind that enabled him to steer his case, like a canoe in rough water, stroke by stroke through the cross-currents of unexpected answers and on into the calmer stream that he could generally expect from police evidence. He made a fluid progress to the conclusion he wanted to reach.

In a murder hearing this is often most difficult. The characteristic murder is not witnessed. People may arrive on the scene very soon, but the shock or passion of the moment may make them very unreliable witnesses afterwards. In a murder hearing the Prosecuting Solicitor must mainly rely on these immediate witnesses, and the cooler observation of the police officers who are called. To construct these accounts into logical and convincing indictment can be a matter of great expertise. It is probable that this tribute can be paid to Pugh's handling of the prosecution following the death of Sidney Marston. But it can also be held that the prosecution finally lost the case in the higher court because of the way Pugh had been instructed to handle it, and that incautious admiration for the manner in which Pugh had conducted his earlier examinations brought on the Birmingham Police severe censure from Mr Justice Humphreys.

Sidney Marston, a young grocer's assistant, died in October 1932 at 63 Willows Crescent, Cannon Hill, then a suburban slum by the side of the Warwickshire County Cricket Ground. The first word that was spoken after he was struck was "Murder!" A girl of sixteen, a factory worker named Emily Eleanor Thay, ran out of the doorway screaming, "Murder! Murder! Fetch the police." A passer-by ran up to her. Another woman came out of the house. She looked almost as young as the first, though she was really six years older—her married sister, named Marjorie Kathleen Yellow. Marjorie said to the passer-by, a dentist called Harry Thompson, "Come here and get this man out of the house." "What man?" asked Thompson. Marjorie Yellow replied, "I have never seen him in my life before. He hit me in the mouth. There was a ten-shilling note on the table but now it is gone."

Thompson went into the house. In the hallway a man was leaning against the wall. His face was damaged as if he had been in a fight. Thompson got hold of him and shouted, "What's your game?" Instead of struggling, the man seemed to collapse. "I've done nothing," he said. Thompson tried to get him out

Lord Ilkeston

Birmingham Stipendiary Magistrate for forty years

"The shrewdest dandy in Birmingham"

Herbert Willison, criminal advocate

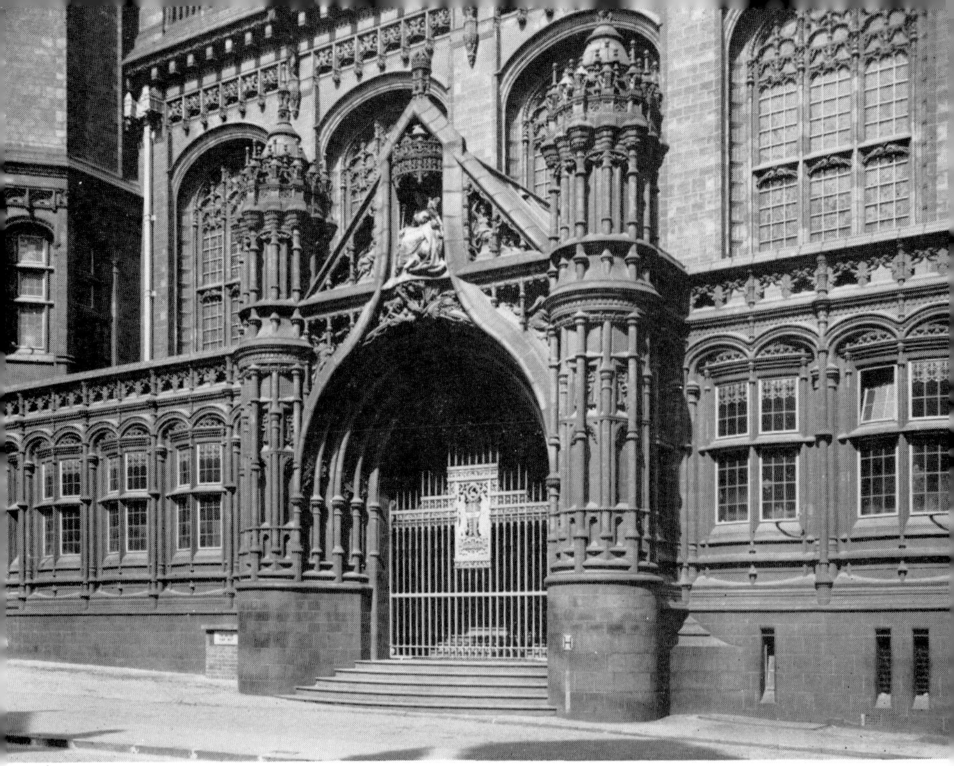

The Victoria Law Courts, Birmingham

Photo Lewis Brown Associates

No. 1 Court, the Victoria Law Courts

of the house, but he could not support his weight and the man sagged to the floor. Marjorie Yellow seemed to be furious with him. "He's only shamming," she said. And then she made a curious remark for one who had "never seen him in my life before". She said, "He has done that before."

The man lay in his overcoat, and Thompson tried to move him, but decided he must be unconscious. He was, in fact, dead. Thompson sent someone to fetch the police and stayed by the body. Marjorie Yellow was talkative. She said that she was making up her face in a bedroom upstairs, and Emily came in from the street and joined her there. They went downstairs, and she saw a man in the living-room. He attacked her, and she resisted. In the struggle she realized that he was trying to stab her with a knife.

The police arrived and examined the body. The man had been stabbed downward in the breast, and the blade of the knife was found in his overcoat pocket. A handle belonging to the knife was on the floor of the hallway. A crumpled ten-shilling note was in a waistcoat pocket. A notebook had the pencilled reminder: "Miss Gwinne"—a mis-spelled version of the name by which Marjorie Yellow was then known. The dead man was identified as Sidney Marston, and shortly before his death he had been sitting in a neighbouring café with two other young men.

The police knew Marjorie Yellow and her family well. She was separated from her husband, and was living in Willows Crescent with another man, named Gwinnell. In the course of fairly jocular remarks during the immediate investigation the police made a note that Marjorie had said, "They don't hang women, do they? Well, you only have to die once. Women go to prison for life, don't they?"

The murder was a Birmingham sensation, but no arrest was made for some time, and the young men with whom Marston had been seen in the café never came forward and were never traced. At the inquest Marjorie Yellow explained the notebook entry which seemed to indicate her name by saying that a young man called Sid had picked her and her sister up some time previously, and had asked them to go dancing with him and a friend, so she had told him where she could be found.

The police still hesitated to make an arrest. What was in fact happening was that M. P. Pugh had sent the files to the Director of Public Prosecutions—as he was bound to do in the early stages of a charge of "causing death", and more rarely before a charge was made—and he had an appointment to consult with the Director in London. He kept this appointment, and was instructed to proceed against both sisters on a charge of murder and to handle the case as the Director's agent. The sisters were therefore arrested and charged, and Pugh prepared the prosecution.

In the Stipendiary's Court, with Willison appearing for the sisters, Pugh opened very strongly and supported his vigorous line through the examinations, exposing the inconsistencies of Marjorie Yellow's story. He gratuitously added that though it was never necessary for the prosecution to advance a motive he adduced a clear motive in this instance. Marjorie Yellow had said that there was a struggle, and that a ten-shilling note which was on the table had disappeared. A screwed-up note was found in Marston's waistcoat pocket, but it had been proved that Marston, a methodical shop assistant, habitually carried paper money in his wallet. Whatever the antecedents of the struggle, it had occurred, and Marston was dead after it, and the two sisters had been in the room with him when the mortal blow was struck. He claimed that there was a *prima facie* case against them, and the magistrate, concurring, committed them for trial.

Pugh was acting on instructions, and it is not unusual for two putative accomplices to be prosecuted on the maximum charge on the assumption that 'something will turn up' to clarify the issue later. But there is no doubt that he was worried by the case. For the first time his wife, who was pregnant, sensed that the office was intruding into the home. The Marjorie Yellow case became a domestic preoccupation.

Herbert Willison got in touch with A. E. Bowker, clerk to Norman Birkett, K.C. When Birkett, who had always been happy in Birmingham, took silk Willison, in his Brummie accent, had blustered to Bowker, "I suppose this will go to your head. You'll soon be asking fifty guineas to come here." But shortly Willison was agreeing to 250 guineas. Now Willison told Bowker that he had obtained a certificate for counsel to defend the two sisters under the Poor Persons Defence Act: would Birkett take the brief for the statutory nominal sum of fifteen guineas? Birkett agreed.

The Birmingham police were still extraordinarily confident. When Birkett, according to his custom, asked to see the scene of the crime he was escorted to Willows Crescent by Superintendent Whitehouse, the officer in charge of the case—viewing a revoltingly squalid bed-sitting room, the only furnished room in the house, which left remarkably poor accommodation for Marjorie Yellow to have made up her face upstairs. The police officer asked Bowker, "Why in the world have you taken this defence? Your chief has the reputation of never having been on the losing side in a murder case. Mark my words, he will lose his record here. This is a certain conviction."[1]

Pugh had briefed Maurice Healy, K.C., to lead Donald (later Mr Justice) Finnemore for the prosecution. Some of the prosecution witnesses gave evidence that seemed to be following almost verbatim the depositions they had signed as a result of Pugh's examinations-in-chief in the lower court. At one point Birkett queried this. At a later point a witness seemed to refresh his memory from a paper he took from his pocket. The judge, Mr Justice Humphreys, asked what it was. The witness revealed that it was a copy of his earlier statement which a police officer had given him on the previous day, and it became clear that these 'cribs' had been widely distributed among the lay witnesses. It was a tribute to Pugh which he did not relish.

The expert witness for the prosecution was the pathologist Sir Bernard Spilsbury, who described the death wound as curving downward and outward, a very difficult wound for Marston himself to have imposed, with the reverse direction making it almost impossible for Marston to have withdrawn the knife which had been found in his overcoat pocket. In his cross-examination Birkett asked Spilsbury how he thought Marston had received the thrust, and the witness said that it would have been from someone face to face with him. Therefore, Spilsbury agreed with Birkett, if Marjorie Yellow had struck the blow Marston and she must have been looking at each other at extremely close quarters.

Birkett seized on this aspect at the conclusion of the prosecution's case, arguing that there was no case to go to the jury. He said that, since the evidence given showed that Marston and Marjorie Yellow knew each other, if Marjorie had struck the blow Marston would have known it, and he would have told Thompson with his dying breath immediately he was questioned, instead of saying, "I have done nothing". He then submitted that

[1] A. E. Bowker, *A Lifetime with the Law* (W. H. Allen, 1961).

there was no evidence at all against Emily Thay. Only one blow had been struck. Only one person had struck it. Both had been charged with the murder itself, without qualification about being accessories before or after the fact. He summarized his submission: "The Crown cannot put a finger on either of them."

The judge upheld him. He directed the jury to find both the prisoners Not Guilty. He then made strong criticism of the practice whereby the police supplied witnesses with copies of their previous evidence—a custom which was not exclusive to Birmingham, nor the rule there, but which ceased after these particular comments. In the turmoil within the Birmingham Police Force following this criticism one police officer ended his life. Pugh had had no part in this method of official prompting, but altogether it had been an unhappy case. He had followed his instructions to proceed against both sisters—and, indeed, the judge had said that there was a *prima facie* case that one of the two struck the fatal blow; but that was not enough for a conviction. At least Pugh could be satisfied that, to twist the maxim, injustice had *not* been seen to be done, but the publicity about the prompting had been deeply disturbing.

Both judges and advocates generally know more about people in the dock than do the members of the jury, but in this case any alert juryman was speedily enlightened. Within weeks of her acquittal Marjorie Yellow was jailed for keeping a disorderly house, and she was later sentenced for stabbing a man with whom she was living.

Pugh had a habit of dropping into the Assize Courts, even during cases on which he was not active, and assessing the form of the counsel engaged. He could be sardonic. "He'll get no bloody place," he would mutter to a newspaper-man of a barrister in action. He could not say this of Birkett, who had conducted an unexpected but extremely sound defence on the point of law. But he had no great opinion of Birkett, though he had retained him in the Power case, and was to serve under him on the Committee on Abortion. Nor, in retrospect, did he give great praise to Marshall Hall. It was a curious antipathy for the nationally acclaimed advocates with whom he showed certain resemblances in style: Birkett, for his painstaking attention to detail, and Marshall Hall, for his gimmickry and occasional theatricality—there was an incident during a flick-knife case when the defence contended that the weapon was only a toy, and Pugh grabbed the exhibit, flicked it, and plunged the blade deep into the desk in front of him, exclaiming scornfully, "A toy!" "I really don't see the need for that," remonstrated the Stipendiary, concerned for the court furniture. It is possible that Pugh, as a big fish in a comparatively small pool, resented the range and impact of the others: there was an occasion when he contemplated making the astonishing leap from Prosecuting Solicitor to Chief Constable of Birmingham. He was at least frank in his enjoyment of publicity. He would cynically justify the adjournment of a case which the defence thought could be disposed of in one sitting by claiming that it would be doubly reported. "Harry," he said to Harry Faber, a solicitor who began to be active in the Birmingham courts in the 1930's and who had reproached him on this count, "you like to see your name in the papers? So do I."

But he still wanted to see his name on the winning side. "Diabolical!" he yelled at Faber when the defence had unexpectedly taken the case. "How did you get her off?" "Don't get excited," urged Faber. "It's all in a day's work. You'll get paid at the end of the week." But Pugh saw the decision as an affront to justice. Pugh, in the main, was remarkably encouraging to promising young solicitors like Faber, and went out of his way to bring them on. Not so Willison, who gave them a rough baptism of fire when they appeared against him, as Faber might in a husband-and-wife case. The interruptions and imprecations flew like grape-shot: "Why? Shut up! Sit down! Oh, siddown, lad!"—all in broadest Brummie tones—with the occasional grinning expiation flung nonchalantly across the court: "Oh, I've got nothing against you, boy, really. You're only the mouthpiece,"[1] jerking his hand towards Faber's client; and the explanation afterwards when Willison excused his simulated indignation: "Faber, my lad, that's where the money comes."

[1] Curiously, the word 'mouthpiece', with its connotation of a bent American attorney, was used without any disparaging implication by Sir Norman Birkett, then Lord Justice of Appeal, in his presidential address to the Holdsworth Club of the Faculty of Law of Birmingham University on the 7th of May, 1954: "The disfavour in which the advocate is sometimes held arises almost wholly from the grave misconception of the advocate's true function. He does not profess to present his own point of view or his own beliefs to the Court. He is there as the mouthpiece of the client to say for him what he would wish to say for himself, were he able to do so with knowledge and understanding."

Pugh saw himself, much more seriously, as an agent of justice. He knew the underworld, and had no mercy on the professional criminal families who were the trigger-spring of much of Birmingham's crime. If his prosecution failed in a higher court he would still give a deterrent warning. One afternoon at the Sessions he watched a man get acquitted on a charge of metal-stealing—he learned accidentally afterwards that one friend had swung the entire jury to record a verdict of Not Guilty, and they were much ashamed later. Pugh sternly called the man as he stepped from the dock: "Half a minute, Jones. You've been a very lucky man. Now, remember. Just be careful!" If Pugh intended to be ruthless he would often warn the defending solicitor: "Your man's a professional receiver, Harry. We've only caught him once, but I'm going to throw everything at him." On the other hand, if having studied a case he thought that, in justice, the charge was severe, he would make the first approach to the defence to reduce it, removing it from trial at the Assize Court to be disposed of in summary jurisdiction: "I shall help you today, boy. Maybe wounding with intent is a bit strong for this chap. You plead unlawful wounding and I'll not press it." And if a revelation occurred during his prosecution examinations that altered the weight of the accusation or exposed a fault in the preparation of the case by his office he would not—as self-important prosecutors do—flannel round the leak in his case and keep the defendant in suspense by asking for a remand for reconsideration. "I withdraw this case," he would say shortly. "The facts do not warrant it."

Advocates in Birmingham claimed that the Prosecuting Solicitor could make a better speech in mitigation than any of them. If he saw factors which could explain the prisoner's behaviour and might affect the sentence, he would persuasively draw them to the attention of the Stipendiary, and the more powerfully if the accused was not represented; if there was an advocate opposite, Pugh appreciated the tactful acknowledgment: "You have heard Mr Pugh say in his usual fair manner . . . and coming from him. . . ." He would advance this mitigation even if the case was to go to the higher court. He had to prosecute a servant girl for infanticide. She had had her baby in her room and wrapped it in paper and put it outside on the window-sill. He told Faber: "Harry, I've been going into this case and I'm inclined to be sympathetic. The girl has been let down. Her employers didn't know she was pregnant, and if she had told them she would have been sacked. She delivered the child herself. She must have had a hell of a time. Anything I can do to help I will." Which meant that after the inevitable committal Pugh would give instructions to counsel to urge these features, and, given a judge of reasonable temper, he could expect the prisoner to be bound over.

It was no real disparagement to Pugh to sneer that he was 'the law man' on the model of the American political district attorney, or to carp that he relished—as he undoubtedly did—this imperial power to proceed with the utmost severity against inveterate criminals, while moderating the crunch of the law on the victims of circumstances. This fatherly discretion was a part of the appurtenances of power that he himself had built up. The Aliens Department of the C.I.D. passed over to him the prosecution of a Danish woman for failing to register as an alien, and for entering the country without the permission of an emigration officer. Mr Charles Ladds, one of the strong solicitor-advocates of the Birmingham courts, defended. The story he elicited in court was pathetic. The woman had fallen in love with a Birmingham man who could not get a divorce. She lived legally in Birmingham for a time, went home to Copenhagen to have her baby, but when she tried to come back was twice refused entry because her lover's divorce had not been obtained. Finally she brought the baby over via Ostend on a weekend ticket, and the divorce was secured, but this time she was refused permission to marry because she had no passport. So the couple lived together until they were caught. Pugh, for his part, declared that the woman had an irreproachable character, and apart from the immigration offence there was nothing against her. He asked for a remand to see what could be done. In the interval he got in touch with the Home Office and received from them the assurance that if he did not press for deportation the Home Office would not exercise its power to expel her, and if he would see that the couple got married—which was all they wanted—a residence permit would be granted.

Frequently Pugh would have to prosecute minors for false declarations of age in order to get married. "They were in love, and this made them do these things" was his theme, and if he could announce that the parents now approved the marriage they had opposed he would make great point of it. Taking the case against a man accused of stabbing his wife's lover, Pugh began, "Whatever one may think about the association of the accused's wife with the wounded man, however one may disapprove of it—and one's sympathy goes out to the prisoner—it has no bearing on the case, although at the proper time I hope it will be brought before the judge who will have to deal with the matter." On Pugh's instructions counsel did bring it before the judge, who sentenced the man to one day's imprisonment. A woman was charged with the attempted murder of her eight-year-old daughter and with attempted suicide. She was trying to shock her husband, who had brought his mistress and baby to live in their home. "One is not anxious to take a woman who has been treated in this abominable and callous manner to the Assizes," said Pugh, and when the husband was called for the prosecution Pugh told him, "You can absolutely and entirely please yourself whether or not you give evidence. What do you want to do?" The husband declined to give evidence and left the box, and at the Assizes made the same decision. No evidence at all was called by the prosecution, and the woman was acquitted. A mother tried to gas her two-year-old baby who was dying of cancer. "I idolized him," she said, "and it was breaking my heart to see him suffer and live." Pugh pleaded: "There is no doubt that this is a case of attempted murder, but it comes within the category of what is known as a mercy killing." At the Assizes the judge bound her over, saying, "You have suffered greatly, and it is quite unthinkable that I should add to that suffering even in the smallest degree."

Even in a minor case Pugh went out of his way to soothe the unnecessary scandal which the most innocent court appearance can breed. He prosecuted a fifteen-year-old boy in the Juvenile Court for a telephone slander. The boy, out of some pique against a neighbour, telephoned the neighbour's wife while the man was out with his dogs, and said, "I think you ought to know what is going on when your husband is supposed to be taking the dogs for a walk. You ought to know that he goes into lanes with a girl." Pugh wanted to be sure that the mud did not stick. He called the wife into the witness-box and asked her, "You don't now believe this allegation against your husband?" "I hope not," she said. "I want to assure you," said Pugh, "from investigations made that there is no truth in it." But he had taken the trouble to have the investigations made.

Pugh's case files show scores of instances of this consideration for ravaged human feelings, and when he drew from the evidence of police officers some indication of the copper's humanity he would look towards the Press and emphasize it: their finding employment for vagrants as they came out of prison; or releasing a reputed thief, imploring him to go straight for Christmas and provide for his wife and family, and, when they had had to take him in again for picking pockets on Christmas Eve, going round to his house to give their own money to his wife and children.

But Pugh never hesitated to use the sword as well as the scales of justice. He could be bitterly tough, even on small matters. When Willison once asked for bail for a man accused of multiple false pretences Pugh rasped, "We don't want the money. We want his body." Prosecuting in a drunken driving charge, Pugh was challenged by the defence Counsel, Peter Thorneycroft, when he asked a lay witness, a bus-driver, what was the condition of the accused after the accident. Mr Thorneycroft objected, "Mr Justice Hawke ruled in the High Court recently that a lay witness is not a proper person to decide between sobriety and drunkenness." He turned to the Stipendiary: "I ask you to uphold that decision." "I have never heard such a ridiculous submission," said Pugh with heat. "It happened at the recent Shrewsbury Assizes," Thorneycroft interjected. "You are not casting aspersions on the judge, are you?" "Oh, no!" said Pugh airily. "Mr Justice Hawke has made a ruling on Euclid." Lord Ilkeston allowed the question, and the bus-driver said the accused was hopelessly drunk. The defendant's passenger was then called. When Pugh asked him the man's condition he replied, "Oh, he was quite sober." Pugh glared at Thorneycroft. "You don't object to that question, do you?" he challenged.

Pugh developed a system of give and take with the Press. He always told a local reporter in advance, "Got a good one for you today", if he thought he had a headline; and if he was aiming for the national Press he would even consult with Ray Hill of the *Daily Mirror* how best to phrase a comment in his opening statement for maximum news value—"Couldn't you put it this way?" Hill would suggest. In return he looked to the Press for space for the deterrent publicity which is one of the policeman's chief aids: the public knowledge available to villains that other villains are being caught. Before Christmas the Chief Constable always organized a very necessary round-up of shop-lifters. Pugh warned the Press, took twenty-six cases in a batch, urging exemplary sentences and securing terms of imprisonment up to six weeks. Then he spoke his sermon: "After these sentences of imprisonment and heavy fines, it is hoped that, as a result of publicity, there will be recognition of the intention to continue to inflict heavy punishment until the menace to traders is stamped out. Shop-lifting in the city is causing the Chief Constable great concern. He feels his responsibility in trying to stamp out what has become a local evil. Most of the thefts are committed, not by poor persons driven to thieve on the impulse of the moment or because they badly need articles for their children and homes, but they are the results of systematic expeditions by people of seemingly good character, of respectable parents and generally earning substantial wages." In a drive against indecent assaults on children—cases which generally require a lengthy hearing—Pugh said, "I am taking two cases today. There have been six such cases in the list this week, ten are to be heard, and there are sixteen pending. I think some public mention should be made of this, in the hope that parents will keep a stricter eye on their children."

In a curious case Pugh prosecuted a motorist for careless driving, after he had lost control of his car, which mounted the footpath and killed a pedestrian. The mildness of the charge was explained when medical evidence was given that the driver suffered from a rare disease called laryngeal vertigo which was incurable, but harmless in itself. Its only effect was that on occasion a cough or a sneeze could make the sufferer black out in a faint for about ten seconds. The driver had experienced this only once before, when he coughed as he lit a cigarette, and he did not then know that it was an abnormal condition. Because it was now diagnosed, and the man could not forecast his next black-out, he had agreed never to drive a motor-car again. "I have no wish to press this case," said Pugh, accepting the medical evidence. "But I have brought it to show that there must be strong confirmatory evidence in such cases, and that a defendant cannot merely say 'I fainted' and expect the case to be dismissed."

But there were some charges which Pugh could never take seriously: fortune-telling, gaming machines—on which he always registered fantastic wins in open court whenever he tried to demonstrate that they were fraudulently fixed—and prosecutions under the old laws regulating drinking clubs and street betting which the police were cynically required to sustain. And it was not always easy to take bigamy seriously. Pugh once prosecuted a woman for bigamy after she had initiated a farcical rearrangement of the marriage laws of the country. On her twenty-first wedding anniversary, after she had borne her husband eleven children, she went to live with another man. Within days the deserted husband and all the surviving children had also migrated to the other home. They thought they had better make it legal, and a bigamous marriage seemed cheaper than a divorce. They therefore went through a ceremony at the Birmingham Register Office at which the husband was the official witness and their nineteen-year-old daughter was the bridesmaid. When later questioned over this Eskimo-style hospitality the original wife said she had done it to give the children a home, while her genuine husband, also happily rehoused, said warmly, "It's the best thing she ever did."

Willison attacked the constant necessity of the police force to put in *agents provocateurs* to prove their charges of street betting and serving liquor to non-members of clubs. But there was no provocation, only sheer daredevil high spirits, behind one licensing prosecution which Pugh took. A charity organizer had used the hall of the Birmingham and District Oddfellows Club in Livery Street for a film show in aid of the Spanish Relief Fund. At the end of the performance the organizer, who was not a member of the Oddfellows Club, told the audience, "If anybody would like a drink you can get one downstairs. If you have any difficulty, just mention my name." This invitation was accepted by some of the audience who did not belong to the club, including two officers of the Customs and Excise.

"I want to emphasize," said Pugh in his statement, "that the Oddfellows Club, which has no fewer than 11,947 members, is a highly respectable institution and has been properly conducted over a long period. The secretary was not present when this remarkable invitation was made to the audience. But the Customs and Excise officers went down to the bar and asked for two beers. They tendered a two-shilling piece, and they got 1*s.* 6*d.* change.

"Which may be one of the reasons," said Pugh thoughtfully, "why the club has 11,947 members."

CHAPTER

5

The Smile on the Face of the Jury

JOHN Bruce Thornton notched a private claim to fame. He boasted that he was the only hard drinker ever to have survived five separate attacks of delirium tremens, and impressively declared that in his most serious bout he had not come to the surface for a month. More publicly, in M. P. Pugh's records, he was the man who planned to kidnap the millionaire Lord Nuffield, hold him to ransom for £100,000, and, if his complicated plot went wrong, dump the industrialist in the North Sea, where he was not intended to come to the surface for ever. What foiled the mechanics of Thornton's scheme was the fact that at the time he intended to complete it he had such an alcoholic hang-over that his nerve failed. And, since Lord Nuffield and two dozen armed policemen were awaiting him anyhow, this spoilt the roundness of the operation from the police viewpoint as well; for instead of Thornton coming to them they had to go and fetch him; and this in turn made the case for the prosecution more difficult than it would otherwise have been. The scheme was so fantastic that it really needed the malefactor to be caught in the act for a jury to be utterly convinced. At Thornton's trial at Birmingham Assizes an extremely able defence counsel had the jury smiling at the apparent absurdity of the plot. M. P. Pugh, asked by the Director of Public Prosecutions to take charge of the case in Birmingham (although the preliminary hearing had been at Oxford), took the smile on the face of the jury very seriously, and determined to wipe it off. The success with which Pugh changed the tone of the trial illustrates the sort of generalship he was expected to display in the final stages of a major trial when, although he had no right of audience at the Assizes, he was still called on to direct the prosecution from the solicitor's bench.

The case began in the police archives on the 10th of May, 1938, when Major Arthur Geoffrey Francis Ramsden drove the dozen miles upstream to Henley from his Thames-side home at Bourne End and told a remarkable story to Superintendent Hudson of the Oxfordshire Police.

Major Geoffrey Ramsden had retired from the Army with a reputation for courage which he kept to himself, though it was known that he had won the D.S.O. and the Cross of the Legion of Honour. There was little else over which he was reticent, and he freely revealed to Superintendent Hudson that, with a wife and six children to support (five of them still at private schools), he was not prosperous. He was a keen and skilful yachtsman, and ten years previously he had had a three-year spell at Cannes carrying on business as a yacht broker, and being also local agent for the Royal Thames Yacht Club. It was at this time, Major Ramsden's story continued, that he met Bruce Thornton.

Thornton occupied a spacious villa at Cap d'Antibes, and was also the owner of a luxurious 52-ton yacht. Both the men and their wives became very friendly, said Ramsden, but when he had to return to England in 1930 the relationship ended. Thornton made a number of visits to Australia, but it appeared that he had not forgotten Major Ramsden. In December 1937 he wrote from Melbourne to his old friend, care of the secretary of the Royal Thames Yacht Club.

"My dear Ramsden," he wrote, "Will be in Europe in the spring of 1938, and if you drop me a line at the Club we might have one or two. Much water has flown beneath the bridge since last we met, and perhaps I may know of something which may interest you." By mischance this letter was not forwarded until the spring, and in the meantime Thornton, having arrived in London, advertised in the *Daily Telegraph* of the 1st of April: "RAMSDEN, Major G., late of Cannes. Please communicate with B. T. of Antibes. Box —." The Major did communicate, and on the 11th of April Thornton came down to see him at Bourne End. They drove around to a few country pubs in Major

Ramsden's small eight-horse-power car, and on the way passed Huntercombe, the country house of Lord Nuffield. Thornton said he would like Ramsden to take him sightseeing in England, and they really ought to have a larger car. If Ramsden would put in his small car towards it, and Thornton paid the difference for a better car, Ramsden could keep the car when Thornton left the country.

Thornton stayed the night at Bourne End, and the next day the two men went about again, through the delightful riverside villages. At the King's Arms in Cookham they had "one or two" and passed on to Bray. Then they went to Reading to find a better car, and selected a Ford V8 which they agreed to collect in a week. They continued in the old car, and in the afternoon passed Huntercombe again. It was at this point, Ramsden related, that Thornton first suggested his strange enterprise.

"Well, Ramsden," he said, "how are you off financially?"

"Oh, pretty hard up," replied the Major. He had been reduced, in fact, to making pin-tables in a workroom in his house and trying to sell them to clubs. But he had not been successful.

"Laddie," said Thornton, "I can put you in the way of making a lot of money. Thousands!"

Ramsden thanked him and waited for elaboration.

"I have nothing like as much money myself as I had when we knew each other at Cannes," Thornton continued. "I've got enough to exist on, but existence is not good enough for me. Unless I have a lot of money I would rather be dead."

Thornton then revealed that he had been considering for a long time the possibility of kidnapping Lord Nuffield. He said he had once travelled in a ship with him, and knew the type of man he was. Kidnapping ought to be quite easy in England because it was rarely attempted, and millionaires were not in a state of constant suspicion. Thornton then hinted at the part that might be played in such a coup by Major Ramsden. He was an experienced and capable yachtsman, and if Nuffield were kidnapped a yacht might be the best way of keeping him safe.

Having implanted the suggestion, Thornton took it no further for the moment. They were to meet again in a week to pick up the new car. "But in future," he said, "we shall never mention the name of Nuffield. We shall refer to him as 'Kelly', since it will not be safe to talk about him by name."

In the following week the two men met and went to Reading

to pick up the car. Ramsden traded in his baby Austin, and Thornton paid over £200 as the balance for the V8. Since Thornton did not want to discuss his further plans in a pub, they drove to a field at Turner's Court where Major Ramsden had some rough shooting. There Thornton elaborated his design. He said that he favoured a yacht for the kidnapping, since it would not be so easy to trace as if they used a house to hold Kelly. "Do you know of a quiet place on the coast where yachts can go and where Kelly can be loaded?" he asked. Ramsden said that Pin Mill, half a dozen miles from Ipswich, would be as good a place as any. Thornton said that Kelly would have to be watched, and Ramsden was the man for that. "We must find out what Kelly's movements are. If once I can get into his presence I can guarantee to bring him out," he promised. Ramsden asked how he would manage that. Thornton said he might get into Kelly's presence by pretending to be a Special Branch detective from Scotland Yard. "If I can get him alone," he declared, "I can bring him out at the point of a pistol, and then, if we get him into a car, you can drive him down to Pin Mill, or wherever it is. Once he is on the yacht it is easy enough."

Thornton then told Major Ramsden that he would have some surgical instruments aboard the yacht, and he would threaten to perform an operation on Kelly without an anæsthetic. "Then he will have to sign what I want." Thornton planned that three documents should be signed. One would be a letter to his wife or secretary saying that he, Kelly, had been unavoidably called away and his engagements for the immediate future must be cancelled. The second would be a letter to Kelly's bankers telling them that a Dr Webb would call the next day, and they were to give him a letter of credit for £100,000. Thornton's signature as Dr Webb was to be put on that letter so that the bankers could identify it when he called for the credit. The third letter would be one from Kelly introducing Dr Webb to the bankers.

In further elaboration Thornton said that he would have to disguise himself. He had a red wig, which he would wear, and four gold caps which could be fitted on to his front teeth. He would get corsets to slim his somewhat bulky figure. He would apply peroxide to lighten any part of his hair not covered by the wig, and he would put the same bleach on his eyebrows and moustache.

"You can guard Kelly while I get the letter of credit from the bankers," Thornton told Ramsden. "I shall have to go to France to cash the credit, because French banknotes are far less easy to trace than British notes. You keep Kelly on the yacht for a week, then take him back to land and release him. Put adhesive tape over his eyes so that he can't see where he is going. Drop him off in a field somewhere and drive away. It had better be a field," he added solicitously, "because if he's staggering about in a road at night trying to get the tape off his eyes he might be run over.

"Then you can meet me in Tréport"—Le Tréport is on the coast of France, between Le Touquet and Dieppe—"and we can share up.

"But," he added, "I suppose it's always possible that Kelly can play us false. You had better get a wireless set so that you can listen in on the day I go to get the letter of credit. If you hear that I have been arrested you will know that Kelly has not played the game with us. Take him out to sea and dump him. But otherwise, if all goes well, meet me at Tréport." And with this distinct reversal of concern for the safety of the victim, Thornton ended the outline.

It was a fantastic proposal, none the less unrealistic, from Major Ramsden's point of view, in the consideration that once he was lumped with Kelly on the yacht there was no mortise in the plan requiring that Thornton ever needed to see him again. But the next day the two men drove to Suffolk and inspected Pin Mill, in the Orwell estuary, and later made inquiries about craft. Within two days they had approved an eleven-ton yacht called *Pierrette*, and made arrangements to charter it for a month at eight guineas a week. At this point Major Ramsden became ill, and it was not until the 3rd of May that he met Thornton again. There was a wealth of new suggestions to assimilate. Thornton thought that the car they had bought, and which was to be used for the kidnapping, should carry false number-plates, and told Ramsden it was his job to get them. He was also to acquire some writing paper with the Morris Motors heading, as used by Kelly's company. It would be necessary to remove the internal mirror in the kidnap car so that Kelly could not recognize anyone in the back. In order to disguise Ramsden while he was guarding Kelly on the yacht, he was to go into his presence only when wearing a potato sack over his head, through the mesh of which he could see his victim but not be identified. Chains and padlocks would also be necessary to bind their captive, and Ramsden began the ploy by immediately going out and buying a dog-chain. But the next morning he went to Scotland Yard.

Major Ramsden was listened to, but, inexplicably, no action was taken following his disclosure. Ramsden had an appointment with Thornton in six days' time, and excusably thought that there would be developments within that period. But on the 10th of May (when he was to keep a further appointment with Thornton that evening) he drove to Henley and told his story again, this time to the Oxfordshire Police. He met Thornton later in the day and tried to dissuade him from going on with the plot. Thornton's only reaction was, "My dear man, you are not pulling your weight."

Superintendent Hudson at Henley was not pooh-poohing the conspiracy, and Major Ramsden was soon repeating his story to Captain Arbuthnot, the Chief Constable of Oxfordshire. The captain got in touch with Lord Nuffield (who was most exhilarated at the prospect of being kidnapped), and a meeting was arranged between the Chief Constable, Lord Nuffield, his secretary Mr Alfred Hobbs, and Major Ramsden. Lord Nuffield was keen to go through with the kidnapping, providing he could be given in advance as many details as possible. For the sake of his wife, whom he did not want to be worried, he asked if the operation could be done at the Morris Works at Cowley, rather than at his home, Huntercombe. Since Thornton had not yet decided on what pretext he should gain admission to Nuffield's office, "Kelly" himself suggested to Major Ramsden that Thornton should say he was a doctor who wanted to talk about the special children's orthopædic hospital which Nuffield had founded near Oxford. Ramsden thanked him for the thought, and added that he was supposed to get hold of some Morris Motors writing-paper, and, as things now stood, he would rather be given it than have to steal it. Mr Hobbs promptly gave Major Ramsden a sheaf of notepaper and envelopes.

Lord Nuffield's decision to be kidnapped at Cowley rather than at Huntercombe was a disappointment to Captain Arbuthnot, who found that the climax of the plot was being transferred out of his administrative area. He immediately got in touch with Mr C. R. Fox, the Chief Constable of Oxford City, and begged the privilege of being in at the death. Mr Fox ordered inquiries at

Scotland Yard's Criminal Records Office for any dossier on Thornton, and received most interesting information in return.

Thornton had no convictions, but the Metropolitan Police held the details of a most interesting life. He had been born Patrick Boyle Tuellman, the son of a German watch-maker and his British wife. Soon after leaving school he emigrated to America. In 1915, at the age of twenty-five, he returned to England, and was engaged as a male nurse to an invalid in Blackpool. Soon he had married a relative of his employer. The marriage was unhappy, he was drafted into the wartime army, but was soon discharged and remarried his wife in Birmingham, this time under the name of John Bruce Thornton. Within months he had left her, and she shortly afterwards died, leaving a considerable fortune which Thornton could not claim because it was tied up in Chancery. Thornton married again in 1919 and was divorced four years later. By now he was a member of the Royal Thames Yacht Club, and successively the owner of expensive yachts. He was, in fact, living on blackmail. He had demanded the sum of £170,000 from an Indian prince, and the man had paid up about half this sum, including an annuity of £500 a year. The victim was willing to allow the police to prosecute for blackmail, but the India Office had stepped in and forbidden the action on the grounds that, however camouflaged in court, the prince would be recognized, and the consequent repercussions would be politically too severe. Eventually the prince had bought the incriminating documents for which he was being blackmailed by payment of a lump sum, and Thornton had promptly blackmailed him with photostat copies. But the annuity had been stopped in 1937, which was the reason for Thornton's comparative poverty at the moment. Since his divorce in 1923 Thornton had married twice more, making his fourth wife and fifth ceremony, but when he left Melbourne he had been living with another woman. In his general habits he was a drunkard.

This was the man who, on the 19th of May, was vacating the flat he had taken at 8 Knaresborough Place, Earls Court, and preparing for his coup with Ramsden. The Major picked up Thornton with his heavy cases in the big Ford, and on the drive to Oxford passed on Lord Nuffield's suggestion that he should seek an interview posing as a doctor. "What!" exclaimed Thornton scornfully. "Every doctor in England is trying to get hold of Nuffield to get money out of him. Sheer madness! No,

I shall say I am a journalist writing for the American papers on commercial magnates in Europe. I will ask him for an interview, and when I get it I will talk about my interest in orthopædic work. I will try to get Nuffield to say that he will take me over the orthopædic hospital near the Morris works. If I can get him in the car peacefully in that way it will be excellent. If I can't I shall have to threaten him with my pistol. Once we get him in the car I can keep him quiet with my pistol, and you can drive us down to Pin Mill." The pseudonym 'Kelly' was abandoned.

Major Ramsden drove Thornton past the Morris works so that he could have a look at the site, and turned east for the Essex coast. On the next day they hired a typewriter. Thornton sat in the car in a lane near Colchester and, using driving gloves so that there should be no fingerprints on the paper, wrote a letter to Lord Nuffield asking for an interview and saying that, in two days' time, "I will take the liberty of 'phoning you asking when you can grant me an interview". He assured Lord Nuffield, "I am not interested in seeking financial assistance in any shape or form, either for business or charitable purposes."

That night the two men stayed at a hotel in West Mersea, the Essex haven where the yacht *Pierrette* was moored. In the bedroom which they shared Thornton unpacked his red wig and put it on, showing where he would need to bleach any hair that showed. He fitted the gold caps on his front teeth. He had now urged that Ramsden too should be disguised, in chauffeur's uniform, and that any hair which showed under his driver's cap should be darkened, not peroxided, and Ramsden's eyebrows and moustache also. He produced the tints and eyebrow pencil to do this. Thornton then played with two automatic pistols which he had along with three ammunition clips in his luggage. The next day, whipped on by Thornton, Ramsden bought a chauffeur's peaked cap, a white collar and black tie, and padlocks and stronger dog-chains to replace the chains he had already bought, which Thornton said were too weak. After making these purchases Major Ramsden said he was going out to buy some tobacco; instead he telephoned the Oxfordshire Police to report progress, and to try to pinpoint the date of the interview between Thornton and Lord Nuffield.

On Sunday the 22nd of May Ramsden sailed the boat *Pierrette* from West Mersea to Pin Mill, and Thornton made the journey by car. The next day they set out to drive towards Oxford. Both men were on edge. As Ramsden later said, "I was travelling about with a man carrying a couple of guns, and I was getting jumpy." Thornton told him he was in no state to drive, and took the wheel. But, when it came to the pitch of telephoning Lord Nuffield, as had been arranged for this day, Thornton said, "I'm no good on the telephone. You telephone Nuffield. Put on a trace of an American accent. But don't overdo it."

Major Ramsden went to a public telephone, called Lord Nuffield's secretary, announced his true identity, and was told that the letter requesting an interview had been received and an appointment was fixed for 6 P.M. the next night. A heavily armed party was detailed to receive the kidnappers, and for this reason Nuffield had fixed the time of the interception at the Morris factory after working hours.

Ramsden rejoined Thornton in the car, and they drove to Thame, where they booked in at the famous Spread Eagle Hotel. It was still afternoon, and Thornton said he had to start peroxiding the fringes of his hair. He tossed across to Major Ramsden a remarkable document, and asked him to type it while Thornton bleached his hair. This script (which Thornton planned to place on Lord Nuffield's desk under his eyes if there was anyone else in the office at the time) read:

> To Viscount Nuffield. Read this carefully before passing any remark and do not show it to any other person.
>
> 1. I am packing two automatic pistols of large calibre and will immediately shoot you through the guts if you attempt to raise alarm or suspicion. *Any help will be too late to help you.*
> 2. You will ask me to come and see your children's hospital.
> 3. Cancel any appointments which you may have for today.
> 4. Walk out with me to my car and my chauffeur will do the rest. Do not on your way out attempt to make a run for it. It means instant death to you and anyone who attempts to interfere.
> 5. Smile, chat and be cheery even if it hurts. Do not raise suspicion anywhere, or ——.
> 6. I am a quick and accurate shot with a gun, but do exactly what you have been told and you have nothing to fear.
> 7. Place this letter on your desk with the remark: "The writer of this letter is a close personal friend of mine."
> 8. Dismiss anyone who may be in your office.
> 9. Do not attempt to leave me under any pretext whatsoever.

10. Offer me a cigarette before the car starts, and light one yourself.
11. Make sure we are not followed by anyone of your folk. It is fatal for you.
12. Jump to it. I am in a hurry.

When Ramsden had painfully typed this long ultimatum Thornton, still busy with his make-up, dictated a draft telegram which was to be sent after the kidnapping. It was addressed to Nuffield's secretary and read: "Hobbs, Morris Motors, Cowley. Unavoidably called away. Cancel all appointments for next week. Writing. Nuffield."

Thornton decided it was time to have a few drinks.

Back in their bedroom before dinner, Thornton demonstrated to Ramsden with some pride the body harness worn underneath his waistoat, which held a Browning automatic in an open-ended holster under his left armpit. "The beauty of this," he claimed, "is that it is easy to draw for ordinary use, but if I am suddenly attacked from behind I can fire the pistol under my arm still in its holster and only singe the back of my jacket." He examined his other pistol, a Mélior automatic, but slipped the clip out before he put it away. He had tried on his corsets in order to adjust his body harness correctly. Now, somewhat exhilarated, he put on his wig to match his bleached fringes, adjusted the gold caps on his teeth, and ran rapidly through the material requirements for the morrow. "Number-plates!" he snapped to Ramsden. "What are the new numbers?" Major Ramsden had given to the Oxfordshire Police the task of getting false number-plates, and he had arranged to pick them up in the morning; but, fortunately, he remembered the number that had been ordered, and smoothly told Thornton "UD 9850." "Where's the licence disc?" asked Thornton. He found the road taxation licence which had been taken from the windscreen of the Ford V8, dropped on ink eraser to delete the genuine number, ADD 963, and passed the paper to Ramsden to write in the false number. "Now, your props," he said to Ramsden. "Check: chauffeur's rig." "At home," said Ramsden. "Cap." "Yes." "Grease-paint"—for Thornton had now decided that Ramsden should tint his face darker as well as deepening the colour of his hair and moustache. "Yes," said Ramsden. "Hair-dye, eyebrow pencil, chains, padlocks, adhesive plaster. . . ." Everything was declared in order.

"Now, dinner," said Thornton.

They dined extremely well, in the tradition of the Spread Eagle at Thame. Thornton wined even more definitively, and finished with half a bottle of port. He was dead drunk when he went to bed, and he woke with a colossal hangover which pick-me-ups could not touch. Groaning, and little more than half-conscious, he allowed Ramsden to drive him to the Clarendon Hotel in Oxford and went straight to bed. Ramsden took the car towards his home, and was helped by the police at Henley to attach the false number-plates that had been procured over the top of the Ford's genuine plates. Then he went to Bourne End, tinted his face and darkened his hair and moustache, donned a chauffeur's double-breasted jacket, cap, and black tie, and drove to Oxford in the late afternoon.

Chief Constable Fox had drafted a powerful reception party to deal with the kidnapping at the Morris works at Cowley. Two dozen of what he described as the 'toughest nuts' among his detectives had arrived at the factory. All were armed. One was dressed as the commissionaire, one sat at the reception desk, and another strong man waited behind the door of the room into which Thornton was to be shown. Lord Nuffield had pleaded that the kidnapping should be allowed to go through as far as the actual hold-up. He said that, being on the alert, he could give Thornton what he termed his "mechanic's punch", of which he was very proud, which ought to settle him. Mr Fox replied that it only needed one detail to go wrong with Nuffield's suggestion and there would be a Chief Constable walking around looking for a job. He had already consulted the Director of Public Prosecutions about the extent of evidence needed to prove a kidnapping, and was assured that it was only necessary for Thornton to enter the works for the file to be complete. But, in case Thornton did manage to shoot his way out, Mr Fox sent armed detectives in two cars to set up road blocks outside the factory, which could be closed as soon as the Ford car had driven in.

At the Clarendon Hotel Thornton had awoken from a wretched sleep, still trembling and dazed from his alcoholic bout, and found that he was in no condition to perform the slightest feat of daring. Miserably, he dressed. Even the thought of putting on the corset filled him with nausea, and he packed it in a case. He pushed into an attaché-case the Mélior automatic, the ammunition, the wig, and the gold tooth-caps. But there was nowhere to pack his Browning, so he donned his body harness and put the pistol, unloaded, into its armpit holster. At 5.30 P.M. he left the Clarendon to keep his appointment in the street with Ramsden. As he got into the car Ramsden, fully made up as a swarthy chauffeur, noticed that though the edges of Thornton's hair were lightened he was not wearing the red wig. "The wig got burnt, by accident," said Thornton. "A candle fell on it. It's all off. Drive away fast, and we'll have to change those number-plates quickly."

Ramsden talked as he drove, but drove towards Cowley, some three miles from the Clarendon Hotel. "If we do not keep the appointment with Nuffield tonight," he said, "we are not likely to get another." "Then telephone him and make some excuse," said Thornton. "Say that the car has broken down and we cannot get along tonight."

Ramsden drove towards Cowley for as long as he dared, but when Thornton saw a telephone kiosk he had to get out and use it. Ramsden called the Morris works, was put on to the Chief Constable, and said, "Thornton has got a hangover. He won't do it. He's in no condition to, anyway."

Mr Fox let out a howl of dismay. "Where are you?" he asked. Ramsden gave the position of the kiosk. "You're not even inside our road blocks," said the Chief Constable. And then, with remarkably quick thought, he said, "Tell Thornton this kiosk was out of order and you have to drive to another. Go to . . ." and he detailed the position of another kiosk in the Oxford Road 350 yards from the works which was plain enough for a stranger like Ramsden to find. "Get inside that kiosk and stay inside. We are coming to get him, and there may be some shooting."

Ramsden rang off and obeyed. Mr Fox turned to Captain Arbuthnot, who had insisted on being in at the death, though Cowley was out of his territory. "A car, quick," said Mr Fox.

Swiftly the drama changed to farce. The police of 1938 were not so mobile as they later became, and all the cars had been sent away to form road blocks. None of the senior officers had brought his private vehicle, and the car park was empty. They were in the middle of the biggest motor-car factory in Britain and entirely without transport. "Well, you'd better take mine," said Lord Nuffield, whose car was invisible, in a private garage. The police ran after Lord Nuffield to where it was kept. It was a Wolseley with a strange and ornate fascia board. "Who is going to drive this?" asked Mr Fox. "I'll have a go," said Inspector W. J. Barnett,[1] and got into the driver's seat. The Deputy Chief Constable, Superintendent Goodchild,[2] got in beside him. Mr Fox and Captain Arbuthnot got into the back. All had their arms at the ready, but Captain Arbuthnot, instead of carrying a revolver, had insisted on bearing a 12-bore shotgun, the muzzle of which protruded to Mr Goodchild's backside and concentrated his thoughts during the hectic journey on the position of the Captain's trigger-finger.

The Wolseley came up behind the stationary Ford. The police burst out, simultaneously opened both rear doors of the Ford, and threw themselves on Thornton in the back seat. They pinioned his arms and searched him for weapons, finding only the empty Browning. They drove him into the Morris works for preliminary questioning, and brought Ramsden separately in Nuffield's car. Lord Nuffield showed Ramsden a lavatory where he could wash off his make-up, and came to have a look at Thornton in the waiting-room where he was held while the Ford was thoroughly searched. Thornton was not aggressive, but seemed almost too shaken to recognize his intended victim. "I am the man you came to collect," said Nuffield. In the car and its baggage the police found the Mélior pistol and much ammunition, the corsets, wig, and tooth-caps, make-up and hair-dye, the chains and padlocks and sticking-plaster, and the amazing twelve-point letter announcing that Lord Nuffield would be shot through the guts unless he co-operated. Mr Fox, after cautioning Thornton but not charging him, began to question him. Thornton was too nervous to answer very coherently. "I have been ill," he said. "I had too much to drink last night. Listen," he begged, "there was half a bottle of whisky in my car. Let me just have one drink from it, and I'll be much better." Recognizing the alcoholic withdrawal symptoms, Mr Fox allowed him to have a couple of tots for recovery. (Thornton subsequently alleged at the preliminary hearing that he had been plied with liquor to induce him to talk, and thus became the last prisoner Mr Fox ever gave a drink to.) Whether the whisky raised Thornton's condition from four drinks below par to two below, or to par, or even above par, he was refreshed and coherent enough to give a positive statement in explanation of

[1] Now Chief Constable of Lincolnshire.
[2] Later Chief Constable of the West Midlands.

his present position, and one which he clung to throughout his trial. He said that an appointment had been made with Lord Nuffield in order to interest him in a revolutionary carburettor which Ramsden was trying to market. He habitually carried firearms, and had nowhere but the holster to put the Browning. When Mr Fox suggested that Thornton had intended to kidnap Lord Nuffield (and the twelve-point ultimatum strongly supported that premise) Thornton said the suggestion was completely untrue, and the letter was a part of a cinema script he was writing. Fox said, "Isn't the reason you telephoned Lord Nuffield to put off the interview because you had lost your nerve?" Thornton replied, "Do I look nervous? Not at all!" And at that time he seemed to be telling the truth. Fox asked, of Thornton and Ramsden, "Are you two fellows afraid of each other?" Thornton said, "No, Ramsden is not afraid of anything or anybody. He is a good scout, but I think he is half mad."

The carburettor theme, the film-script ultimatum, and the suggestion that a half-crazed Ramsden had invented the whole incredible kidnap plot remained the bulwarks of Bruce Thornton's defence, and the subsequent discovery aboard the well-stocked boat *Pierrette* of further chains and padlocks and the surgical instruments with which, according to Major Ramsden, Lord Nuffield was to be threatened with vivisection did nothing to damp the theme. Thornton was committed from the Oxford Police Court to take his trial at Birmingham Assizes on four charges which virtually boiled down to two: possessing firearms and ammunition with intent to endanger life, and inciting Major Ramsden to conspire with him to kidnap Lord Nuffield and hold him to ransom. He had been vigorously defended at Oxford by Mr A. J. Flint, and for the trial Mr Norman Birkett had been retained to lead Mr Flint. But Birkett was detained on the Barbara Hutton/Count Reventlow marital case and Mr Arthur Ward took over the defence. "And a damned good job he is making of it" was the gloomy tribute, after the first day, of M. P. Pugh, who had been asked by the Director of Public Prosecutions to take charge of the case in Birmingham and instruct counsel for the prosecution, Mr W. H. Cartwright Sharp, K.C., and Mr John Foster. "He is making bricks without straw," Pugh added, "but he is making a very clever defence."

The preposterous extravagance of the alleged plot could be used as one of the defence's principal weapons, and Mr Ward was taking full advantage of it. The prosecution had done something to prepare the jury for absurdities to follow. "The facts I have to reveal to you are not common in regard to crime in this country," commented Mr Sharp in his opening. "They sound far-fetched, fantastic, more fit for melodrama or the penny dreadful than fitting the facts of crime as we know it ordinarily in this country. The methods of the gangster are not usual in this country, and a crime so desperate in its nature seems foreign to the English criminal. But an attempt to kidnap is a serious and desperate crime, and the facts I must reveal to you are, in my submission, of a desperate effort to kidnap Lord Nuffield and extort from him by threats £100,000."

The impressive summary of the facts which followed, as stately as the drift of a Spanish galleon, was inevitably pushed periodically off course by the almost unacceptable burlesque of some of the incidents that had to be narrated: the Kelly references, the threatened vivisection, the wig and corsets, and the twelve-point 'letter of introduction'. And when, towards the end of the day, the first witnesses were put up, Mr Ward, as nimble as an English man-o'-war, was able almost to dance around them, firing in a burst of ridicule first from one quarter, then from another. With the owner of the yacht *Pierrette*, who gave brief evidence for the prosecution, Mr Ward was able to discuss "that popular yachting station, Pin Mill: it is not the sort of place you would choose to take a manacled viscount in a dinghy from the shore to a yacht about a hundred yards out?" "I should think not," replied the yachtsman.

When Mr Hobbs, Lord Nuffield's secretary, submitted to cross-examination he contributed as freely as Mr Ward to the air of hilarity that was creeping over the court. Mr Ward established that Nuffield was inundated with begging letters, all of which were "dealt with under a microscope", and anyone wishing to see him would have the greatest difficulty in getting past the protective screen of guards and aides.

"So was not the kidnapping plot in reality personally arranged by Lord Nuffield and Major Ramsden?" Mr Ward asked.

Mr Hobbs paused. "I think the idea was that if someone was coming to see Lord Nuffield with loaded guns it would be as well if he came on a day when he was expected," he said. The court rocked with laughter.

Mr Ward continued, "Lord Nuffield was asked, 'Will next

Tuesday, at six o'clock, suit for you to be kidnapped?' "

"I think Lord Nuffield felt it would be as well to have his defences ready," Mr Hobbs commented.

The laughter was unabated when Mr Ward went on to suggest the conspicuous incongruity of a Ford car being used by kidnappers inside a Morris factory. "If a Ford V8 car should stop outside the offices of the Morris works, that would be a matter that anyone seeing it would have impressed on his mind with horror?"

The atmosphere grew more serious when Major Ramsden, the principal witness for the prosecution, was called. But he had completed only a fraction of his evidence in chief when proceedings were ended for the day. In conference afterwards with prosecution counsel and the Oxford senior police officers M. P. Pugh made disconsolate prophecies of the treatment Ramsden would suffer from Ward.

When Ramsden continued his evidence next day Arthur Ward took the opportunity to make a point—which he was to hammer at by reference through the day—that Thornton, although he carried firearms, had never been known to use them. Ramsden was describing the scene in the hotel at West Mersea when Thornton put on the red wig, "completely altering his appearance", and displayed the two pistols. The wig was shown in court, and at the sight of it Thornton was observed to smile broadly as if to indicate "How ridiculous!" When the automatic pistols were produced as exhibits for identification by Ramsden the judge observed, with a not unexpected wry caution, "Somebody has taken the trouble to see that these are unloaded?"

Ward burst in like a sprinter. "They never have been loaded, my Lord," he said. "If the pistol has been loaded it has been done since it left our possession." He found more than one opportunity later to refer to Thornton's virginal record with weapons.

Mr Ward began his cross-examination by an outright attack on Ramsden's credibility. He obtained admissions of a number of judgments for debt which had been secured against the witness, and declared, "I suggest that shows you to be a dishonourable man." The judge, Mr Justice Wrottesley, discounted this. "I think all that is a matter of comment," he said. Incisively Mr Ward brought up the subject of smuggling—it was Thornton's explanation that he had come from Australia to seek reacquaintance with Major Ramsden, as a practical yachtsman who with Thornton could smuggle cigarettes into France and bring brandy, wines, and silk stockings back. Major Ramsden admitted that a smuggling proposition had been discussed.

Again and again Mr Ward came back to the sheer incredibility of the alleged kidnapping plot. Lord Nuffield was to be taken on a four-hour car journey through towns as large as Ipswich and Colchester in a motor-car that had no blinds to its windows. "And if you got in a traffic jam, there would be the man chained and with adhesive tape over his eyes. . . . At a public place in the open at Pin Mill you are going to leave the two in the motor-car; you are going round to get the dinghy, and then you have to bring it back, and all the time this man is to remain with Lord Nuffield sitting in a motor-car; then you have to get him from the motor-car into the dinghy? The whole thing is so ridiculously fantastic that one cannot imagine it in this country or anywhere else. As for the ransom, do you think it is possible for a prisoner in a yacht to sit down and ask his bankers to pay to a man, 'Dr Webb', £100,000? Do you think that when the man goes as 'Dr Webb' the bankers are going to make out a letter of credit for £100,000? The whole thing is so fantastic that no-one would dream of putting forward such a scheme at all. I suggest it is false from start to finish."

"I say," replied Major Ramsden, "that it is definitely true in every word I have said."

"*You* suggested Pin Mill," Mr Ward told Ramsden. "You went to Pin Mill to find a yacht; you got the false number-plates for the car; you bought the chains and the padlocks; you bought the chauffeur's cap; you telephoned to make the appointment with Lord Nuffield; you typed the twelve-point letter; you wrote the telegram for Hobbs; you altered the figures on the motor-licence; and you altered the name of the motor-car on the licence. Is that true?"

"Yes, I did all these things at Thornton's request."

"Every document in this case from start to finish, with the exception of the signature to the first letter [requesting an interview from Nuffield] and one other exhibit in this case—every document of any sort or kind in this case was all prepared by you. Am I right?"

"You are," said Ramsden. "It was my object to frustrate Thornton's plan."

"And it would be a very nice thing, having frustrated this scheme, to see Lord Nuffield then and say, 'See what I have saved you from!' "

"I did not think of that at any time."

"It would be very nice for you to get a cheque with the full name of Lord Nuffield at the bottom of it?"

"I had no idea that the police were going to mention my name to Lord Nuffield."

Then Mr Ward, as a final, visual demonstration of the fantasy in the kidnapping plot, turned from the passionate and eloquent clash of facts to which the duel had mounted, and reduced the whole proceedings once more to pantomime.

"Stand up," he told Thornton. The prisoner rose to his feet in the dock.

"You ask us to believe that this man," Mr Ward told Ramsden, "intended to execute a serious and desperate kidnapping, seriously disguised in a wig like *that*." And he stepped and reached and brought the red wig down on Thornton's head. "Is the wig on Thornton the same way as when you saw it in the hotel?"

"Yes," said Ramsden, "as far as I recollect."

But many in the court were laughing. And, even as M. P. Pugh scowled at them from his seat, the jury were undoubtedly laughing, too. Thornton was facing Ramsden, and the Major did not notice any strange effect. But Thornton was wearing the red wig far forward of his natural hairline, and from any other angle but straight ahead the hair-piece looked indescribably comic.

The judge interposed and stifled the ripple of laughter and relief. "From where I sit," he observed, "Thornton's grey hair is showing. Was there any grey hair visible when Thornton tried on the wig at the hotel?"

"No, my Lord," said Major Ramsden, "I don't think there was."

Mr Ward put no more questions, and the charade was virtually the end of the day's hearing. M. P. Pugh was livid with anger as he strode into the library at the Victoria Courts for the conference he had called for the end of the day. He took the incident of the wig far more seriously than counsel or Chief Constable Fox. "The jury were laughing!" he exclaimed in horror. "We've got to knock that laugh off their —— faces." And he used an alliterative adjective. "As for all this business about Thornton never firing a shot, we've been caught short. What about Southampton? We knew about Southampton. Well, we've got to take immediate steps about that. The trouble is, can we get the woman, and can we get her here on time?"

But it was the wig, the wig, that he kept coming back to as he paced restlessly across the library. "Can we get an actor?" he asked. "Get an actor to show us how to fit it so that it appears to be natural hair. We can put him in the box and wipe that smile . . . BARNETT ! ! ! . . ." he exploded. "Are you wearing it?"

Inspector Barnett had come into the library to speak to Chief Constable Fox. He had been fooling with the exhibits while checking them, and had put the wig on, to find that it fitted him perfectly.

The group in the library pressed round the Inspector to examine him for traces of his own hair.

"This is what we'll do . . ." said M. P. Pugh.

Next morning it was the turn of the police officers to give evidence. Before the hearing began Inspector Barnett, wearing the red wig, walked about the precincts of the court in and out of the crowd which, as was normal, hung about the hall and corridor waiting for proceedings to start. He was alert for any expression that there was anything peculiar about him, but he observed no undue curiosity. The case was resumed. Mr Fox was the first witness. He described the arrest, the prisoner's statements, and his answers when charged. Then Mr Cartwright Sharp said, "Call Inspector Barnett."

The Inspector entered the courtroom, bareheaded but wearing the wig. He went into the box and took the oath. He gave his name and rank and Force.

Mr Cartwright Sharp's first question captured the jury's interest. "What size hat do you wear?"

"Six and seven-eighths," said Barnett.

"What size hat does the prisoner wear?"

"Six and seven-eighths."

"Are you wearing the wig, exhibit 37?"

"Yes, sir."

"Have you been wearing it all this morning about the court precincts?"

"Yes, sir."

"And have you attracted any unusual attention?"

"No, sir."

"Please remove it."

The gasp of astonishment throughout the court as the police officer took off the wig and demonstrated that he had looked perfectly normal both with it and without it was extremely heartening to the prosecution. M. P. Pugh had had his eyes fixed in concentration on the jury, which included one woman, and he was nodding with grim satisfaction now that he saw that they were at last convinced that the notion of disguise was not ridiculous. He had wiped the smile off their faces. There remained one other mine to spring under the defence.

At the end of the police evidence Mr Ward put Bruce Thornton into the witness-box as the only defence witness. Thornton told of his long yachting experience and his villa at Cap d'Antibes, which had been the forcing-ground of his friendship with Ramsden. He said that the only reason for any attempt to see Lord Nuffield was to introduce a project which Ramsden said he had invented, a device by which petrol consumption in any car could be reduced by 40 per cent. There was scarcely a time when he met Ramsden and the Major did not bring up the petrol device, complaining that he found it difficult to get any kind of interview with Lord Nuffield. If Thornton could get the interview Ramsden had promised him 25 per cent of the profits. But Thornton could not give a credible reason why anyone should wear gloves to avoid fingerprints when typing a simple letter asking for an opportunity to introduce the carburettor. "It was Ramsden's idea," he said.

He explained his possession of the two automatic pistols by declaring that he had always carried firearms during his seagoing life and had not got out of the habit; but he never used them, only threatened with them. As an example, he cited an incident when the engine-room of his yacht blew up off Barcelona. "The boat was insured for £5000, and a Spanish trawler came alongside and threw a rope, which I ordered to be ignored. They wanted to get easy money for salvage. I kept telling the trawler skipper to go away, and eventually I only persuaded him to leave by brandishing my gun at him. I have carried firearms for years. One of the pistols exhibited I have had for over twelve years, and the other, the Browning, for about two years. The Browning has never been fired by me, even in practice," said Thornton.

He had bought the gold tooth-caps because he wanted to get work in films. As for his possession of the wig, Thornton explained that he had trouble with the lease of his house at Antibes, which his first wife had not given up when she remarried. (He was in truth referring to his third wife, but no catalogue of wives had then been listed.) There was a legal dispute about it, but he was very anxious to see his property. "I told Ramsden that I was going down to Antibes to have a look at my house, but because I was well known there and might not get in, if I was recognized, I had this disguise which would be useful."

Ramsden's disguise as a chauffeur was the Major's own idea, though Thornton had provided the make-up. "I told him you will have to use this stuff if you want to do it." Thornton himself had peroxided his hair at the Spread Eagle Hotel only because Ramsden asked him how it was done. As for the surgical instruments, he had had them for years. They had come in useful when he had to perform emergency operations aboard windjammers.

Thornton declared that he had specifically sought out Ramsden from Australia because he had a scheme to take tobacco over to France and sell it to fishing-boats outside the three-mile limit. That, said Thornton, would be within the law. But Ramsden wickedly suggested that, rather than come back light, they should bring French brandy, "and that probably would be smuggling."

As for the twelve-point letter—which did not have the superscription "To Viscount Nuffield" when he had seen it—Ramsden had written it, but it seemed only a friendly effort to help Thornton out of an impasse in a cinema script he was writing. "At the time I thought it would fit in excellently with my story. For two years I had been puzzled over one problem of my plot. The story always stuck on this one point—how a man can be got out of a room by a woman when he was all the time fairly well guarded. I was very grateful to Major Ramsden for solving this difficulty."

The judge intervened. "Clause Two of the letter states, 'You will ask me to come and see your children's hospital.' In the cinema story you were preparing, did the character have a children's hospital?"

"Yes, my Lord," said Thornton.

Thornton was strongly cross-examined, and conveyed with apparent regret the impression that any inconsistencies in the story were due to Ramsden's idiocy. "Can you suggest to the jury," asked Mr Sharp, "any honest scheme which would require the avoidance of leaving fingerprints?" "No," said Thornton. "I honestly thought Ramsden was not well. He showed every indication of it."

"Ramsden never told you how the petrol-saving with the new carburettor was to be effected. This invention must have been worth millions, and he was to give you 25 per cent, if you would introduce him to Lord Nuffield! You agree that Major Ramsden knows nothing about carburettors?"

"I am beginning to fear so," said Thornton sadly.

"It sounds flimsy, doesn't it?"

"The whole thing sounds flimsy."

Mr Sharp got Thornton to agree that he was "comparatively on the rocks" by contrast to his previous wealth. There was a dark reminder that both the prosecution and the judge knew—if the jury did not—that he was missing the £500 blackmail annuity recently stopped. Then Mr Sharp asked leave to address questions which might justify the prosecution's case that Thornton was a man whose use of firearms had to be taken seriously. It was the end of the afternoon, and a police officer had ushered a woman into the body of the court and come over to speak to Pugh.

"Did you," Mr Sharp asked Thornton, "on one occasion at your villa in the South of France, draw a pistol and threaten to shoot your wife with it while you were the worse for drink?"

"I did not—never," replied Thornton vehemently.

"She ran round the room trying to escape?" asked Mr Sharp.

"No. That is . . . I was going to say that is a lie, but wherever the information came from, it is more than a lie."

"Perhaps you would give the jury your version of the incident."

"I had been out," Thornton recalled. "When I came back home I had the pistol in my hip-pocket. When I went to take it out it flicked off and the bullet went into my leg.

"I was very drunk," he added in humorous self-deprecation.

"But was your wife unfortunately in the house at the time that this gun went off?"

"She was."

"She was in the room?"

"She was."

"Did she run round the room?"

"It was rather a large room," said Thornton in complete exposition of the situation, "and she was at the top end."

"In the spring of 1922," continued Cartwright Sharp, "you

stayed for some months in a boarding-house at 22 Cumberland Place, Southampton?"

"Yes."

"Was a private-inquiry agent, Captain Marter, trying to obtain documents you had in your possession?"

"He was."

"The night before you finally ceased to live in that boarding-house you had your gun with you?"

"I don't know that I had."

"I am coming to something which, if it is right, you will not have forgotten. You strongly objected to Captain Marter following you and trying to get these documents?"

"I certainly did."

"The night before you finally left the boarding-house had your landlady found you on the landing, gun in hand?"

"I remember that," said Thornton with an air of dawning candour. "There was somebody at the bedroom window, late at night after dark, and I wanted to see who was there."

"Had you your gun with you?"

"Yes."

"You said, 'Look at him!' and pointed through the open window to a man who was by the wall at the bottom of the garden?"

"Yes."

"Did you think it was Captain Marter?"

"I didn't know who it was. I had seen somebody climbing up outside the window."

"Did you fire the pistol, duck down, and say 'I think I have got him'?"

"I did not," said Thornton indignantly. "I have never fired a pistol through a window."

Mr Sharp turned into the court and asked, "Is Mrs Helena Bath here?"

A middle-aged woman stood and said, "Yes."

"Would you mind standing there?" And Mr Sharp pointed to a spot in front of the witness-box. The woman walked to the place.

Mr Sharp turned to Thornton and asked, "Do you recognize this lady?"

"I am not sure," said Thornton, completely surprised.

"I suggest this is the lady who was your landlady at that time?"

"I remember now," said Thornton. But he was mumbling, and entirely nonplussed.

"Did you not in her presence take a pot-shot at the man in the garden?"

"I don't think so," breathed Thornton. "And I say that in all sincerity."

Pugh was again gazing fixedly at the jury. They were undoubtedly impressed by Thornton's obvious confusion when confronted with the landlady who had given him notice on the spot after that shooting incident long ago. It would be quite unnecessary, Pugh decided, to prolong proceedings by calling the lady from Southampton as an additional witness.

Mr Arthur Ward made his final address to the jury. He said the onus was on the prosecution to prove this fantastic, impossible story. Major Ramsden was a lying, cunning traitor. "I can suggest a reason for Ramsden's actions, if he is not mad. He was hard up. He arranged the whole thing, and then he went to the police. Afterwards he could turn to Lord Nuffield and say, 'Look what unpleasantness I have saved you from'."

Mr Cartwright Sharp asked the jury, "Have you noticed that the fantastic and melodramatic points now turn out to be those things which are common ground to the stories you have heard from both sides? You have two utterly different stories before you. Major Ramsden tells you that all these fantastic circumstances are to be accounted for by the one thing consistent with them—a wicked plot to kidnap Lord Nuffield and hold him to ransom. Thornton speaks of a scheme to save petrol which would be worth millions, but in a hundred and one other things—the gloves, the wig, the letter, the guns—gives not a single rational explanation to account for them."

Mr Justice Wrottesley, summing up, said, "There are certain things which have not been challenged, and they are of great importance. It is not challenged that on the 4th of May Ramsden went to Scotland Yard, and on the 10th he was in touch with the Oxfordshire Police. The importance of that is to show that this is not a case of an accomplice. It is not suggested that this is one of those difficult cases where two persons plot a crime, and one gives the other away."

The jury found Thornton Guilty. He was given seven years. Ironically, the case brought him some financial advantage. For all beneficiaries to the estate of his first wife—the woman he had espoused five marriages ago—had died; Thornton had been advertised for, as Tuellman, three years previously, but, not having been traced to Australia, was officially presumed dead, and the estate was in Chancery. The publicity of the trial was enough to verify Thornton's identity. He claimed the money, and when he came out of gaol spent it on drink, from which he died. But the wryest comment on the futility of the plot came from Lord Nuffield. "It didn't really matter, did it?" he asked. "After all, I shouldn't have noticed £100,000 from the account."

CHAPTER

6

The Carnal Cases

DETECTIVE Inspector Hewins came into the outer office, exchanged glances with Miss Selwyn to check that it was tactful to go farther, and knocked at the door of the Prosecuting Solicitor. "I've got another sex assault," he told M. P. P.

Pugh grimaced and asked, "Is it a strong one?" Hewins answered, "I've seen the man in the presence of the girl. He said, 'I'm sorry for what I did. I must have lost my head. These scratches on my face I got in the struggle.' " Hewins's voice tailed off.

"Yes?" demanded Pugh.

"But when I read that statement over to him at the station he refused to sign."

Pugh sighed. "Let's have a look at the statements," he said. Some time later he telephoned Hewins. "That man of yours," he said. "I'm throwing the book at him." The man was charged with unlawfully having carnal knowledge of the girl, and with attempting to suffocate her with intent to commit the criminal offence.

In the Stipendiary's Court Pugh opened strongly. "Under the Offences against the Person Act the Court has power to order the defendant to be flogged" was his menacing initial gloss on the case. He narrated the events with his customary stern condemnation. The woman in the case was aged twenty. "A girl of exceptionally good character," Pugh declared. "The defendant recently came to work at the firm where she was already working. He asked her to go out with him. She refused, twice. Then she consented to go to the pictures with him, believing that she could trust him. He looks a decent upright, straight young man." The defendant was in fact slightly younger than the girl.

"At the pictures he held her hand, bought her a box of chocolates, and acted in a perfectly gentlemanly manner towards her. They came out of the cinema at about 10.45. He led her to a piece of waste ground which he told her was a short cut to the trams. He here put his arm round her and tried to kiss her. She protested, and asked that he should take her home properly. She said, 'I don't want to stop here; I came to the pictures with you.'

"She started to walk ahead, but he came up behind her and put his arms round her waist. She hit him on the head with her umbrella. The blow was of considerable force, so strong that it broke the umbrella. The man said, 'You have asked for it now', and he attacked her. She struggled. She scratched his face and hit him again with her umbrella. There is no doubt that this girl put forward a very serious resistance against the intentions of this youth, and made a magnificent fight. She screamed for help. The man stuffed a handkerchief into her mouth. She pulled it out. He stuffed in a second one. He raped her and then walked off, saying that he was going to see a friend of his who had a car, to see if he would drive her home.

"The girl was in a very distressed condition. She was crying. Her clothes were torn and covered with mud. A dastardly thing about the affair is that the young man left the girl where she was, practically out of her mind, not caring a snap of the fingers what became of her. The girl was demented. She walked round. She did not know the district. Eventually she saw a police officer. He directed her home, and she arrived there at about 1.50 in the morning. Her mother was waiting for her, and the girl, very distressed, exhausted and crying, told her what had happened. There can be no doubt that she put up a fierce fight in defence of her honour. . . ."

It was not an uncommon story. The mother had informed the police. Next day Inspector Hewins, with the girl, supported by a woman detective sergeant, saw the man at his place of work. There he made the statement Hewins had first quoted, refusing to sign it later at the police station; and Mr Howard Baker, for the defence, now vainly objected to that statement being put in.

The girl went into the witness-box. She declared that she was struggling and screaming all the time, and what had happened was without her consent. She had torn the man's tie away from his collar and scratched him. While trying to escape from him she had climbed some railings. In cross-examination she denied that the scratches on the man's face were the result of her becoming hysterical after the event.

The girl's mother gave evidence. She described her daughter's return at two in the morning, weeping, with thick lips, a swollen face, and a bruised body beneath her torn clothing. The police gave evidence. Even the mother of the accused gave evidence of discussing the scratches on her son's face next morning. He had said, "The cat must have been upstairs." Pugh asked for committal to the Assizes, and this was ordered.

The Assize trial took place three months later, with Mr A. P. Marshall prosecuting. Mr D. L. Finnemore, for the defence, emphasized that the girl had said nothing to the policeman who had directed her home. The man said in the witness-box that the girl did not resent his advances, nor struggle at the time, but afterwards she became very excited, caught him round the neck, scratched him, and told him that she ought not to have done it because he would tell other people at work. The jury brought in a verdict of Not Guilty.

After discharging the prisoner Mr Justice Singleton called the girl into the witness-box once more. He told her, "I wish you to understand that, so far as I think, you have nothing to be ashamed of in this matter at all. I believe you are an honest girl." The girl blushed and went away, not perhaps realizing the rarity of this tribute to her integrity, which was the only trophy she could flourish after fourteen weeks of anxiety. Pugh, as piqued as ever that he had lost the case, called on the special resignation he reserved for the consideration of all carnal cases—notoriously the most difficult to prove, when common experience demands that one woman's unsupported testimony must be weighed against the passion, and the remorse, that exist in the most virtuous hearts. Yet the case in question had come within the rules he had laid down as governing any decision to prosecute in such offences.

He had mentioned these rules to Jimmy Webster on the first day they had met. It was in the spring of 1937 that Dr James M. Webster, a big, untidy, bald Scot, arrived in Birmingham with a retinue of only one specialist Sheffield police sergeant chancing his promotion in Brum, to set up from nothing the West Midlands

Forensic Science Laboratory. Very early during Webster's introductory visits around the Victoria Courts the Deputy Chief Constable, Mr W. C. Johnson, had suggested that he ought to see Pugh. Webster called on the Prosecuting Solicitor. He took in the pace of the work being done in the small unpretentious office by Pugh and his quartet—secretary Miss Selwyn, clerks A. E. Field and Norman Brown, and handyman Massey. He noted the choler with which Pugh often used the telephone, and the peremptory way in which he rebuked police officers. And Webster thought, "This gentleman and I are going to clash without a doubt."

"What sort of assistance do you think you can give me?" asked the Prosecuting Solicitor.

"That depends," said Webster, "on the ability and the willingness of the Police Force to do what I want: to bring things in for examination and to invite me to the scene of a crime. To begin with, I doubt whether we shall be of much assistance to you in as many as 20 per cent of your cases. But I think—if we're asked—we ought to be of some help in such cases as breaking and entry, criminal abortion, and carnal cases; quite apart from murder, where, of course, you will get all the pathological help you would expect."

"That will certainly be useful," said Pugh. "Did you mention carnal cases?"

"Yes," said Webster. "Are you having much success with them here?"

"I won't undertake any prosecution unless I get a confession from the accused," Pugh declared dogmatically. "Otherwise I lay my police open to prosecution for wrongful arrest. And," he added, "the way things are going, the actions will start. Look!" He threw a book across the desk. Webster examined it. "It's a complaints book," said Pugh. "All carnal cases are set down here and the parents are entered as the complainants."

"But what's the idea of this comic thing?" asked Webster.

"Comic!" retorted Pugh. "It's armour plate. That book protects my police from any action if the case fails."

"It's a lot of balls," said Webster. It could be said that, if he foresaw that he and Pugh would clash, he was doing nothing to sidestep the impact. "In the past," Webster continued, "I have done very well with a scientific examination of the witness, of any relevant clothing, and of the scene of the crime."

"I shouldn't have noticed £100,000"
Lord Nuffield after his attempted kidnapping
Photo Keystone Press Agency Ltd

"The Prof"
Professor J. M. Webster, head of the West Midlands Forensic Science Laboratory

Principal Solicitor-advocates of Birmingham at Pugh's Farewell Party
Left to right: Alec Evans, Charles Ladds, Mervyn Pugh, Howard Baker

University of B'ham Medical Society

The Medical Practitioner as witness in Criminal Cases

Some people think it necessary and even desirable to formulate rules respecting:-

(a) the manner in which a medical witness should give his evidence,

(b) how he is to act on cross-examination, and

(c) in what way he is to recover himself on re-examination.

I agree with the principles laid down in Taylor's Principles and Practice of Medical Jurisprude[nce] that such advice is superfluous and these rules, like those given to prevent drowning, are invariably forgotten at the very moment when the person concerned is in the situation when he requires them most. Technically speaking you should never have any trouble if you are speaking the truth, the whole truth and nothing but the truth but in order to enable you to carry this out, there are a few tips I can give you which will enable you to the best of your ability to testify to the truth.

Firstly, always be well prepared on all aspects of the subject on which you are to give evidence. Your demeanour should be suitable to the serious occasion upon which you appear. Although you may feel annoyed, insulted or irritated by cross-examination, never let it show. A medical witness ought not to evince any resentment because his professional qualifications, his experience, his means of knowledge or the grounds for his opinion are investigated very closely. Rather he should prepare himself to meet with good humour, the attempts of an opposing counsel to involve him in contradiction and he should clearly demonstrate to all who hear him that his sole desire is to state the truth.

Very few people can shake the evidence of a little child.

(Miss Ann Ballantine) - over -

Do not regard the cross-examining lawyer as your enemy. Do not be flippant. Do not try to be clever. The lawyer is on his own ground and in Court will have the same advantage over you as you would have over him if he was the patient in Hospital.

Lose your temper, lose your case. An advocate loses his temper, he jeopardises his own case.

Take an example from the lawyers, who after abusing each other in Court, are afterwards seen in friendly intercourse and if there is any drink handy are buying each other one.

I don't like giving rules but I think those that have been given in the text books are as good as any as long as you interpret them liberally and do not try to be too highbound.

(1) Have the subject-matter clear in your own mind.

(2) Give direct answers to simple questions and answer the question asked. Most questions ad mit of an answer "yes" or "no".

(3) Beware of vague terms, like "undoubted traces of poison". If it is there, measure it, if you cannot measure it, say a slight trace but do not leave it vague.

(4) Beware of double or involved questions. If you are embarrassed by the duplicity of the question, ask for a severance and give separate replies.

(5) Do not argue with Counsel.

(6) Speak slowly, audibly and distinctly - someone deaf.

(7) Give your replies as far as possible in simple, non-technical language.

(8) Avoid exaggeration.

(9) Don't lose your temper.

dence given by Doctors

M. P. Pugh, back in Private Practice

Pugh was interested but noncommittal.

"Can I ask you something?" said Webster. "I thought you pricked your ears up when I mentioned criminal abortion. Was I right in that impression?"

Pugh had, in fact, a double concern with that subject at the time. He had just been appointed to the Inter-Departmental Committee on Abortion set up by the Ministry of Health and the Home Office with Mr W. Norman Birkett, K.C., as chairman. Pugh, who in effect represented the Director of Public Prosecutions on the committee, had two particular preoccupations relating to the exposure and punishment of criminal abortion. (The committee came to the conclusion that 40 per cent of the then presumed annual number of 110,000–150,000 abortions in Britain were criminal abortions.) As a prosecutor Pugh urgently favoured new legislation to permit the police to obtain a search warrant for the examination of the premises of a suspected abortionist, to reform the situation whereby they had no power of search unless they had entered the premises to effect an arrest. Pugh's other crusade on the committee was to change the attitude of doctors who had to deal with the human debris of criminal abortion, and by so doing became the recipients of vital information and even identification of abortionists, but because of their feeling for medical privilege passed no word on to the police. Pugh signed, with Lady Baldwin of Bewdley, the gynæcologist Sir Comyns Berkeley, the coroner W. Bentley Purchase, and others, a reservation to the final report declaring that a doctor had a legal duty to report instances where he knew that criminal abortion had been procured or attempted. This group of the committee expressed

> the hope that the Royal College of Physicians will find it possible to consider afresh the position and duty of a doctor, at any rate in those cases in which he knows for certain that criminal abortion has been attempted or procured, and to revise their recommendation, made in 1916, which has had the effect of limiting the power of a doctor to assist justice to those rare cases in which the patient consents to disclosure. We believe that a restatement of the position by the College . . . would not only help to promote a better administration of the law relating to criminal abortion, and thus be of benefit to the community, but would also give an impetus of great value to the advancement of Preventive Medicine.[1]

[1] *Report of the Inter-Departmental Committee on Abortion* (H.M. Stationery Office, 1939), page 138.

It was on this subject that M. P. Pugh now irritatedly relieved his mind to Dr Webster. "The doctors here are too frightened to get involved. They ought to get hold of the police and say, 'We've got a criminal abortion here and you ought to come in.' But they hide behind the B.M.A. The specialists are as bad. When we do get a case we can't get them to go into the box. And if they do give evidence they won't even say outright, 'This is a drug which may cause abortion.'"

"As far as drugs are concerned," said Webster reassuringly, "I will be perfectly prepared to go into the box and say of many of them that they are drugs that *have* caused abortion and *may* cause abortion.

"But be careful how you push me," he continued, giving advance notice of a concern for qualitative accuracy which was to exasperate the eager Pugh many times in the future, "to say that such and such a drug undoubtedly *will* cause abortion or will undoubtedly endanger the life of an expectant mother."

Pugh said nothing, thinking perhaps that, while he was still feeling his way with Webster, he must occasionally take a chance in his opening statements; shortly afterwards he prosecuted a man for supplying a young woman with "certain things" with the intention of procuring abortion; the drug concerned was five grains of quinine sulphate made up as pills, which, Pugh said, "clearly constituted a noxious thing and would be dangerous for a woman in her condition to take". But all that his committee in London could say of quinine was that "serious ill-health sometimes follows its use in excessive quantities for improper purposes". However much, for purposes of publicity, Pugh exaggerated the effect of drugs reputed to be abortifacients, there was a practical preventive aim behind his drive against their sale. No backstreet shop selling 'female pills' would handle a true abortifacient such as ergot, the drug legitimately used to contract the uterus after childbirth in some cases of hæmorrhage: the drug was firmly restricted in the Poisons List. But Pugh was concerned with the fraudulent exploitation of the mental distress of pregnant women who paid large sums for worthless pills which would have been priced sixpence a box if bought openly at the chemist's. Moreover, he believed that once a woman had taken a drug to induce an abortion, and predictably failed, she was more likely either to use an instrument on herself or to consent to its use by a professional abortionist—because her state of mind was at once more desperate and more permissive of abortion.

Meanwhile Pugh was kept busy with his London meetings—the Abortion Committee met forty-seven times in all—and with the cut and thrust of crime in Birmingham. The crowning of King George VI in Westminster Abbey was to have been celebrated at Ward End by what a Pype Hayes man called his "Coronation Murder" of a former mistress who had ended their association. He had kept a detailed diary of his intentions and recorded sharpening his butcher's knife a fortnight before he meant to use it. But on the chosen day he had to write: "I have been foiled by a few minutes. Involved in slight motor accident on way back from town . . ." He accordingly wielded the knife on the next day, but only wounded the girl. Pugh's prosecution for attempted murder had to be delayed while the victim recovered.

Through this time also Dr Webster, with Sergeant E. S. Burgess, was setting up his Home Office laboratory above the mortuary by the Coroner's Office in Newton Street, only the other side of the road from Pugh's office in the Victoria Courts. Webster had already put his foot down when he had been asked by the Chief Constable, Mr C. C. H. Moriarty, editor of the "policeman's bible", *Police Law,* and of *Police Procedure and Administration,* to undertake what could be construed as the routine duties of a local police surgeon. There was at the corner of Newton Street a hostel which, as part of its service, catered for the reception of girls picked up wandering in need of care and protection. Occasionally it was necessary for a girl who had been placed there to be medically examined. It was put to Webster that Pugh was embarrassed in his duties because the resident doctor at the hostel refused to go into the witness-box and report on oath on the condition of a girl. Would Webster take over this responsibility? "No!" declared Dr Webster. Pugh personally pressed him. Webster exploded. "You've already told me," he said, "that you personally refused to take work home. Why shouldn't I get my night's sleep, too?" It was a disingenuous protest, for one thing above all that Webster was noted for was the fact that he would work on a case at any hour of the day or night, and it was confidently asserted that he often looked so untidy because his labours had forced him to sleep in his clothes. But eventually, in spite of his protests, he was, as he put it, "framed" by Pugh (but also by his own zeal) into doing much of the investigation that he was resisting.

It happened that a girl had been taken into the hostel for wandering, and the story she told was that her father had committed incest against her. Dame Geraldine Cadbury, who ran the hostel as a social service, was told, and a report came through to the Chief Constable and to Pugh, with the intimation that the girl was at least not a virgin. The father was brought to court for incest. Pugh presented the charge, and outlined the case. At this stage the father (who was not legally represented) interrupted and said, "Before you go any further, I deny this charge absolutely. This girl is a liar, and has caused a lot of trouble so far. I demand an independent medical examination."

Pugh was temporarily nonplussed. Then he suavely rose to seize his opportunity. "There is one person," he told the magistrates, "whom you will regard as being truly independent in this matter. He has much experience in this type of offence. Moreover, he is not paid by the local authority and stands above all parties here. He is the new director of the Home Office Forensic Science Laboratory." Shortly afterwards Pugh presented himself to Dr Webster. "I'm afraid there's no help for it, Jimmy," he said. "The magistrates have made an order for you to examine the girl."

Webster gazed malevolently at Pugh. "Then fetch both the father and the girl," he said shortly. The appointment was arranged, and Dr Webster spoke first, as in law he was bound to do, to the father. "Father," he said, "this girl is your daughter, and she is a minor. Do you give your consent for me to examine her?" "Certainly," said the man. The doctor turned to the girl and explained the examination. "Since you have already given your consent for one examination . . ." he continued, but the girl quickly said, "I never! I was just told that I was going to be examined." "Well," said the doctor, "since you have already been examined once, do you take any exception to my examining you?" "No," said the girl. A policewoman was called in and the examination was made.

"She is *virgo intacta,*" Dr Webster later reported to Pugh. The Prosecuting Solicitor speedily withdrew the case, and the charge of incest was dismissed. In the subsequent reaction Dr Webster found all the cases from the girls' hostel being assigned to him, and, gradually, all carnal cases that the Birmingham Police handled. He declared that he was not pleased with the outcome. "M. P., you ran a fast one on me," he told Pugh. "I am not happy."

There was, in any case, a little more sorting out of temperament to be completed before happiness could be said to be settled on either side. Once Webster had opened his lab there was far more frequent communication between the two men, by telephone or personal contact. But at first it was always on Pugh's terms. The telephone would ring on the desk of Miss Smith, Webster's secretary. Miss Selwyn would be on the other end. Would she please get the Doctor for Mr Pugh? Webster would come to the phone, and on occasion he would be kept waiting while Pugh disposed of another call or other business. But the occasions were not many. After a running-in period Miss Smith was instructed not to pass a call until Pugh was on the line. Since she was a sensitive soul, the ordeals were painful for her. Webster would be mouthing with grim joy at her across the desk while she was made to demand, "Then get Mr Pugh, please. I'm not going to get the Doctor until Mr Pugh is on. You put Mr Pugh on . . . ." Despair from Miss Smith. Grimaces from Dr Webster. Miss Smith puts the telephone on the desk in surrender. Webster firmly replaces it in her hand. Mouthing, "It's your call, Miss Selwyn. Put Mr Pugh on, and I'll get the Doctor." And once that revolt was established as successful there was only the question of the leg-work to be straightened out. Pugh began by following his usual habit, and requesting Webster's attendance at his office. Webster told him, "Let's get this straight. My time is as valuable as yours. The distance between us is the same. When I want you I'll come. When you want me—you come. I'm not a copper, and I'm not going to be treated like one."

And Pugh acquiesced, though not so fully as Webster believed. For the Doctor's aide was a copper—Sergeant Burgess rose through the years to the rank of Chief Superintendent, always as the senior police officer in the lab. And Pugh had a way with coppers. So, when Webster was incommunicado there might still be a telephone call to the Forensic Science Lab, and the sharp voice of the Prosecuting Solicitor might wheedle, "Eddie, I'm not sure about the medical description we're going to use for the cause of death. Eddie, come across here for a minute, will you? And bring your medical books."

Once boundaries had been defined and respected, Pugh and

Webster were colleagues and sparring partners for twenty years. Apart from friendship, Pugh needed the dependability of a number of people who could be relied on to take the shafts of his sometimes droll, sometimes schoolboy, teasing wit. Pugh would very often refer to Webster by his full name, which he misaccented as James Ma*thew*son Webster. This was all very well in private, but Pugh occasionally took the habit into court with him. There was more than one time when the Prosecuting Solicitor began his examination of his expert witness with, "You are James Ma*thew*son Webster?" And the irritated expert fired back, in broader Scots than usual, "You know very well my name is James *Matheson* Webster," not sounding the W.[1]

Webster, though exchanging knock for knock, still credited and reported Mervyn Pugh as being "the best and most efficient police court prosecutor I have ever known". He declared that the Prosecuting Solicitor really mastered his briefs; he interviewed every police officer who was to give evidence, and saw that every man knew what he was going to say; he knew his law; and he could put it across.

But Pugh also, like a good general, knew how to use the ability and enthusiasm of his colleagues to the hilt. If he would not work after office hours, he relied on them to. One Sunday afternoon in Ward End a commercial traveller left his house in his car in order to be out of the way while a woman came to perform an abortion on his young wife, who already had three children. The visitor was not working for money, but for friendship: she had performed a successful abortion on the wife two years previously. But in the interval the couple had had twins who were now only eight months old. The abortionist left the house immediately after the operation—which was the common use of the syringe—saying that everything was all right. Within minutes the commercial traveller was being telephoned by his mother-in-law that if he wanted to see his wife alive he must hurry home. But she died before he came. Five minutes after her death the family doctor arrived, but he declined to certify the cause of death and informed the police. Superintendent Baguley of the C.I.D. arrived, and in his company was none other than Dr James Mathewson Webster, pathologist for the Home Office,

[1] But there was the occasion when Pugh, questioning the mother of a girl in a carnal case, asked, "And of course you had your daughter examined as soon afterwards as possible?" "Oh, yes," said the mother, "Webster Booth did her."

and not the Birmingham Police, regardless whether he was working nights or weekends, and on this occasion doing both. Webster made an external examination on the spot, and conducted a post mortem next day. He could not be said to be slacking! The abortionist was traced. M. P. Pugh, for the Director of Public Prosecutions, charged her with causing death, but in the lower court asked that the woman should be committed to take her trial at the next Assizes on a charge of murder; and this extreme course was taken. Dr Webster gave unequivocal evidence, both as to the cause of death and the agent responsible: "In my opinion death was due to an attempt at abortion by local violence. I don't think the woman was responsible for her own death." Herbert Willison, as strenuous as ever for the defence, had clear evidence that the dead woman had bought the syringe herself, and was urging that the accused woman had only given advice but not used the instrument. But Webster, while he would never inflate his evidence to suit Pugh, would not bend it either to aid a somewhat pitiful defendant. He replied to Willison, "While it is a possibility that the woman brought about her own death, from the result of my examinations I do not regard it as a reasonable possibility." He had no sooner said this than the accused woman fainted, and Webster had to leave the box to bring her round. When she had recovered she sat in the dock, sobbing, "What have I done to deserve all this?" She was indicted for murder, and tried before Mr Justice Macnaghten. Mr Cartwright Sharp, K.C., appearing for the woman, successfully submitted that the jury should not be asked to consider the murder charge, which the judge allowed on the ground that medical evidence indicated that it was most unusual for death to result from this particular use of the instrument. Mr Sharp called no evidence for the defence, but pleaded in mitigation that the woman had not done it for money but as a mistaken kindness, and the judge sent her to penal servitude for three years for manslaughter.

With the development of the two Midlands Home Office Forensic Science Laboratories—the East Midlands organization had been established at Nottingham under Dr Holden—Pugh was beginning to boast in the court of "the great value of science in apprehending criminals", and there were cases unconnected with any offences against the person which Pugh presented relying almost entirely on scientific evidence. After an office-breaking in which three safes had been either forced or sawn, and the ballast from the safes strewn all over the premises, the only remaining clues were a handprint pointing downward below a broken window—indicating that the intruder had come in head-first—and blood presumably caused by a cut from the broken window. When the police cornered their suspects later, they used the scientific experts to make two major points: a cut on one prisoner's hand, which he said was caused by his wife biting him during a quarrel, corresponded conclusively with the indentations of the broken glass; and dust found in the men's clothing contained two varieties of safe ballast of an obsolete type which had been used in the safes that were forced. In another case, a smash-and-grab raid on a jeweller's in Worcester Street, Birmingham, a suspect was eventually detained, and the prosecution relied on the identification by Webster's laboratory of silk threads used for jewellers' price tickets, broken glass of the identical specific gravity of the shop-window, and paint from the window grille, all found on the man's clothing or in his trouser turn-ups.

But it was natural that in view of Dr Webster's medical expertise in carnal cases, his deep knowledge of poisons, and his skill as a pathologist—he was to become Professor of Forensic Medicine and Toxicology at Birmingham University—Pugh relied on him principally in cases of sexual assault, criminal abortion, and murder. Yet Webster, with his pawky, independent character and a concern for scientific advocacy which overbore any wish-fulfilment of advocacy, found himself in frequent tussles with the Prosecuting Solicitor. "The work of any investigation is done," he maintained, "by the police and the scientific witnesses. It is the task of the prosecuting solicitor to weld these findings into a continuous and logical progression, step by step from the crime to the accused. At this accomplishment, M. P., you are an ace. If you see that there is a weak link in the chain of evidence that the defence can or may attack, you're on it at once: you send for the officer in the case and tell him what additional confirmation he must get. But, my word, M. P. when I'm in the box I've got to watch you. You'll never accept an inch. You always want an ell."

Pugh would never accept defeat. When he lost a struggle with Webster at the conference before the hearing he would bring it up again in the court. "Now, Jimmy," he would say at the conference, "you're going to say that it would take this man five minutes to die?" "Yes." "And then you're going to say that in that time he could have picked up that overcoat, put . . ." "NO!" Webster would roar. "I'm not going to have that in the depositions. I'll be torn to pieces for that at the trial."

"All right, Jimmy."

But in the witness-box it would not be all right. The examination would begin with the jaunty "You are James Ma*thew*son Webster. . . ?" It would proceed: "Now, Dr Webster, you have detailed the injuries received by the deceased. In your opinion, how long would it take for the man to die?"

"He could die in a matter of approximately five minutes."

"But, Dr Webster, during those five minutes the deceased would be able to carry out such voluntary acts as . . ."

"No, sir. I cannot say that he could carry out any voluntary acts. In some circumstances it has been known, but I cannot say for certain that he was capable of anything."

Pugh would pass smoothly on to the next question, without betraying that he had not got the progression he wanted. And Webster would continue to watch him, as he always watched him.

The conflict would become keenest in a prosecution for supplying drugs to procure an abortion:

"Dr Webster, this drug is what is termed as ecbolic?"

"Yes."

"Will you explain to the Bench what an ecbolic is?"

"An ecbolic is a drug which stimulates contraction of the womb."

"And that is applicable to the pregnant woman?"

"Yes."

"What is the action of an ecbolic on a pregnant woman?"

"She runs the risk of an abortion."

"And therefore such a drug is noxious in a pregnancy?"

"Yes."

"And in your opinion the use of an ecbolic would most certainly cause a criminal abortion?"

However carefully led up to, the culminating question would crash on Webster's defensive rocks if it was opposed to his tenets. "No, sir. It *could* cause an abortion, but not in one hundred per cent of the cases."

What was remarkable about the depositions built up by the question-and-answer ploy of Pugh and Webster was their outstanding simplicity and clarity. To the lawyer's ear they were works of art. And they served the highest interests of justice, because they were always completely understandable to the defendant. By contrast there was an occasion when an expert witness gave his evidence in a jumble of medical jargon. The magistrate, Lord Ilkeston, turned to him and said, "I understand all that you have said, and Mr Pugh understands it. But would you kindly translate it into English, so that the prisoner will know what you are talking about?"

M. P. Pugh had a justifiable anxiety compelling him to nail down Webster to the extreme of what could be extracted from him regarding the toxicity of pills commonly supplied for abortion. He was hampered in his prosecutions on this count by a judicial decision[1] that, when the substance administered is not a poison, it must be of a noxious character with regard to the *quantity* administered in order to bring the administration or supply within section 58 of the Offences against the Person Act. It was for this reason that he was always trying to gain from a medical witness the admission that the pills were a "noxious substance". The Inter-Departmental Committee recommended—though the report was blanketed out by the Second World War—that "the obligation imposed by section 58 to prove that it must be poisonous or noxious appears to be unnecessary. . . . We recommend, therefore, that the words 'any poison or other noxious thing' should be deleted and replaced by some such expression as 'any substance whatever', wherever they appear in sections 58 and 59."[2] The reasoning behind this sweeping suggested change was the conviction that women who began by sanctioning the use of drugs for abortion would, when the drugs almost inevitably failed, be more prepared than before to go to a backstreet abortionist. Webster was by no means out of sympathy with Pugh's propaganda, and, whenever he felt justified, would contribute to it. Soon after he took his Chair at Birmingham University he gave evidence at the trial of two widows who were indicted for conspiracy to procure a poison or other noxious thing knowing that it was intended to be used to procure a miscarriage;

[1] R. *v.* Hennah, 1877 (13 Cox 547).

[2] *Report of the Inter-Departmental Committee on Abortion* (H.M. Stationery Office, 1939), page 51.

and of causing it to be taken. The substance on this occasion was aloes. Mr Justice Humphries asked Webster, "Is there no means by which the sale of these noxious things to pregnant women can be stopped?"

Webster replied, "At the present moment this is probably the most nefarious trade in the country, and there is no legal means of stopping it. The amount of profit made is colossal. I have conducted post-mortem examinations on girls who have taken pills of this nature and have died as a result of their abortion. On the boxes is 'Not to be taken by pregnant women', but, so far from acting as a deterrent, it is simply an advertisement."

The judge commented, "I do not often ask the Press to take the trouble to put anything in their papers, but I do feel disposed to say in this case that I think these remarks by this gentleman, who is an eminent authority, ought to be published, in order that those who have the power to make laws may consider them, and may consider whether steps ought not to be taken to put an end to this open invitation to women to procure the abortion of themselves or others (for that is what it is), and so that persons who occupy the responsible positions of chemists and druggists, and as such have many privileges not open to ordinary tradesmen, may be prevented from carrying on this nefarious trade, as Professor Webster has most rightly described it."

Meanwhile Webster worked extremely closely with the police to convict known abortionists. While the home of one of them, a sixty-six-year-old Small Heath widow, was being watched a girl was seen to call. She was followed home and traced as a barmaid aged twenty-five. The widow's house was kept under observation. Four days later she went to the barmaid's home. The police followed, and after an interval knocked at the door. They told the widow, "We have reason to believe that you are here in connection with this young woman's condition." The widow said, "I have done nothing yet. I have only seen the lady twice." The barmaid declared—probably in less stilted language than the official report—that all that had occurred was that she had asked the widow to "demonstrate to her the proper use of an instrument of hygiene". When a chief inspector asked to speak to the barmaid privately the widow said, "Remember, I haven't touched you yet. We were only talking." After her private interview the barmaid consented to go with the police to the laboratory, where Webster was waiting. He declared in evidence that he had examined her, and found that her condition was consistent with an operation having been performed. At the Assizes Mr Justice Oliver sentenced the widow to fifteen months' imprisonment. It would be difficult to conceive more effective liaison than the sequence through which the conviction was obtained.

War, as is always very noticeable in a provincial city, has the civil consequences of an increase in bigamy, sexual assault, and abortion. In the main the bigamists were leniently treated in Birmingham, but there was no *détente* in the campaign against abortion. Pugh was handed a file on a young doctor of Acock's Green whose case had come to the police quite out of the blue: the parents of the doctor's girl friend, after a quarrel, had reported that he had arranged an abortion for her. When the police saw the doctor he exclaimed, "I am in a jam!" and mentioned that he had helped some sixteen women in Birmingham, because they had told him that if he would not do something for them they would do something to themselves. The police could get no evidence on the other women, but, three days after their visit and before he was charged, the doctor married his girl friend. A nurse told the police, "The doctor has been advised to marry her to clamp her tongue." The wife did not give evidence, but some incriminating letters were discovered, and the doctor was sent to prison for twelve months. The cumulative tragedies ran on. An Erdington woman died of septicæmia, and a Handsworth woman was indicted for the manslaughter and labelled as a professional abortionist. She was a devoted worker for the Methodist Church, and her husband committed suicide when he learned of the scandal. The woman said, "I wouldn't care if I had done it for gain, but I have only done it to help people out." She had kept a list of her patients, and the code used by people asking for her services was a letter asking, "Could you do a day's cleaning for me?" She went down for four years' penal servitude. A twenty-nine-year-old typist died in the Queen's Hospital of general septicæmia following an abortion. Pugh prosecuted both the abortionist and the man with whom the victim had lived for eleven years, the father of her nine-year-old son. The charge was unlawful killing. When charged the man said, "Kill her? I only wish she was here now." Evidence was given by the couple's doctor (and not contested by the prosecution) that the man had done his utmost to go through with the pregnancy. He said, "We have one child; we can have another." She said, "I would rather kill myself than have another child. I am going to get rid of it." Under the threat of suicide the man drove her to an abortionist's door, waited for her, and drove her back. Mr Justice Asquith bound the man over and sentenced the abortionist to fifteen months.

Wartime inevitably meant also more assault and rape, but more false accusations, too. In one tragi-comedy handled by Pugh even the name "Professor Webster" had been enough to save him from an embarrassing prosecution. A Kingstanding prostitute ran across an American army sergeant, had drinks with him in several pubs, and then offered: "I wouldn't mind doing something for you, Yank, for a pound." The eager sergeant produced the pound note and conducted her to a bomb-site, where they had intercourse. At the end of the exercise the sergeant found his virility unimpaired, and asked for more. The woman objected, but the soldier was in no state to take a refusal, and became more pressing. The woman screamed. A policeman came up, and the woman accused the soldier of rape. The man said he had paid a pound for his entertainment, but the woman denied that she had had the money. The soldier was arrested, and soon handed over to the American military police. Under American military law the penalty for rape was death, and the sergeant, not wishing to face the rope, said to his military escort, "If you will leave your revolver and go out of the room for a moment, I will take the gentleman's way out." The guard refused him this opportunity.

In the meantime the woman had gone to the police station to file details of the complaint. She demanded a medical examination, and was conducted to Professor Webster. When she realized who was examining her she objected to going on with it, and said she wanted to drop the case, though previously, even when told that the sergeant was liable to the death penalty, she had persisted in the accusation. The police knew her as a recognized prostitute and the associate of thieves and brothel-keepers, but this, of course, did not mean that she could not be raped. Pugh prosecuted her on a charge of causing a public mischief and rendering a sergeant in the American Forces subject to arrest. He said that her complaint had caused investigations which occupied just under thirty hours of the time of the police and Professor Webster. The woman was committed to Birmingham Sessions, and got twelve months' hard labour.

But there were periods when Pugh and Webster, even in the fullest collaboration, ran into difficult weather. Most outstanding was the astonishing series of prosecutions of no fewer than four doctors, all coloured, charged at different times with serious offences, either indecent assault or abortion, where conviction meant the end of their career. The fact that these prosecutions of medical men, coming in sequence, all involved coloured practitioners was not only a fortuitous occurrence, but a distinct embarrassment to M. P. Pugh, who sensitively felt that his motives might be impugned. Long before the post-war 'colour problem' in Britain, Birmingham, along with the other great cities, had had a proportion of coloured doctors, mainly Indian, who spent their lives in general practice—mostly in working-class areas—and were extremely affectionately regarded. Indeed, one of the factors of these particular prosecutions by Pugh was that ministers of the Church were virtually clamouring to testify to the excellent characters of the accused, and there was generally a gallery of admiring white patients sitting in the public seats and waiting to applaud the acquittal of their medicine man.

The acquittals came (to Pugh's agonized disgust). Of the first two cases, of doctors charged with indecent assaults on their patients, Pugh had said to Webster before the Assize hearing, "This is going to be dodgy." "I know," replied Webster. "And I know who is going to carry the can," he continued. "*I* could put up a better defence, and get the jury to believe it, than what I am going to say in the box—never mind if it is the truth."

"Well," said Pugh, "we'll get the best silk possible." They engaged a notable King's Counsel and briefed him profoundly. But the case was lost. The next trial came up. Again there was the most careful preparation. Again the case went down the drain.

There was very much of a wake in Pugh's office after the failure of the second prosecution. "But there are two more of them in, and they are already committed," he moaned. "Should we offer no evidence? If we go on like this it will get around that there is a persecution from this office." Pugh was always sensitive to reactions in the Council House, and on a rare occasion when he had made a complete misstatement about the alleged subversive activities of a Birmingham official he had gone to the Watch Committee to read a prepared statement in a three-quarter-hour session from which the Press had been excluded.

"We'll go ahead," he finally decided. "But we'll run the case our way. We've got nothing to lose. In the last two cases our counsel have been top-notchers. But they wouldn't put the questions we asked them to. We want someone who will listen when we are prompting. We don't want someone with his own ideas of how to run the prosecution, we'll have a B.F. We'll have Seamus O'Riordan."[1]

Pugh was giving vent to his frequent irritation at any deviation from the method in which he thought the prosecution should be conducted. It was an aspect of his perfectionism that made him choose very carefully even among the witnesses he decided to call, particularly the experts. Before one infanticide trial Professor Webster said to him, "Look, Mervyn"—Pugh had always been referred to by his initials, but he was coming to be called by his first name—"if the defence are sensible they'll attack me. They will ask me how long it is since I delivered a baby. I will have to tell them 'twenty years'. In fairness we ought to call a consultant obstetrician." "Very well," said Pugh, "whom do you suggest?" Webster mentioned a name and added, "He's a decent chap." "I don't CARE if he's a decent chap," shouted Pugh. "We don't want to kiss him. Is he *efficient*?" "Well," said Webster, "he's an efficient gynæcologist." "But I want an efficient *witness*," growled Pugh.

The third trial came up at the Assizes. This time Pugh had chosen a man who could not only hear what was being whispered to him but would take some notice of his prompting: "Ask him this . . ." "Put it to him that . . ." The case went smoothly, and a conviction was obtained. Pugh was jubilant. "This is marvellous," he said. "Now we're only one down with one to play. No change of tactics. The same team for the next case." And when the fourth prosecution was upheld he declared to Webster, "We owe it to ourselves to sink a few pints tonight."

This series of four similar trials was extraordinary. But it proved to be only the curtain-raiser to one of the most remarkable criminal trials in legal history. Yet another doctor—and again he was an Indian—was accused. But the details of the charge seem entirely unique. It was alleged that he had committed rape on a woman patient in the course of a gynæcological examination

[1] A pseudonym.

while the husband was present in the room, but the other side of a screen, and without the slightest objection by the woman because, it was alleged, she did not know until too late that she was being raped. The doctor was sixty-eight years old.

Pugh continually cited the case afterwards as important from a completely different standpoint. He was always a champion of the Press, and strongly opposed any exclusion of public reporting from the court except under the Official Secrets Act. When suggestions were made—as they are now increasingly made, and occasionally acceded to—that the Press should be barred from preliminary hearings, particularly on charges involving indecency, because a subsequent jury's mind might be prejudiced by a memory of the sordid details, Pugh would constantly quote the Pardhy case as an instance when the public reporting of all but the most grossly scandalous details of a judicial proceeding was the direct cause of an unexpected interpolation at the trial proper which worked solely to the benefit of the defence.

On the evening of Thursday the 10th of June, 1943, Professor Webster received a telephone call from a general practitioner in Shirley. "I have a very sticky medico-legal problem," said the doctor. He said that a patient of his had gone for examination to Dr K. M. Pardhy, who in the past had performed a therapeutic abortion on her, and was concerned with fitting a contraceptive appliance, and that this patient had now come to him, her family doctor, and reported that she had been the subject of intercourse even though her husband was in Pardhy's surgery at the time.

When Pardhy's name was mentioned Webster had two swift reactions: first, he recognized him as one of the most clever and able surgeons who ever operated in Birmingham; second, he remembered that many years before this Pardhy had stood his trial at the Assizes for interfering with a young female patient in circumstances which made the details the Shirley doctor was telling him almost a replica of the first case, except for the additional incredibility of the man's presence in the room. On the previous occasion the surgeon had been acquitted.

Webster spoke urgently to his caller. "You can't tackle this on your own. Report it to the police straight away. I'll make myself ready immediately against their wanting me to make a further examination." This course of action was followed, and at half-past eight that night Webster examined the patient. He found that she was pregnant, and that intercourse had been had with her during the last few hours. As soon as he got his report back to the police a conference was held as a result of which a warrant was issued for Pardhy's arrest. Seven police officers arrived at Pardhy's house at ten minutes to midnight, and interviewed him in circumstances of truculence that were later criticized by the defence at the trial, before examining and photographing his consulting-room. The brusqueness of the arrest was mainly the effect of the hour at which it was made, Pardhy having to be knocked up out of bed. But from the point of view of a scientific witness like Professor Webster it was essential to get hold of the clothes Pardhy had been wearing that day, and also (according to the story of the patient and her husband) of a towel with which he had masked himself; and if the linen was not impounded that night it could have been laundered by the morning.

M. P. Pugh naturally knew nothing of the case until the next day, and he immediately put it in the list for the morrow, a Saturday morning, when he briefly presented the facts and asked for a remand. The defence had already retained Mr J. F. Bourke, who closely questioned Chief Detective Inspector John Davies about the arrest, and established that there had been no search warrant. A remand of a little over a fortnight was ordered. When the main hearing began Pugh now found against him, in the lower court, both Mr G. D. ("Khaki") Roberts, K.C., and Mr J. F. Bourke, a defence team which had recently been successful in one of the doctor cases. Pugh had taken the greatest care in preparing his presentation, and a model of Pardhy's Edgbaston house and consulting-room, fitted with miniature furniture, had been previously placed in the courtroom.

For Birmingham the prosecution was a sensational light relief from the drabness of war: the details of the allegations were so fantastic that they provoked discussion among men, a frisson of apprehension among women, and a prurient amusement among sections of all classes. On the Monday morning of the resumed hearing a queue had formed outside Number One Court three-quarters of an hour before proceedings began. The majority were women.

Pugh's advance-guard of secretary and aides was at full

strength, but he himself made no dramatic entry. The accused surgeon,[1] Krishna Morishwar Pardhy, took his place in the dock, clearly carrying all of his sixty-eight years. The charge was read and the plea made. The Stipendiary, Lord Ilkeston, addressed the public benches.

"Respectable women would not care to hear the details in this case. They have an opportunity now of leaving the court."

Nobody stirred.

Pugh was torn between his normal liking for publicity, his theoretical support for unhindered reporting, and the position which he had acquired as the repository of law for the Stipendiary. Breaking the uncomfortable silence, he said, "The details are very delicate. You have power to clear the court if you wish."

Lord Ilkeston pondered. "People who like to stay can," he pronounced, with some distaste.

M. P. Pugh made his opening statement without his characteristic 'dastardly' adjectives or any assurance that this was the most disgusting case he had handled. It was not an occasion for superlatives. "No-one appreciates better than I do," he said gravely, "the serious implication of a case of this nature with respect to Dr Pardhy, and no-one appreciates better than you the implication with regard to the public. If it were true that a surgeon carrying out so intimate and delicate an examination—which he would do with a number of women in the ordinary course of his profession—committed an offence of this sort when the woman was not in a position to resist, or even to see what was taking place, the implication with regard to the public could not be more serious.

"The complainant is a married woman aged thirty-five. She was married about thirteen years ago, and has a child eleven years of age. Her husband holds a responsible position as an engineer with a salary of about £800 a year. When you see the husband and wife in the witness-box you will form an impression which is favourable to them, and I think you will be struck by their candour and honesty of purpose in coming here. For, indeed, it is no pleasant experience for a woman to have to come and testify on a matter of this nature in the witness-box. At the same time, one appreciates that if this sort of thing has happened anyone who comes forward is performing a public service."

[1] Except by professionals like Webster he was generally called 'Dr', not 'Mr'.

Pugh outlined the patient's relationship with the accused surgeon, to whom she had been sent by her family doctor, from the time of his operation on her five years previously through the treatment he subsequently recommended. The families were on good terms socially, and the surgeon had treated two of the husband's relatives. In January 1943 the patient had visited Pardhy's consulting-room, and again in May; on the latter occasion her husband came with her, and she was examined while he sat in the same room on the other side of a screen. This was also the arrangement on the day when the offence was alleged to have taken place, the 10th of June.

The prosecuting solicitor explained clearly that for the gynæcological treatment the patient was receiving she had to lie on her side on a surgical table while the doctor (who was behind her) penetrated with his fingers. At a certain moment she became aware, not of the doctor's finger but of his flesh. "Immediately she realized this she sat up and called her husband. He came round from behind the screen and saw Dr Pardhy standing there with a towel in front of his trousers, which were unbuttoned. The patient told her husband what had happened, and he spoke to Dr Pardhy in language which could not have been mistaken as to its meaning. He called him a —— swine."

M. P. Pugh then recounted the visit of the husband and wife to their family doctor, and the subsequent examination by Professor Webster, as a result of which it was confirmed that intercourse had recently taken place; and this was the ground for Pardhy's arrest. But it was not essential to the charge.

"There is no need in law for this woman's story to be corroborated," Pugh declared. "If you believe her story alone it justifies you sending Dr Pardhy for trial. But on top of that you have the story of the husband—of how he caught him more or less in the act, certainly within a couple of seconds of his wife calling out—and you have also the medical evidence, including that of Dr Webster."

Pugh then recounted the midnight arrest, the examination and photographing of the consulting-room, and the confiscation of the accused surgeon's clothing and linen. When Pardhy was charged at Steelhouse Lane Police Station he said, "It is all false. Any statement I want to give I will give in the presence of my solicitor."

Having presented his facts, Pugh justified their credibility.

"In a matter of this nature," he said, "one may wonder what *can* happen. People who do not think are apt to say 'Fantastic, for a woman to be raped with her husband in the room'."

He paused, and added grimly:

"Matters of an indecent nature can take place in such circumstances, and, indeed, in circumstances much more public.

"Where does the truth lie in this case? Is this woman suffering from hallucinations? If so, the husband is suffering from them too. Is it a conspiracy by the husband and wife to ruin the doctor or to get money from him? Those are the only other explanations for the woman's story if it is not true. But we say that it is true, that she was raped in the way she says.

"I submit that the evidence here is conclusive and that the case could not be proved with any more certainty. If you accept that evidence there cannot be the slightest doubt that a *prima facie* case has been made out, and that the prisoner should be committed to take his trial at the Court of Assize."

Pugh paused until the last echoes of his gravity had faded. Then in a very business-like manner he called the police—not yet to give the evidence of arrest on which they were likely to be severely cross-examined, but to swear to the authenticity of the model of the consulting-room and of the plans and photographs of it that had been put in. These were the important props to credibility that were to set the scene, the boundaries, and even the measurements from floor to table-top, which the prosecution needed to present its fantastic case. Lord Ilkeston, the magistrate, said that additionally he would use the luncheon adjournment to go to Edgbaston and inspect the consulting-room. This was not a rare excursion. Ilkeston and Pugh would often go out on field work when the evidence was disputed, even in a brothel case: when the fiery Herbert Willison had declared that a police witness could never have seen the indecency he alleged from his position behind a high garden fence, it was Ilkeston who found the hole in the fence the officer had used to get a clear view of the window.

After the long luncheon adjournment the woman complainant was the only witness in the afternoon. She was allowed to sit, and given a glass of water which she frequently sipped. She said that she had first consulted Dr Pardhy eight years previously, and in the interim there had been social calls between the two families. "I looked upon him as a friend," she said. Mentioning her previous visits to the surgeon that year, she said she had begun to be suspicious of him on a former occasion. She was taken through the events of the afternoon of the 10th of June. "I was aware that something was wrong and I called to my husband behind the screen. I told him what had happened and he called Dr Pardhy a swine. Dr Pardhy said, 'I have done nothing.' After my husband had said other things to him he said, 'I have a beautiful wife and two lovely children.' My husband answered, 'I also have a wife and child.' As we were leaving the doctor said, 'Think kindly of me; I was good to you when you were in trouble.' "

Mr G. D. Roberts, K.C., rose to cross-examine, and quickly fastened on the patient's previous suspicions of the doctor:

"You say that on a previous occasion Dr Pardhy committed the same kind of offence against you?"

"Yes."

"With your husband sitting within a couple of feet of you?"

"Yes."

"You are a married woman with ten years' experience?"

"Thirteen and a half years now."

"Are you right in the head?" asked Mr Roberts.

"Yes."

"Would you believe any sane married woman would tell a story like that?"

But the magistrate intervened in this robust line of questioning, and counsel did not insist on an answer.

"Why did you want your husband present at the examination on the 10th of June?" he resumed.

"I felt more comfortable when he was there."

"Don't mince words," rapped Mr Roberts. "Would you agree that you did not go to the June interview expecting something wrong to happen?"

"Yes," said the woman.

"Were you in a very nervous condition that day?"

"No."

Mr Roberts was reserving the major assaults in his cross-examination for the next day, and the hearing was adjourned when the patient had already spent three and a half hours in the witness-box. Before the proceedings began next morning the Stipendiary announced, "The court must be cleared of all persons lacking a satisfactory reason to be present for the remainder of this woman's evidence." In the consternation that followed the Clerk added, "This order does not apply to relatives, but to all gapers and others." Under the challenging gaze of the court police, the majority of the men and women on the public benches rose and left. Mr Roberts was about to resume when, after an officer had conferred with him, the Clerk intervened and told the magistrate, "Some members of the medical profession are interested in the case and wish to enter the public gallery." "They can go to their own medical school for the knowledge," retorted Lord Ilkeston. "They can't come here."

Mr Roberts addressed himself to the witness. "I suggest immediately," he said, "that it would have been impossible for Dr Pardhy to have committed the offence."

"No."

"When you called to your husband, did he come round the screen and say, 'What are you doing to my wife?' "

"No."

"Did you not hear your husband say, 'I will make you pay for this. This has cost me twenty guineas already'?"

"No."

"Did he threaten to go to the police?"

"Yes."

Mr Roberts passed a piece of paper to the witness. "On this paper," he said, "there is the name of a woman. Do you know the lady's husband?"

"They are friends of the family."

Pugh rose quickly. "I object to the name of the woman not being given," he said.

The magistrate ruled, "The name of the woman must be given." Mr Roberts mentioned her name.

"Did her husband pay a very great deal of attention to you?" he asked the witness.

"Not that I know of. He was friendly," she conceded.

"Did the lady complain frequently to you that you were alienating the affections of her husband from her?"

"No."

The magistrate intervened. "Never?" he asked.

"She did come round to my house on one occasion and did say something about her husband. She thought he was paying too much attention to me."

"I suggest that she complained many times," said Mr Roberts.

"No."

"Perhaps you will say what did happen?"

"As far as I can remember—it was a long time ago—I told her, 'We are friendly, and there is no need for you to worry.'"

Mr Roberts changed the emphasis. "Did she complain that *you* were paying too much attention to her husband?"

"No."

"Or encouraging him?" pursued the magistrate.

"No."

Mr Roberts resumed, "Did her husband leave her and come to live with you and your husband?"

"No," said the witness promptly. She added, "The lady went to live with an aunt. She and her husband were in financial difficulties. My husband offered to her husband to come and stay with us. He got him a job at his works."

"How long did he stay with you and your husband?"

"I should say about six months."

"Was the lady very unhappy in consequence? Did she tell you that?"

"No."

Mr Roberts pursued another line: "Have you ever reported any other man to the police for rape, or attempted rape?"

"No. Three years ago I reported a man who kissed me and pushed me into a chair."

"What were the circumstances of this assault?"

"The man was a stranger. He came to look over our house because he was thinking of buying a similar house near by which was being built."

"Where did the assault occur?"

"In the kitchen."

"You say you were suspicious of Dr Pardhy's conduct on a previous occasion. What did you do about that?"

"Nothing," said the witness.

Mr Roberts sat down.

M. P. Pugh rose to make a swift re-examination. "You say you did nothing on the previous occasion. Did you not mention it to anyone?"

"Yes. I told my husband."

"What did he say?"

"He said, 'Dr Pardhy has too big a reputation to do anything like that.'"

"And then?"

"After that I put the thought away from my mind."

M. P. Pugh then called the patient's husband, who recounted how he had sat behind a screen during the examination. "I heard my wife say, 'I must get up.' Dr Pardhy replied, 'No, no! Lie down. You are quite all right.' My wife persisted that she must get up, and called me by my name.

"I immediately went round the screen. My wife said 'Look!' and pointed to Dr Pardhy. I saw Dr Pardhy fumbling with a white towel in front of himself. His trousers were undone.

"I grabbed his two wrists with my hands. I released his left wrist and raised my own right fist threatening him, and I called him a —— swine. He was in an agitated state and said, 'No, no. I have not done anything.' I said, 'You have never even examined my wife.' He said, 'Yes, your wife is neurotic and imagines that she is pregnant.' I accused Dr Pardhy of having had intercourse, and he said, 'No, no. You do not understand. I am an old man, and suffer from an enlarged prostatic gland.' "

At this point Pugh interrupted the sequence and asked permission to suspend this examination and call Professor Webster, who had to attend to give evidence in other cases at Assize Courts on the following day. The husband stood down, with his evidence in chief incomplete.

Webster described his examination of the complainant at 8.30 in the evening after the incident.

Pugh asked, "Having regard to what you found, what opinion did you form?"

"I formed the opinion (1) that this woman was pregnant; (2) that someone had had intimacy with her a few hours prior to my examination."

"You found that she was pregnant?"

"Yes."

"And what would you have thought if the accused had remarked, as he is alleged to have remarked, 'Your wife is neurotic and imagines she is pregnant'?"

"I am not an expert in gynæcology," the Scot replied with his cautious candour, "but I had no difficulty in diagnosing pregnancy in this case, and I cannot understand, if the complainant's evidence is true, why Mr Pardhy failed to diagnose pregnancy if he examined her for that purpose."

Pugh then asked Webster clearly if rape were possible in the circumstances of this particular gynæcological examination.

"In the position in which it is stated the woman was lying on the consulting-room couch she would not be able to see what was going on. There is no reason that I can see why Mr Pardhy, if he were so minded, could not have committed the offence in the circumstances alleged."

Mr Roberts rose. "I suggest," he said, "that the story that has been told is an utterly impossible one."

"I don't agree," said Professor Webster. And the hearing was adjourned for the day.

On the next morning the public were readmitted to the court, but the benches were not crowded. The husband continued his evidence from the moment of confrontation. "My wife said, 'Take me away', and I said, 'Very well, then, come along.' Dr Pardhy said, 'I have a beautiful wife and children, and a very high reputation, and I would not do such a thing.' I said, 'Dr Pardhy, if you did do such a thing you are a fool, and I know that you did it.' Dr Pardhy tried to shake hands with me. I brushed him aside, opened the front door, and went out. When we got to my car outside Dr Pardhy said, 'Remember, I have been a very good friend to you when you were in trouble, and you must think kindly of me.' I said, 'Dr Pardhy, your very attitude confirms your guilt.' I then wished him 'Good afternoon' and he said, 'Go home, and think kindly of me, and remember my wife and children.' I then said, 'You may hear more about this. Good afternoon.'"

The couple, said the witness, drove straight to their family doctor, found that he was out, and left a message. He came to their home at 5.45, about an hour and a half after they had left Dr Pardhy. He made a telephone call and accompanied the husband to the police station. A police inspector came back with them, and later he consented that his wife be examined by Professor Webster at Newton Street.

In his cross-examination Mr Roberts quickly came to the wife's discussion of her suspicions of the doctor on a previous occasion, after the January examination.

The husband said he replied, "Darling, that's absurd. He would not do such a thing. Why do you think that?" His wife had answered, "Because I felt his coat," and he had said, "It must have been his sleeve." "I laughed her fears away and forgot the whole question," he concluded.

I

"On the afternoon of June the 10th, did you tell Dr Pardhy, 'I will make you pay for this'?" asked Mr Roberts.

"No."

"Did you threaten to take action against him?"

"Yes."

"Did you say to Dr Pardhy, 'I understand a similar charge has been brought against you before'?"

"Yes."

"How did you understand that?"

"I heard of it from business friends about eighteen months ago."

"Did you mention it to your wife?"

"Yes."

After a total of two and a half hours in the box the husband stood down. The family doctor, the next witness, was not cross-examined, but on the presentation of the evidence of arrest Mr Roberts spent almost the rest of the day questioning the "bullying and domineering" attitude adopted.

The defence counsel then submitted that no case had been made out.

"On the case as it stands," he told the Stipendiary "no jury would be likely to convict. Here is a charge of rape in perhaps the most remarkable circumstances in which such a charge has ever been brought—the rape of a woman who has not been intimidated by threats or violence, a woman who says she did not know that she was being raped. Her husband, who sat within two feet of her at the time, had no idea either that the offence of rape was being committed."

Lord Ilkeston pronounced that a *prima facie* case had been established.

"Having regard to the length of the prosecution's evidence," said Mr Roberts, "and the close proximity of the Assizes, it has been decided not to call evidence for the defence, as this would take several days. The charge has been brought, and at the first moment it was indignantly denied by Dr Pardhy. That is the attitude he has taken up now. Through me, the defendant emphatically asserts his innocence, and reserves his defence until the proper time."

The Assizes began, in fact, nine days later, but the very heavy list delayed Pardhy's trial until the 26th of July, 1943.

According to Pugh's later judgment, this delay had a vital

bearing on the outcome of the case. For a woman who lived at Great Barr and knew the Pardhys read of the case in the newspapers and wrote about it to her son, who was serving a sentence in Lincoln Prison for a military offence. He too knew the doctor's family, and wanted to give them some information. But he was limited to writing one letter a fortnight, and could not write until the 15th of July. On that date he wrote a long letter to Mrs Pardhy which reads, in part:

E—— B. B——
Reg. No. 3337
Lincoln Prison
15th [July] /43

DEAR MRS PARDHY,

In the first instance, please forgive my present residential address, for I assure you, in spite of the present handicaps and "Temporary lodgings", I am quite a respectable person . . . [The writer spent three paragraphs identifying himself to Mrs Pardhy.]

. . . I trust this letter will reach you in time or prove to be of some value to you if only as an interesting epistle.

I understand you know or have reasons for knowing one "Ann Anderson"[1] who resides in Shirley, on August 10th I met Ann, we became very intimate friends, and although it only proved to be a "Flash of Romance" the incidents, and the times are forever present.

I met Ann Anderson at "Greys" [café] during a little shopping expedition, we passed the time of day, in the Cafe over afternoon lunch. We finally went to the "Paramount Cinema" in the evening after which I escorted her home, or very nearly home.

August 12th 42 we met again by appointment, just after lunch! and went as far as "Barnt Green" on the bus, from Station Street where we spent the afternoon in a pleasant state of comatose.

Our third meeting proved to be the last for I volunteered for the "Royal Engineers", and had received my papers however, we enjoyed an evening at the "Grand Casino", New Street or is it Corporation Street? and then went to a small hotel where we spent the night, just off Bromsgrove Street.

So you see it was very short, but very real, and Im confident its the same, it is definitely, the same Ann your husband knows, to be lying, according to my mothers letter.

I hope that your reply, will prove to me, that which I feel certain is correct, let me assure you also, I shall be only too

[1] The name has been falsified—*Author.*

pleased to help you in any way, theres not much I can do in here, but one never knows.

If you appreciate this effort, I am repaid already, in conclusion I beg you a favour.

Will you please tell mother [name and address given] in a short note the reason I have not written to her, you see we are allowed only one letter per fortnight and mother will be worried over the long delay, Thanks awfully,

In conclusion I wish you and yours
Every possible bit of Good fortune.
Remaining yours Sincerely,
E. B. B——

P.S.

Hoping you will reply, for I shall naturally be intrigued, to know if this is any value to you, unfortunately I failed to settle down in the army, and Im at present suffering for "Individuality" which is not appreciated in this free thinking country, anyway you can rely on Ann Anderson being identical girl, in your dilemma.

E.B.

Mrs Pardhy naturally passed this letter immediately to her solicitor. The prisoner was interviewed and sub-poena'ed, and was brought to Birmingham under guard on the first day of the trial.

In the Assize Court the public doors were barred once the benches were filled, and no further queueing was allowed for any seats that might be relinquished. The waiting gallery buzzed as the model of the Edgbaston consulting-room with its scaled-down furniture was carried into court. Counsel entered. For the prosecution Mr Gilbert Paull, K.C.,[1] led Mr Norman Winning. The defence retained the same team of Mr G. D. Roberts, K.C., and Mr John Bourke. A wartime jury of eight was sworn, three of the members being women.

Mr Paull made an interesting development of his exhortation to the jury to forget absolutely anything they might have heard or read of the case. Though newspaper reports were scrupulously fair, nothing might be more misleading, he said, when, as was the case in this prosecution, they could not give all the facts.

Outlining the case, Mr Paull said the woman was first sent to Dr Pardhy in 1938,[2] and on his advice she underwent an operation. Subsequently a friendship grew between the husband and wife and the doctor. In the previous October the wife decided

[1] Now Mr Justice Paull.

[1] The date 1935 mentioned at the Police Court was clearly a slip.

on a course which made periodical gynæcological examinations necessary. In March the wife began to suspect that she was pregnant. Her husband telephoned Dr Pardhy, who told him, "If your wife is pregnant it is a miracle." There had been an examination in January, and there were further ones in May and on June the 10th. Counsel then recounted the scene in the consulting-room and the verbal exchanges there and outside. When the husband accused the doctor of never having examined his wife Pardhy said, "Yes, I have. Your wife is not pregnant. She is neurotic." But Professor Webster would give evidence that a proper examination at that moment would easily have disclosed that she was pregnant. When the husband snatched away the towel Pardhy was holding in front of him and saw that his trousers were unbuttoned he raised his fist and called him a —— swine. The doctor, agitated and somewhat exhausted, said, "I have done nothing. I suffer from an enlarged prostate. My wife is always telling me I leave my trousers undone."

"There are two questions," Mr Paull told the jury, "which you will be asking yourselves. Might not the husband and wife have been mistaken; moreover, how do we know this is not a deliberately invented story?

"If for some evil motive you were going to accuse wrongly a doctor of a matter like this, who are the people you would avoid? The first would be another doctor, and the second the police. And, if you honestly thought this had occurred, who would be the two persons you would go to first? Would you not go first to another doctor to make sure as to your suspicions? Then, if he corroborated your suspicions, would you not go to the police?

"That," he continued, "is exactly what the husband and wife did." And he recounted their search for the family doctor, his subsequent call, the visit to the police, and the examination by Professor Webster. "And what the Professor found was consistent with intercourse having taken place between some man and the wife within a few hours previously. Moreover, he said that there was no reason why intimacy should not have taken place between the defendant and the wife without the woman realizing it."

Mr Paull said that Professor Webster had found traces of semen on some of the linen taken from Dr Pardhy's house. "If we prove all these facts," he concluded, "we shall invite you to say that there can be no reasonable doubt as to what occurred that afternoon."

After Mr Roberts had obtained the agreement of the judge, Mr Justice Wrottesley, that the jury should see the actual consulting-room, the complainant was called. She told of the events in the consulting-room. She said that after she had dressed Dr Pardhy wanted her to lie on the couch again, but her husband refused to allow this.

Seated, she turned for Mr Roberts's cross-examination.

He took her back to her suspicions after the January examination. "Are you saying that in January 1943 Dr Pardhy had connection with you?"

"No," she said. "I am not saying that."

"Are you saying that he did not have connection with you?"

"Well, as far as I know he did not."

"Had you any suspicion after that visit that anything wrong had taken place?"

"I mentioned to my husband that I felt his clothes against me."

"What did he say?"

"He said, 'It must have been the sleeve of his coat. Dr. Pardhy has too big a reputation to do anything like that.'"

"I suggest your story is utterly false?"

"No."

Mr Roberts asked a series of questions arising from the wife's admission that another woman had complained that her husband was paying the witness too much attention. He traced the occasion when the witness reported a man to the Shirley police for making indecent advances to her.

Counsel then called for the presence of a man whom he named. A young man was brought up from the cells and into the dock by a warder. The judge remarked to the jury, "It can be seen where he comes from. He is now in prison." Mr Roberts asked the witness to look at the convict. "Do you know that man?" he asked.

"No," she replied.

"Have you seen him before?"

"Not that I know of."

"Did you meet him in Grey's café in August 1942?"

"No."

"I suggest that you have slept a night with that man?"

"I have never met that man before."

"Did you hear that a letter had been received from him?"

"No."

"It is quite news to you?"

"Yes."

"It was a commercial hotel just off Bromsgrove Street on the 15th of August, 1942?"

"I have never seen that man in my life."

"I suggest that you met him three times altogether, and at one of your meetings you gave him a handkerchief?"

"I never met him."

The convict was taken away. Mr Paull, rising to re-examine, asked, "Did you ever sleep in a commercial hotel with any man?"

The woman replied, "Only with my husband when we came back from Scotland." She gave the details of an occasion in January 1942.

"Is there the slightest truth in the suggestion that has been made regarding you and that man produced from prison?"

"No."

"Is there any truth in the suggestion that Mr —— [Mr Paull named the man friend who had been mentioned] paid too much attention to you?"

"No, and the matter has been cleared up with the wife."

When the husband was called Mr Paull asked him too about the suggestion that his wife and the friend had been intimate. "I think that is absurd," he said. The judge questioned him about the alleged visit of his wife with a strange man to a commercial hotel. He declared that it was absolutely impossible for his wife to spend a night in Birmingham without his knowledge. In reply to Mr Roberts, he said his wife could not have misconducted herself with any man on the night of the 15th of August, 1942, because she was in his company.

The second day of the trial began with a resumption of the husband's cross-examination. He admitted that in the consulting-room he had told Dr Pardhy that he had not even examined his wife.[1] Mr Roberts continued: "Did you accuse him of having connection with her?"

"I did not use that word."

[1] An enigmatic point, one of several, which was not taken further. The judge, in his summing up, said, "I do not think there has been any suggestion, from first to last, that [the husband] on this occasion acted as a kind of Peeping Tom."

"Did you say to him, 'My wife says you did the same thing last time'?"

"No."

"Did you say, 'I understand a similar charge was brought against you before'?"

"Yes."

"What were you referring to?"

"I had been informed by business associates that that was so, but I had dismissed it, because all doctors, some time in their lives, are liable to that sort of rumour."

"Did that refer to an action for seduction brought against Dr Pardhy about nineteen years ago?"

"I don't know how long ago it was."

"Did you know that the jury found for Dr Pardhy and that the judge agreed with their verdict?"

"I was not interested. I did not discuss it."

"Did you mention it to your wife?"

"Yes, at the time I was told about it—about eighteen months or two years ago."

"Have you discussed the matter with her since?"

"No."

"Did Dr Pardhy say on the matter that it was pooh-poohed by the judge and jury?"

"Yes, something like that, and that it was laughed out of court."

"Did he tell you to think carefully before you made any allegations against him?"

"No."

"Did you threaten him with your fist?"

"Yes."

"Did you say, 'I will have you up'?"

"No."

"Did you say, 'I will make you pay'?"

"No. Definitely not."

"Did you consider you will have a good action for damages if this charge is established?"

"I do not wish to make any money out of it. I have a solicitor here watching the case on my behalf, and I am leaving the question of any possible action to him. If damages should be secured the money will go to the Red Cross or other charities after meeting expenses."

"Then you are clearly contemplating an action?"

"I have already answered that question. That matter is in the hands of my solicitor. I shall not give instructions for any action to be taken."

"Did you say, 'It has cost me twenty guineas and now I get this on top of it'?"

"No."

"Did Dr Pardhy say that he was tired out after six operations?"

"No."

"Did he point out that you were in the room on both occasions, and that it was ridiculous that such a thing could be done within a few feet of you?"

"No, he did not."

"Did you take some coins out of your pocket and rattle them in your hands?"

"No. Definitely not."

"Did you say, looking at him, 'Dr Pardhy, you are not a psychologist'?"

"No."

In his re-examination Mr Paull dealt with the final implication: "You realize that the suggestion that you rattled some money in your pocket, and that you are supposed to have said, 'You are not a good psychologist' is to suggest that there was some sort of conspiracy between you and your wife? Is there a word of truth in that suggestion?"

"No," replied the husband. He gave assurances of his salary, standing, and *bona fides* and left the box.

The police gave evidence of arrest, and Professor Webster gave an account similar to his evidence in the police court, again strongly resisting Mr Roberts's challenge that the accusation was impossible. Webster had in fact consulted earlier with Mervyn Pugh, and agreed that if necessary he would give a demonstration in court of the practicability of the feat with which the doctor was charged. Accordingly, Pugh had arranged for the consulting-room couch to be available in court; but he had to observe a delicate schedule of time-keeping and furniture-removing since the judge and jury visited the consulting-room at lunch, and the couch was required at the afternoon session. An extraordinary scene then occurred, when the couch was man-handled right up to the judge's bench, on the wing nearer the jury, and the complainant's family doctor lay down on the couch in the position adopted by the wife for examination while Professor Webster, perched on a footstool by the side of the couch, went through restrained motions of rape.

Medical evidence was then called, including the assurance of a Harley Street consultant that he saw no reason why the act could not have taken place. This concluded the evidence for the prosecution.

The last witness had been an eminent surgeon who had written a book called *The Physiology of Sex,* but he was not a gynæcologist, and Mr Roberts, at the outset of his preliminary address to the jury, stressed this, and asked them to draw "a reasonable inference" from the fact that the prosecution had not called a gynæcologist to substantiate the medical evidence. "I am going to call a gynæcologist from London," he assured them, "as well as two or three other witnesses, who will say that in their opinion the alleged offence is either impossible, or is so difficult to perform without the woman knowing what was happening that it is almost impossible."

Mr Roberts stressed the gravity of the case. "It is a matter of life or death to the defendant. In defending this man it is impossible to spare people's feelings . . ." and he gave details of Pardhy's poor sexual performance. "We are dealing with the most intimate possible thing in the world. In courts of law we can discuss the facts of life without any false modesty, without any giggling or sniggering. I am going to suggest to you that the act alleged against this man is an absolute impossibility. Have you ever heard of such a thing? This is a man of nearly seventy who can with difficulty achieve an erection, but living happily with his wife, with children who are brilliant in their careers; a man who has given his life to the service of his fellow-men. On the morning of the alleged offence Dr Pardhy, though he had been working late the night before and had not gone to bed until 1 A.M., got up at seven o'clock and went to the Midland Hospital, evacuated twelve miles out of the city, and lectured the nurses for about an hour. He performed six considerable operations at the hospital and did not leave until 2.30. He arrived home at about three o'clock and had a hurried lunch before he saw the husband and wife complainants. What more can a doctor do, a doctor so liable to have charges brought against him by women, than to have the woman's husband in the room within four feet of him? Apart from its physical impossibility," Mr

Roberts told the jury, "you may consider this act, said to have been performed by a tired old man on a footstool, as a gymnastic feat of the highest quality. If there is a conviction in this case, then nobody would be safe at all."

At the end of his counsel's address Dr Pardhy was called into the witness-box and gave details of his professional career before the evening adjournment. On the next morning, before he continued, Mr Roberts called his experts into the box. A Harley Street gynæcological surgeon stated, in answer to counsel, that he had known of false charges of sexual interference brought by women against doctors without any motive, but the judge ruled that such a line of examination was irrelevant. The specialist continued that he would have thought that the act alleged would have been impossible with the woman lying in the position which had been described. "I never conceived such a thing was possible until this case was presented to me," he added. He declared that he did not think a woman lying on her side facing away from a man could distinguish whether it was a finger or anything else that was in contact with her.

In what was little less than a squabble which then ensued the proceedings approached the atmosphere of high farce as learned men, none of whom had had any subjective experience, debated a sensitivity which might have been resolved if they had called on the testimony of a woman, and preferably a woman gynæcologist.

The tone of the trial became even more ludicrous as the couch was once more hoisted on to the judge's bench, and first the defence expert, with an aide, demonstrated that rape was impossible, to be followed by Professor Webster and the family doctor repeating their demonstration that it was possible. At this point laughter in the public gallery could not be stilled. The judge stopped the case, said it was an extremely serious trial, and if he heard any more laughter he would have no hesitation in clearing the court.

Dr Pardhy was called to resume his evidence. He gave details of his arduous working day on the 10th of June which bore out his counsel's opening statement. He said that, before seeing the husband and wife that afternoon, he went to the lavatory. He declared that he had got "the bad habit" of sometimes failing to button his trousers. He described the examination and its sequel. While it was in progress the woman suddenly got up and called out. He appealed to her to resume her position so that he could continue the examination, but the husband came from behind the screen and said, "What are you doing to my wife?"

"He then accused me of the offence," Dr Pardhy continued. I replied, 'I did not.' I think I also said, 'Ridiculous!' He said he should report the matter to the police, and asked to use the telephone. I told him the telephone was downstairs, and indicated that he could use it. He did not, of course. Then he said, 'It's already cost me twenty guineas, and I am getting this on top of it.' I said something like this to him, 'My dear man, I have a beautiful wife and lovely children, and do you think a man in my position, with my reputation and the type of patients I have, would do such a thing?' He said, 'Dr Pardhy, you have been accused of a similar thing before,' and I answered, 'Yes, but both the judge and the jury pooh-poohed it.' Once in the conversation he came across to me with his right hand clenched. I told him that I ought to continue the examination, and he said, 'You are not going to touch my wife again.'

"Outside, just before the husband got into his car, the husband said, 'Mr Pardhy, you are going to hear more about this. I am going to see the police.' I said to him, 'Think of the matter carefully. I am a man about seventy years old with a beautiful wife and lovely and brilliant children, and do you think I would do such a thing?' In effect, the husband replied that I should hear more about it. I remember I said, 'Sleep over it.' When he was in the car he put his right hand into his trousers pocket and pulled out a lot of coins. He shook them in his hand and said, 'Mr Pardhy, you do not understand psychology.' I replied that I understood the psychology of my patients. They drove away, and later I went to my solicitors."

Mr Gilbert Paull cross-examined. He asked, "Either the husband and wife have concocted this wicked story, or you are guilty?"

"I don't know," was the answer.

"Do you agree that if a woman thought she had been raped she would be terribly shocked?"

"Yes."

"Did you hear [the family doctor] say that she was extremely upset, that she was trembling all over? Does not that suggest to you that she had that afternoon received a dreadful shock?"

"She could imagine it; that would produce trembling."

"Is that agitation consistent with a deliberately concocted plot against you?"

"I am not sure of that."

"I suggest that the condition of the wife was only consistent with her honestly thinking that she had been raped?"

"I do not. I have seen women simulating nervousness and shock. Every day I examine women who imagine things without having any basis, and it is my opinion the wife is neurotic. I have written a book about that. I will present you with a copy if you like," Dr Pardhy offered.

"Whatever you have written, do you agree that you have written nothing in your notes concerning the wife's case to the effect that she is neurotic?"

"Yes."

"Did you think there was an attempt to blackmail you that afternoon?"

"The word blackmail is rather . . ." said Dr Pardhy indecisively.

"Do you think there was between the husband and wife some form of concocted story to try to get money out of you?"

"From what they said I had my suspicions."

"If that were so, I suggest you would have said to them, 'Get out of my house!' and not have talked about your beautiful wife and lovely children. Do you tell the jury that is the way you would talk to a blackmailer?"

"I said I had suspicions. Even people who have an inclination to blackmail turn round if you appeal to their better senses."

"I suggest you used those words about having a beautiful wife and lovely children because you were guilty?"

"No."

Dr Pardhy left the box. He was followed by a lecturer in forensic medicine who gave evidence for the defence over the space of an hour.

The fourth day of the trial began with evidence from a Sheffield surgeon of an examination he made of Dr Pardhy eleven days after the alleged rape. He said that the condition from which the doctor was suffering was in an advanced stage. [Inflammation of the prostate gland is a painful condition which can lead to a discharge from the urethra.] The witness was further asked his opinion of the practicability of the offence said to have been committed in the consulting-room. He declared, "I should say it was impossible." The judge asked him on what he based such an opinion. He said he based it on physiology. Mrs Pardhy had been called, and testified briefly to her husband's bad habit of failing to adjust his dress after visiting the lavatory, and this concluded the evidence for the defence.

Mr G. D. Roberts made his closing speech to the jury. "I am suggesting to you," he said, "that this is a case on which it would be wholly unsafe to convict. If you convict you would be speculating a wild guess at something that has not been proved. A verdict of Not Guilty will not cast any criticism on [the husband and wife] that they have concocted a wicked story, but will merely indicate that the accusations against Dr Pardhy have not been proved.

"From the beginning Dr Pardhy has denied the charge in the most forcible way. You do not need reminding that doctors examine women patients every day. From that, two things follow. First of all, a doctor becomes so familiar with the human body that he is less likely to be tempted by sexual desire; and, secondly, doctors are peculiarly liable to be made the subject of charges such as this.

"This is why, in my submission, it is important to realize that women, from imagination or from other reasons, frequently make accusations which are found to be quite groundless. That is common knowledge.

"I suggest this case is unreliable and flimsy, and not founded on the solid rock of fact. You have heard the remarkably confident opinions of Professor Webster. He is a Pooh-Bah of the medical profession," declared Mr Roberts. "He will give expert evidence on any subject at all. Some of the evidence he has given is wild speculation. It is impossible to conceive that Dr Pardhy would be so reckless as to do the thing alleged against him when the woman's husband was sitting within a few feet. Moreover, a guilty man would have got rid of a lot of things which have been produced in the case before the police seized them.

"This remarkable case is by no means proved. To fly in the face of all physical and psychological probabilities of the 10th of June is impossible. Those probabilities point one way, and that is against the thought of Dr Pardhy committing such an offence in such circumstances.

Mr Gilbert Paull, in his closing speech, suggested that, if the defence put forward was true, the complainant must be a most despicable woman. He spoke strongly of the production of the convict to confront her. "That was an appalling suggestion to make, that she slept with that man in a commercial hotel, if it was not true. The wife had not the slightest knowledge that any such suggestion was going to be made against her, and the idea that she should be branded as a woman of that character has no foundation at all.

"You have heard Dr Pardhy's suggestion that he was being blackmailed. I leave it to your good sense. If you were being accused by a blackmailer, what would you do? Would you kick the man out of the house, or would you say, 'Go home and sleep it over; you may think differently in the morning?' Is that the sort of language you would use to a person you thought was blackmailing? Those are rather almost the words of a man who thinks, "They have a just suspicion, but they will not take it any further.'

"Do you think that any reason has been produced which would discredit the evidence of the husband? Is there any reason why a respectable man should put his wife into the most appalling position of having to give evidence, unless he thought that what he was saying was true?"

The trial was adjourned, to await the judge's summing up next day. M. P. Pugh went home to his Worcestershire garden with his mind in a rare perplexity. Outwardly he had constantly maintained his normal confident assurance that there was "not the slightest doubt" about Pardhy's guilt. But there were enigmas that had never been resolved throughout the long process. He sat in the evening sun. It was raspberry time, and his wife was gathering the fruit. He could not dismiss the case from his mind. He was irritated by the surface smart of the attack on Professor Webster's credibility, and he was aware that, if it had not been for the routine of immediate investigation that the doctor had built up it might have been impossible to have pressed the charge at all. He went inside and wrote to Webster:

Housmans
Fockbury
Worcestershire

29.7.43

My dear James,

Our labours being over I have been sitting in the sun without having to search my brain for answers that always seem so elusive. I have however thought a lot of the great assistance & help you have rendered in the case & I feel I

> must tell you how I admire the way the matter has been handled by you right from the commencement. It has been a great pleasure for me to be so closely associated with you & I trust and believe that a bond of trust understanding and friendship has been forged between us. Whatever the result I feel that everything humanly possible has been done. I am hoping that the judge will pay you a tribute tomorrow, for I am sure he must appreciate the great value of your services to the administration of Justice.
>
> Yours ever
>
> MERVYN

Mr Justice Wrottesley summed up over a period of three hours. "Only three persons know what went on in that room," he said. "[The wife] is one. [The husband] is another, and the accused is the third. But of those three persons only one is really in a position to say what took place, because, you may remember, [the wife] was placed in such a position that she could not see what was going on, and [the husband] sat with his back to a screen."

He commented on the confrontation of the convict and the wife, and her denial that she had ever slept a night with him or had ever seen him in her life before. "In cases of this kind," he said, "it is allowable in our courts to ask women that kind of question, and it cannot be said to be irrelevant, because it might be established in that way you had to deal with a loose woman. At the same time, our law is quite definite in this: if the witness denies it, the answer must be taken. You may think it a little hard that a witness should be asked that kind of question and not be allowed to call evidence (should it be available) to show that was an unfounded suggestion. But your task in this case is quite hard enough; and it would be an intolerable hardship, amongst other things, on you if we had to pursue that kind of side-issue. In that way one's attention would be distracted from the real point in this case: did that woman impress you as a credible witness? Did she impress you as telling the truth?"

The credibility of the woman was vital, the judge emphasized, because the burden of proof rested on the prosecution. "If you believe [the wife's] evidence and [the husband's] evidence, you need have no hesitation in saying that [the wife] was raped by the accused. Raped by stealth," added his Lordship in a striking phrase.

The judge recalled the evidence given by the accused of what happened in the consulting-room. "If this is true," he said, "there is an end of the case, and you will find him Not Guilty. If there is anything in it which shakes your belief in [the husband's and wife's] story, you must acquit him. You may find it impossible to believe it. That is for you.

"In a case that bristles with improbabilities, this is perhaps the most improbable thing of all: that for some reason [the wife] suddenly thinks there is something wrong, when there is not, suddenly sits up, calls out [the husband's name] and then there follows the scene which he described—when he had done nothing."

After an hour and a half's deliberation the jury returned, and the foreman told the judge that they were not agreed. He asked them to try again, but after a further fifteen minutes the foreman said there was no prospect of their coming to a decision. The judge ordered that the case should be retried at the next Assizes, in five months' time.

Mervyn Pugh was as shattered by the impasse as his colleagues could have anticipated. On mature reflection he drew the consolation that one of the principal factors in the stalemate had been the defence's production of the convict, which could have never been achieved but for previous Press publicity, and that this was a striking instance of the value *to the defence* of the unhampered reporting of preliminary proceedings, a cause which he always upheld. Fourteen years later, at the end of his Birmingham career, when he was asked to give evidence to the Tucker Committee—the Home Secretary's (Mr R. A. Butler's) Departmental Committee on Proceedings Before Examining Magistrates, under the chairmanship of Lord Tucker—he wrote to the secretary an account of the Pardhy trial and the production of the convict from the cells.

"There can be no doubt," he said, "that this dramatic intervention had a great bearing on the result of the case which continued until the 30th July, when the jury failed to agree, and it is generally considered that had it not been for the intervention of B——, Dr Pardhy may well have been convicted. This is a case where considerable help was given to the defence as a result of the proceedings before the magistrates being published."

But in 1943 the tension of the unresolved Pardhy case still bore hardly on Pugh. At the beginning of December, as the

Assizes opened, the Doctor had an acute attack of prostatitis, and was obliged to have a preliminary operation to provide relief. A major operation would soon have to be undergone. But the Doctor took his place in the court on the 13th of December, 1943. Mr Justice Birkett and a jury of seven (one of whom was withdrawn on the third day when it was found that he was a special constable) heard the case argued by Mr Gilbert Paull with Mr Norman Winning, for the prosecution, and Mr J. F. Bourke and Mr W. Field Hunt for the defence. Certain additional points accrued to the body of evidence. The wife denied a defence suggestion that she had deceived two doctors, one of whom was Dr Pardhy, to persuade him to effect an abortion. Dr Pardhy declared that for twelve years, since he had had prostatitis, he had had no sexual desire, and for the past three or four years had been incapable of performing the sexual act. When, during the course of his evidence, Dr Webster, at Mr Paull's suggestion, began again his demonstration on the couch, Mr Bourke complained that the position of the assisting doctor was wrong, and Mr Justice Birkett stopped the display. "It is difficult," he said, "to reconstruct the matter exactly. Unless one could have a naked woman on the couch, which is unthinkable, I do not see how you can get anything on which you can really rely."

The most striking change in the tone of the trial was the character of a brilliant speech made by Mr J. F. Bourke in his opening address to the jury, before he put Dr Pardhy into the box, but putting himself completely into the personality and the voice of the accused.

"Speaking in the rôle of my client," he said, "I affirm that this accusation is entirely untrue. I am a man of long experience in this city, and I am respected. It is acknowledged by the prosecution that I denied and flung back this accusation at once. It is rather suggested that I adopted a cringing attitude and gabbled about my wife and children. It is said that Englishmen in such circumstances would throw the accuser out or do some violent thing. I am an Oriental and I belong to a race with a tradition of oppression; and I did seek to mollify my adversary. I did talk about my family, because I have wit enough to know, when such an accusation is voiced, that it has a menace and an evil about it which makes my world topple. They are everything to me, and in such a supreme moment of menace they sprang to my mind. It is said I am suggesting blackmail against my accuser. I am not; but I have been advised that I should tell exactly what was said. I therefore tell you about this man jingling money and talking about making me pay, with a mention of the police. I leave these facts because I do not understand what he was aiming at. If I were inventing an allegation of blackmail against this man, I should have thought of a clearer story and a more convincing one.

"But from my experience as a surgeon I give my opinion that it was impossible for me to do this thing; and, supposing it were mechanically possible, I would reject and ridicule the suggestion that it could be done without a woman knowing it."

When the jury retired they were out for forty-five minutes, and returned with a verdict of Not Guilty. People who had been awaiting the verdict cheered, and collected outside the courtroom to shake the Doctor's hand as he came out. A crowd followed him out of the Victoria Courts, and cheered as he and his wife and daughter got into a waiting car. People in Corporation Street waved and cheered, and Dr Pardhy responded by waving his hat.

Mervyn Pugh did not withhold his sincere praise for J. F. Bourke. He said philosophically to his colleagues afterwards that the defence in the second trial was markedly different from that in the first, but only on one occasion—when Mrs Pardhy gave a drastically graver account than before of her husband's capacity—did prosecution counsel, who had conducted both trials, draw attention to the change of course. In no major address to the jury did they make an issue of it, but allowed the jury an unconfused view of the case as presented. "And that," Pugh concluded, "is a damned fine tribute to British Justice."

CHAPTER

7

The War Crimes

THE immediate impact of the Second World War on the Birmingham Police Court was that Pugh conducted the first prosecution in the city's history of a driver accused of being drunk in charge of his tramcar. The strain of the novel blackout and the extra hours' work it involved had induced a driver to fortify himself, but when he observed with horror a motor-car reversing at him down Great Charles Street he decided that the world was topsy-turvy, and meekly hit the car. Pugh could find no section in the Road Traffic Act under which to deal with the case, and prosecuted the driver under the Licensing Act of 1872. With regard to the blackout, Pugh and the Chief Constable adopted a very tough attitude from the start, announcing that offenders would be sent for trial at the Assizes, where the maximum penalty was a £500 fine or two years' imprisonment.

During the first fourteen years in which he had held the office of Prosecuting Solicitor Pugh had seen his activities multiply fivefold with no increase in his staff, except for the acquisition of Norman Brown to assist A. E. Field as clerk. Norman Brown got married as war loomed nearer, and was promptly recalled from his honeymoon in Jersey when war broke out. But in the autumn of 1938 Ernest Hooton had joined the office as Assistant Prosecuting Solicitor, and this team saw the department through the War: Pugh and Hooton, Field and Brown, Miss Selwyn and Massey, the one-armed commissionaire who looked after the Law Library and brought Pugh his *Sporting Times.* They were battle-hardened, in fact, before 1939, for they had to deal with the intensive and harrowing trials for many bomb outrages, culminating in murder, of the Irish Republican Army centred in the Midlands. From 1939 Pugh was no longer living in Edgbaston, but took the house where the poet of *A Shropshire Lad* was born, Housmans, at Fockbury, a village near Bromsgrove in Worcestershire. To this address, and not to his office, came the secret and confidential information when Hitler's invasion seemed imminent that as soon as martial law was declared Captain M. P. Pugh, D.S.O., M.C., would be appointed a Military Magistrate with power to conduct a Summary Court and to act as a President and Member of a Military Court, which was empowered to impose any penalty, including the death sentence.

Regardless of martial law, death had already been decreed under emergency powers, as Pugh grimly reminded the court during the heavy bombing of Birmingham, as the ultimate penalty for looting, and some extremely heavy penalties—though never the capital sentence—were recorded for this crime. Death was also the penalty faced by a nineteen-year-old girl munition worker and her boy friend who were tried in great secrecy in the summer of 1942 for offences against the Treachery Act, the Defence Regulations, and the Official Secrets Act.

The girl worked at Kynochs [Imperial Metal Industries (Kynoch) Limited], and her job was assembling incendiary bullets, of a secret design, which were mainly used by the Royal Air Force. Our fighter pilots found that a number of these bullets were dangerously defective, and they were traced back to a particular assembly line. The girls on this line had the task of dipping a small screw into some glue and giving it two or three turns in the assembly. But hundreds of the screws were found to have no glue on them. This could cause a dangerous flashback when the bullet was fired, and it was possible—though this did not happen—for the aircraft firing the incendiaries itself to catch fire. When the defective assembly was traced to one girl secret investigations were made to determine whether she was merely day-dreaming, or kept at such a fast rate of work that she left out the glue operation occasionally in order to keep up with the line, or was deliberately sabotaging the incendiaries. The investigators found that the girl was known in the factory for remarks ridiculing the war effort, and for odd anti-Churchill and anti-Semitic propaganda on the general burden of "Hitler was right". They therefore investigated her contacts, and found that her boy friend was a Mosley supporter who had been released from detention under Regulation 18B, and when they raided his lodgings they found several of the incendiary bullets along with Fascist and anti-Semitic propaganda. In the girl's lodgings they found mild propaganda letters, and also a cup and saucer from the Kynoch canteen. They therefore arrested the pair and charged them under the Official Secrets Act with possession of the bullets.

Pugh handled the case, which meant an almost certain conviction; for under the Official Secrets Act the onus was on the defence to show good reason for possession of the bullets, and this was virtually impossible. But, after further consultations with the Director of Public Prosecutions, Pugh rang up the couple's solicitor and said, "I've got bad news for you. Taking into account the Mosley photographs and the general pro-Hitler propaganda we have found, we are going to proceed under the Treachery Act. I am going up to Winson Green now, and I think you ought to be present. Come with me if you like." In the car on the way to the prison the defence solicitor said, "I think you have overreached yourself. Under the Treachery Act the onus is no longer on the defence, and it is up to you to prove that the intention was to assist the enemy. I think you are going to find that very difficult." "Well," said Pugh, "the instructions have come from the Director, and we must do what we can."

The hearing in the lower court took nearly a fortnight, and was conducted strictly in camera. When the couple went on to their trial the Press were kept away from the Assize Court, all the frosted windows were blacked out, and every door was guarded. Mr Justice Croom-Johnson, who tried the case, early made it evident that he had little faith in the treachery charge. "If this is the way the prosecution case is going," he told the leading counsel, "I shall make short shrift of it." In the end, neither the treachery charge nor the secrets charge was sustained, and all that could be proved was that the girl had stolen a canteen cup and saucer: the case went down into Birmingham legal history as the Cup and Saucer Case. Binding her over for two years, the judge spoke severely to the girl in a long but perhaps fatherly rebuke, which did not seem to have the slightest effect, for the couple left the court arm-in-arm and laughing.

In the autumn of 1942 Pugh began a long series of prosecutions of building firms charged with defrauding the Birmingham

Corporation over accounts submitted for emergency bomb repairs. Like the case of the Forty Thieves, it entailed detailed, exhaustive, undramatic work, and Pugh earned warm professional appreciation for handling these complicated cases which contained none of the flame of human passion. By contrast, he had to deal with the crimes—as without exception they were then—which become more common in wartime, the tragic love affairs that end in suicide pacts.

In one painful case a private and an A.T.S. girl stationed at the same camp ran away when they heard that the man was to be posted overseas, and agreed that if they were caught they would end their lives together. They wandered about, sleeping in fields, and finally came to Birmingham. In Erdington they were picked up by the police, who questioned them and brought them to the station. But before they went into the building the girl said, "Do it now, Chris," and the man whipped out a razor-blade and cut her throat. As he tried to use the blade on himself a detective sergeant hit him on the chin, and another officer overpowered him. Because they were so near aid in the police station the girl's wound was plugged before she could bleed to death. Pugh prosecuted the man for attempted murder. The girl came out of hospital for the hearing and sat in tears by the side of the dock. The man was inevitably committed, and as he left the dock he asked, "Do you love me, Lydia?" She said, "Yes, and I want to marry you." In the Assize Court Mr Justice Croom-Johnson told the prisoner, "This is more appealing to the morbidity of the Russian novelist than to the common sense of the people of these islands. It is inconceivable that people can be so lacking in courage to face the separations and griefs of this world that they are prepared to do what you did, and apparently this young woman agreed to do. I must make the public understand, and the morbid, over-sentimentalized types of young men and women understand, that this sort of thing cannot be permitted." He sentenced the man to five years' penal servitude for wounding and a concurrent twelve months' imprisonment for attempted suicide.

In another tragedy the active partner was the girl, and Pugh did not press for the young lad who survived to face the judge on a charge of murder. The girl was nineteen, married to a soldier, but infatuated with a boy of seventeen. In a dugout air-raid shelter in the garden she put letters in his pocket before they made love, then shook powder into a glass of water, raised it to his lips, and drank the rest. She died poisoned, and he lived. The letters were to the girl's parents and to her husband asking them not to blame the boy. The lad was charged with murder and attempted suicide, but Pugh told the Stipendiary that there was not sufficient evidence to indicate that the boy had incited the girl to take her own life, and the magistrate dismissed the charge of murder and bound the boy over on a charge of attempted suicide.

But suicide pacts can be fabricated. Pugh read one jointly-signed note to the court in Birmingham and said of the accused, "I don't know whether he regarded this as a passport to murder. I do not put this case before the court as a suicide pact, but as a brutal and callous murder. The accused made no real determined effort to end his own life."

The man, an aircraft inspector, was charged with the murder of a typist. He had led the police to her body in a pond at Northfield. He produced a long letter, which he said they both had signed, referring to the fact the he was married but that he and the girl had lived together until her mother found out about his marriage. It ended: "For God's sake forgive her. She is so happy now. She knows we are going to die together. So good-bye all." The man told the police that they had sat talking in the park at Quinton, and the girl had said she could not face her mother much longer, and it would end their troubles if they died together. He continued, "We went across the fields and I said to her 'I will kill you first and I promise you faithfully I will die with you,' but faithfully I did not keep." He told how he pulled his tie round her neck and dragged her to the pond. "She was then conscious and kept saying 'I love you, I love you,' and then my mind went blank for five or six minutes, and when I came to myself I saw her in the pond. I stood in the pond by her. She did not move. I then got my necktie out of my collar and put it round my neck and pulled it tight until I went dazed, and I fell in the pond face downwards. I shouted 'Joyce, where are you?' and I got up on my feet and stayed there for some time, and made another attempt to strangle myself with my necktie and fell into the pond again. I then got up, took the necktie from round my neck, and stayed in the water from ten until five, I think, because I asked the postman the time. I touched her several times as she lay in the water."

True or imagined, this nightmare story presents one of the most chilling chronicles of mundane death ever narrated. Under an examination by Pugh which was intended to support his bizarre opening complaint that the accused "made no real determined effort to end his own life", Professor Webster said that if a cord, which had been produced in evidence, had been tied round the prisoner's neck as the marks on his flesh indicated, "it had not caused any degree of asphyxiation".

"How soon could a cord cause asphyxiation?"asked Pugh.

"If tied properly it could easily cause asphyxiation and bring about unconsciousness in 60 to 120 seconds."

"Did the accused make any attempt on his own life?"

"In my opinion, either he was interrupted in less than two minutes or the attempt was not serious."

At his trial the man went into the witness-box and amended his earlier statement: "I went dazed, and I fell face downwards into the water, but I managed to pull myself up again and say, 'Joyce, where are you?' I stayed in the water for some time, but later I got out and sat on the bank to have a cigarette. I went into the water again to do myself in. Then a picture came in my mind of my children, and a voice which said, 'Don't do it.' "

Mr Justice Croom-Johnson asked him how he reconciled his statement that he had fallen face downward into the water with the evidence that had been given that the top part of his coat and body was dry except for a little water on the back of his shoulders. He said, "All I can say is they had all dried."

He was found guilty and sentenced to death. Even accepting the most culpable explanation, the interactions of that doomed couple present a grim commentary on the mental turmoil experienced by humanity in crisis.

The war ended, and the men came home, including the prisoners of war. One of them, who had been in a German prison camp for five years, came back to Handsworth to await the knock at the door that since Dunkirk he had known must one day come to him. The moment arrived, and John Mavity, a corporal in the Royal Warwickshire Regiment, was arrested on a charge of having murdered his company commander, Captain Guy Glover, on the 20th of May, 1940, at Colonne, near Tournai, in Belgium. He was brought before the Stipendiary, "being a British subject now within the jurisdiction of the Birmingham Magistrates' Court area", and Pugh, opening the case, said it was the first to be tried in Birmingham in which the alleged murder had been committed outside the country.

"At the time of the alleged murder," Pugh began, "the accused was a corporal in the Royal Warwickshire Regiment and Captain Glover was his company commander. I will call evidence to prove that Mavity and Glover had been in the same company since 1929. In January 1940 the 8th Battalion went to France, and just prior to that the accused had been promoted to lance-sergeant. He was, however, reduced to corporal when disciplinary action was taken against him. A witness whom I shall call noticed this and questioned Mavity about it, and his reply was: 'That —— got me this for being drunk. He needn't think he's going to get away with it. I shall certainly get him when he gets up the line.'

"If," said Pugh to Lord Ilkeston, "you believe that Mavity did make that threatening statement it will help you to form an opinion as to why he eventually did fire a shot from the effects of which Captain Glover died.

"A number of possible witnesses," he continued, "are now dead: killed in battle. Some were suffering from the strain of battle, and I shall not be able to satisfy you as to the exact time of day when the alleged murder took place. They had been conducting a fighting retreat for seven days. They were without food. They had been in action for some considerable time and were worn out and tired. They had retreated to Colonne, on the river near Tournai, and the time as near as I can put it was in the evening of the 20th of May at about 9.30 P.M. There was intermittent shelling by the enemy, and mortar-fire and rifle-fire in the distance.

"Witnesses will say that Captain Glover received a message from a runner and left the company headquarters. Shortly afterwards a rifle-shot was heard near by, and a witness will say he heard Captain Glover shout, 'Help. They have got me.'

"I can call no witness who saw the shot fired, but a Corporal Gough heard the shot and found Captain Glover lying on the pavement with a gunshot wound in the upper part of his chest. He was rapidly losing consciousness, and was heard to say that he had been shot, but did not make any allegation as to who had shot him. The only person he asked for was his mother, and those were the last words this very gallant officer uttered in this world.

"Captain N. S. Robinson, a medical officer, who has since been killed, attended to Captain Glover, and said, 'Why did they have to do this to you? I'll put you out of your misery. There's no hope for you. Captain Robinson gave him an injection, and Captain Glover never regained consciousness, and was buried near company headquarters."

(The newspapers investigated this incident. The *Daily Mail* found former officers of the Royal Warwicks who said, "Glover and Robinson were like brothers. Within a few days of Guy's death Robinson was killed in action while tending wounded. When the battalion went overseas, officer friends of Captain Robinson said to him, 'If anything happens to us, deal with us, Robbie, won't you?' ")

"Shortly after the rifle-shot was heard," Pugh went on, "Mavity appeared at company headquarters and said, 'I've come to report I've shot Captain Glover as a spy.' He repeated this allegation and added, 'You're all —— spies.' He then brought his rifle up as though to shoot, and Captain Sparrow told him to drop it. A struggle ensued, and Mavity received a blow in the mouth from a rifle-butt. Mavity's rifle was inspected, and there was an empty cartridge found in the breech.

"He was handed over to an escort, and on the way to headquarters kept saying, 'I want a fair trial.' When asked why he did it Mavity replied, 'I saw tanks up the road, and I told Lieutenant Potts, but he wouldn't take any notice of me. They are all spies.' A witness will say that Mavity seemed at that time to have gone off his head and his eyes were glaring.

"On the following day the village was taken by the enemy and Mavity was captured. He remained a prisoner until quite recently, when he was repatriated. On December the 4th Mavity was seen at his home at Handsworth by Inspector Foreman of the Birmingham C.I.D. and Detective Inspector Burney of Scotland Yard. Mavity said to the officers, 'I guessed what it was all about.' When charged, Mavity is alleged to have said, 'I remember shooting him, but my mind was a blank at the time. I would like to tell you. It has worried me ever since.' Mavity then made a statement detailing how he had joined the Territorials at an early date, and known Captain Glover, and finally gone to France. In May the regiment moved to the Belgian frontier and Captain Glover was the company commander. While they were holding a sector at Tournai he was tired and ill and kept seeing things in front of him. He 'felt' that Captain Glover was a spy.

"'I saw him coming towards me from just behind the firing-line,'" Pugh continued, quoting the alleged statement. "'I asked him why the messenger sent by me to H.Q. had not returned. He turned around and then went back to H.Q. And then he came back carrying his revolver. I thought he was going to shoot me with his revolver. I had my rifle with me with one bullet up the spout. I put my rifle to my shoulder and shot him.'

"Later in his alleged statement Mavity said he had no grievance against Captain Glover: 'I really thought he was a spy at the time because the messenger had not returned to me. I still think I must have been off my head when I did it. I never made any secret of the incident and told some of my men about it.'

"It is no part of my duty," Pugh concluded, "to deal with the question of insanity, but I intend to put in everything relating to the prisoner's state of mind at the time of the alleged shooting so that the defence can make the fullest possible use of it. But I must emphasize that the dead officer was a man of the highest possible character. He was greatly esteemed by everyone who knew him, and greatly loved and respected in the regiment. He was a true British patriot, and any suggestion that he was a spy is absolutely ridiculous. There is not a scintilla of evidence that he was a spy."

Harry Faber, for the defence, immediately jumped to his feet to support this. "I wish to make it perfectly clear," he said, "that I have never received any instructions from Mavity which suggest in any way that Captain Glover was not a British officer of the highest character. If any friends or relatives are in court, I think I should indicate to them that it is my client's conviction that Captain Glover was a gallant officer and gentleman."

"I am very glad to hear you say that," acknowledged Lord Ilkeston.

The evidence Pugh called veered slightly more to the prisoner's favour even than his sympathetic opening. A burly ex-company-sergeant-major said that Mavity's demotion before the battalion left for France was never taken seriously by him, and entailed no reduction in pay. Pugh contested that there had been no resentment, and urged, "Come, come, you are a soldier." "I'm not," said the witness doggedly. "I'm a civilian." Witnesses said that Mavity, with his comrades, had been fighting and marching for seven days, and had not slept for three. When he was being taken away under arrest he struggled against being confined in a cellar, saying, "Don't put me down there. There's gas down there. I know you're going to kill me—shoot me." He was taken to a schoolroom, where he had to be tied hand and foot, and during heavy shelling through the night he told his guards that they were all in heaven and he would look after them. The only surviving officer told of a court of inquiry he held at which Mavity appeared on a charge of murder. The medical officer, Captain Robinson, said that the man was mad, and as a result of this inquiry the brigadier cancelled his order for a field general court-martial. All this time they were under repeated attack, but the company held on, though Mavity was captured.

Faber finally submitted that this was not a case where the man should be committed to take his trial on a capital charge: "Is there any evidence before the court to show the shot he fired killed this man, or any evidence to show the shot fired caused the death? Not one witness can say, 'I saw this man shoot Captain Glover.' All they can say is 'We heard a shot.' "

"But Mavity has admitted the shooting," interjected the magistrate.

"He may think he did it," said Faber, "but there is no evidence to show the shot he fired caused Captain Glover's death."

Lord Ilkeston replied that he thought there was a case to answer and ordered Mavity's committal. At the Assizes in March 1946 he was found Guilty but Insane and detained.

CHAPTER

"The Great Mr Pugh"

"SAY what you know about the following: Gulf Stream." M. P. Pugh's son John, whose admirable preparatory education at the Dragon School, Oxford, had recently been enlarged by his father's keen discussion on form for the 1946 Derby, picked up his pen in the Bromsgrove School hall and wrote, for his Foundation Scholarship entry, an enthusiastic account of Lord Derby's racehorse Gulf Stream, a full analysis of the breeding and form which had made it the favourite for the Epsom classic, and a regretful report of the unlucky circumstances which had caused it to lose. He came home and told his father with gusto of the great showing he had made in this question. Pugh buried his head in his hands. "My God!" he moaned. "I've bred an idiot." But old Pugh—he was now fifty-three—had never strictly segregated work and play. It was part of the duty of Constable Harry Lowe, dock officer in the Stipendiary's Court for seventeen years, to retire at discreet intervals for the Test score, passing it to Pugh, who remitted it to the Bench. During the cricket season when Don Kenyon, the pride of Worcester and of M. P. P., was in and out of the England team John Sellars, a Bromsgrove solicitor and committee member at Worcester, went into court one day when Pugh was in the middle of a detailed cross-examination. Pugh recognized Sellars, paused, grinned, and said across the court, "Morning, Jack—bloody fools haven't picked Kenyon."

Pugh had settled down at Housmans, his country house at Fockbury. His wife continued the welfare clinics which she had made her career. Pugh, who always got on well with children, took a more technical interest in education, and with his friend the Vicar of Dodford (formerly Sergeant-Major Frank Marks, D.C.M., M.M.) was a manager of Dodford primary school. Then he was elected Dodford's representative at Bromsgrove on the district education committee, and was promptly made vice-chairman, and applied to his part-time administration something of the professional zeal he had seen in his father, so long a director of education. Pugh would show enthusiasts for Housman round his home, and once entertained two American admirers of the poet. They arrived while M. P. P. was out, and Dr Pugh, who was not familiar with the wine pantry, offered them sherry. The Americans liked the drink so much that they pressed for more, and then wrote down the details of the label, so that they could buy bottles to take back to the States. Dr Pugh told her husband about it when he came in. "But we have no sherry," he objected. It came out that the Americans had drunk from a sherry bottle some extremely potent cowslip wine made for the Pughs by a farmer friend, Henry Crawford—and anything with the sherry label which they might buy would never match it. "But we'd better not let on," Pugh chuckled to his wife. Next morning the Americans asked him which room Housman had been born in. Pugh had no idea, but, not wishing to disappoint them, span a great yarn with colourful details that it had been the very room where they had slept. The visitors rushed back to take photographs. "Oh, but the bed is different," Pugh had to point out.

From Fockbury Pugh drove cautiously every morning to the Victoria Law Courts, generally arriving in a flaming temper. "I'm the only bugger in Birmingham doing thirty miles an hour," he would roar at the police as he parked his car in the lock-up. He was a meticulously careful driver, giving exaggerated precedence to pedestrians at crossings; but one Assize morning the waiting policeman could not stomach this consideration. He put his head in the car window. "For God's sake, get on," he urged. "The bloody judges are coming."

For eighteen years after 1945 E. J. Dodd (later Sir Edward, and H. M. Chief Inspector of Constabulary for England and Wales) was Chief Constable of Birmingham, and gradually breaking down parochial police administration until the Midlands began to be called "Dodd's own country". Dodd and Pugh had great respect for each other, and Dodd's subordinates were all old friends of Pugh—the 'two Freds', Richardson and Baguley, and George Blackborow, all of whom eventually served as Assistant Chief Constable. "I love the police," Pugh said at this time, though the fact was not always apparent from the curmudgeonly criticism of senior police officers which he occasionally launched at lunch in the Mess—where he never sat down without checking that there were not thirteen at table. "He can't be much good, he has never brought me much work," he would growl in censure when a name was mentioned. Yet he was a different, almost Santa Claus character, as he relaxed with the recruits at the Birmingham Police Training School at their end-of-term supper party and concert; even here the aura of the schoolmaster still clung, and many a policeman, catching sight of Pugh, would almost automatically mutter one of the formulae he had barked at them: "You can't prove burglary unless you are satisfied on four points—time, place, manner, and intent: The time, between nine at night and six in the morning; the place a dwelling-house; the manner, a break-in; the intent, to steal."

The middle ranks of the police were beginning to refer to him as "the great Mr Pugh", and if this phrase initially masked resentment it developed into a genuine tribute. He fought for them, as he also fought for his department. Much of the struggle behind the scenes at Birmingham Council House was never recorded, but a battle for power was in fact being waged and won. The issue was simple. J. Frank Gregg, the young Town Clerk under whose auspices the Prosecuting Solicitor's department officially came, wanted to control Pugh. Dodd saw the dangers that lay ahead, and a long struggle ensued. As Pugh consolidated, rather than capitulated, the atmosphere grew tenser. "My dear Mervyn" in correspondence became "Dear Pugh", and "My dear Frank" dwindled to "Dear Town Clerk". Both Gregg and Pugh were ambitious men, but the inevitable clash never became an open war, for neither was foolhardy. When the time came for Pugh to retire he extended the olive-branch by pointedly inviting the Town Clerk to his private farewell party, and in his speech paid tribute to Gregg for standing up for what he thought was right.

Pugh gradually enlarged his department. Bernard J. Potter succeeded Ernest Hooton as Assistant Prosecuting Solicitor in 1947, and was succeeded by James Ross, now a Q.C. In 1949 Roy M. Dunstan as Deputy, and Charles A. Smallwood as Senior Assistant, complemented a team which Pugh always managed to dress with the prettiest secretaries in the Corporation. Pugh's empire-building extended to territorial claims in the court offices. When the police surreptitiously installed a printing machine above Pugh's own office he exploded into protests that he was the victim of trespass by noise and vibration. The senior police-officers whom he summoned could hear little noise, and said so. "But look at the vibration!" stormed Pugh, pointing to a wildly swinging electric light. John McKay, Assistant Chief Constable (afterwards Inspector of Constabulary), looked at the light, but also observed the umbrella which Pugh had placed handily at the side of his desk, to give the light an extra swing when he heard the police coming; but Mackay conceded the air space to Pugh.

Pugh still bullied police-officers for their professional and hygienic good. His staff in outer offices would look at each other knowingly as they heard the great roar of "Ait!"—Pugh's pronunciation of "Out!"—and another policeman stumbled out of the door. In this way he would impart hard lessons that might, indeed, teach a detective the careful proof necessary, for instance, before an unpaid loan could be treated as larceny, but which could also be most humiliating. In one such case a workman who had lent money to a workmate could not get it back, and finally complained to the police, who preferred a charge. "Bring your witness," Pugh ordered the detective. When the workman was in his office he rounded on him in apparent fury. "You were going to get this money. He was going to pay it back. You knew you were going to get it back, but you tried to use the police to squeeze him. Not larceny, debt. Ait!" Pugh, even more concerned with his health as he grew older, snarled his formidable "Ait!" at the slightest suspicion of infirmity in anyone opposite him.

Pugh had a particular timidity about mental disease. When a West Indian was accused of the attempted murder of his wife Pugh refused to have him brought into the dock, telling the Stipendiary that since the man was "rather violent" it would not be desirable or even safe to put him in the dock. The court therefore adjourned to a cell on the floor of which the handcuffed man was lying; the magistrate and his clerk, Frank Howarth, stood alongside the guarded prisoner, while Pugh prudently made his opening statement from the cell door. When any firearm was produced in Pugh's office as an exhibit he took exaggerated precautions to order constant reassurance that it was not loaded:

"Is it empty? Are you sure? Look again. It's a remarkable fact that whenever anyone has been shot the revolver was always unloaded."

In his later years the police thought that Pugh was slightly losing his zest for attack in the courts, and that he would try to maintain his record of successful convictions by not fighting the doubtful cases as once he did. Detectives in charge of cases learned to challenge him by bringing in a file and saying, "I don't think you can win this one, Mr Pugh; you've got a tricky one here." "Let's have a look at the statements," Pugh would grunt.

But he warmed to an astute piece of detection, and demonstrated it with care in the court like a father. Detective Inspector W. J. Richards (later Chief Constable of Manchester) investigated a case of assault with an element of indecency. A man who had obviously taken drink called at a house on a municipal estate, behaved extremely freely towards the housewife, assaulted her, and made his escape. Richards came to the house, got a description of the man, hunted the district, and finally found a man whom the housewife picked out at an identification parade. In a somewhat puzzled manner, the man denied the charge, which like all in its category, was extremely difficult to prove without corroborative evidence. The only possible clue Richards had was a tatty piece of newspaper taken from the man's pocket, containing a report of a woman who had been mixed up in an unsavoury affair, and giving the implication that the woman named in the report was of a loose character. Richards took significant notice of the clipping only because the man insisted that he wanted it back after he was searched. But, however deeply Richards thought about it, he could not relate the newspaper cutting to the attack on the woman. Finally he got out a large-scale map of the housing estate. He marked on it the house of the woman who had been assaulted and the house of the woman who had been named. He began to turn the map around. It suddenly occurred to him that the two houses bore the same relationship to the boundary of the estate. He went upstairs. "Look, Mr Pugh," said Richards. "If a man had had a tot or two and came on to the estate intending to call on the loose woman and chance his luck, he would go right, left, second left, et cetera. But if, because he had had a few drinks, he came on the estate by the wrong approach, and went right, left, and so on, he'd finish up at the house of the woman who has complained; and that could explain why, according to what she says, he seemed surprised that she didn't take him in, and that she resented what he did." Pugh was enthusiastic in his congratulations, demanded that the map should be mounted and the cutting copied before he went into court, and had the man sent down.

At the end of 1950 Lord Ilkeston retired from the Bench at the age of eighty-two, voicing to the last his objection to being called the Stipendiary: "Other people do work for money without having to bear such a name. I have always felt it wrong that the material reward for honest work should be so indelicately emphasized." Mr John Frederic Milward was appointed Stipendiary. Pugh had to readjust his schedule as an immediate material mark of the change, for Mr Milward advanced the opening of the court from 10.30 to 10 A.M. But, more fundamentally, it was made clear that this was a different régime. Pugh had pleaded before Lord Ilkeston for twenty-six years, and he now found that he had not the same freedom either to expound the law as he saw it or to override the magistrate with the familiarity that habit had bred. The forceful command from the Bench, "Sit down, Mr Pugh, sit down, I am talking" had to be issued more than once before the older man accepted the fact that the court was not to be run by an advocate.

But the files of the cases continued to come in, always in increasing number, and were set in process through the mills of justice indifferently, whether they concerned murder or obscene publications—though proportionately the incidence of pornography increased more steeply than murder. Of the scores of Pugh's murder cases, few are outstanding either for the ingenuity of their method or their advocacy, though they splashed their usual gore over the front pages at the time. An Indian pedlar murdered his white mistress and his best friend because he believed the woman had put a hoodoo spell on him; the murdered man lived long enough for a court to be convened in the General Hospital, and the man's answers, written down by an interpreter, were claimed by Pugh to constitute a dying declaration—a form of evidence he often mentioned in his lectures to the police but could rarely instance. The Indian, who had been in the habit of spraying water round his room and over his fellow-lodgers to 'get rid of the devil' was at the Assizes found unfit to plead: this, or the drab domestic crime following sexual tension, was the general run of Pugh's murders. Three West Africans knifed a man outside the Clements Arms pub in Gooch Street, Balsall Heath, and the preliminary hearing of the murder charge against them was adjourned over eight weeks owing to Pugh's illness: as Agent for the Director of Public Prosecutions he would not delegate his responsibility for the prosecution. When Pugh returned to duty he told the court that before the fight there had been a scene in the pub when a man—not the victim—had called the accused "black bastard" and "Sambo". "I did not know till now," Pugh acknowledged with characteristic fairness, "that Sambo to West African subjects is a very offensive word indeed. I am satisfied, however, from inquiries I have made, that Sambo is in fact a very insulting word." At the Assizes one of the men was given four months for manslaughter, and the others acquitted. An Irish labourer lodging at Nechells was charged with strangling the Irishwoman with whom he had lived after a quarrel in a pub when the victim had said, "Bill should be more careful of the women he goes out with. He should pay for the child before he goes out drinking with another woman." Pugh, admitting that the prosecution evidence was wholly circumstantial, quoted Lord Hewart: "Circumstantial evidence is very often the best, because it is evidence of surrounding circumstances which is capable of proving a proposition with the accuracy of mathematics." The man eventually got seven years for manslaughter.

The astonishing sequence of deaths which came to be called the Moon Murders could have been prevented from reaching its climax if Professor Webster had been heeded on two separate occasions. In 1943 Allan Dennis Witcomb, picked up at his home at Brookfields for being an Army deserter, a man classified by the Army as a psychopath, confessed to the police that ten years previously he had smothered his little niece to death. Webster advised that an exhumation of the body should be made, but at a hearing before the Stipendiary Pugh, for the Director of Public Prosecutions, said that no evidence would be offered. In 1950 Witcomb was charged with killing a neighbouring widow in her bed, and before the hearing he confessed to the similar murder of another local woman in 1948, the crimes being done when, he said, he was out of control of himself when the moon was up. Pugh, prosecuting before the Stipendiary, said of the 1948 death, "I have been requested to inform the court that at the inquest a verdict of Accidental Death was brought in, and to go through the evidence in detail of Professor Webster and the opinion he formed. Professor Webster's evidence made it perfectly clear that in his opinion the woman did not die of natural causes. I think it is right that it should be made clear that although the verdict of Accidental Death was brought in, it was never the opinion of Professor Webster." Webster himself, giving evidence later, underlined the position he had taken even more strongly, and, with regard to the earlier confession of child-murder, said that he had been consulted by the police, but, against his advice, the child was not exhumed. Witcomb's Assize trial resolved itself virtually into a two-day inquiry into the state of his mind, and he was found Guilty but Insane.

An interesting defence in one of the most pathetic murder cases which Pugh handled was advanced when Francis Wilfred Windle, a Corporation baths attendant from Nechells, was charged with murdering his nagging wife by administering a hundred aspirins. Dr Hans Haas, consultant psychiatrist at Winson Green Mental Hospital, made a remarkable diagnosis. He said Mrs Windle was suffering from manic-depressive psychosis, and she would have been certified because of her suicidal tendencies. Windle was so completely under the influence of his wife that he was unable to judge for himself or to discriminate. He was suffering from communicated insanity. When at the Assizes Mr Justice Devlin sought elaboration of this phrase Dr Haas said it was communicated from Mrs Windle to her husband that it would be a good thing that she should die. Windle was sentenced to death, but after a vigorous struggle (which eventually was refused a hearing in the House of Lords) he was reprieved and given life imprisonment.

The tragedies of violence which so often came into Pugh's files rarely bore any relation either to organized crime or to any war-degenerated mentality, and offered little opportunity for bland, general moral condemnation. They were more a continuing reminder of the extremes to which wretchedness, poverty, and disease drive humanity. A South Yardley painter was accused of the attempted murder of his sister-in-law by strangulation. Pugh recounted that the two had been lovers, the victim having betrayed her elder sister. The man had been barred from the victim's house, but after a year he did call one morning, and said, "I know I should not have come. I have to see you once more. I haven't seen you for twelve months. Shall we be seeing one another for Christmas?" When the sister-in-law refused any further meetings he said, "Give me one kiss. It will be the last kiss." According to the prisoner's own statement (made at the police station after three epileptic fits), "We started to make love; when she suddenly said No, I lost my head and I think I tried to strangle her with my necktie." The man was committed to the Assizes, but on the eve of his trial he hanged himself in his own home while his wife was out shopping. On a Christmas night—a frequent occasion for drunken violence—a sodden boxer who boasted that it took six policemen to lock him up went home to his wife at Billesley. It was almost midnight, and she was in bed, literally waiting to be beaten up. But she heard her grown-up sons, who had been waiting up, say, "You are not going upstairs. You leave Mother alone." She heard her husband's obscene reply, and then a prolonged scuffling. After ten minutes her elder son came upstairs. She asked him what had happened. He said, "Something terrible, Mother—what he has been asking for for a long time. We are going to the police station." In the words of Professor Webster, who conducted the post mortem, the father, who was much more powerful than the sons, had fought until his brain was destroyed. According to the statement of one of the sons, "He said, 'I will murder the three of you.' I tried to hold him and told George to hit him with something. George hit him with the poker and knocked him down. He started to get up. I was scared. I thought if ever he got up he would kill us all. I shouted to George to get the chopper, or anything heavy, and the next thing I remember was hitting him with the chopper. Then I realized what I had done, and I thought, 'Well, we are safe now.'" Pugh prosecuted the brothers for murder. At the Assizes the Crown offered no evidence on this charge, but accepted pleas of Guilty to manslaughter. The police said the young men had had a wretched home life and were devoted to their mother. Mr Justice Lynskey sentenced them to three and five years' penal servitude.

A sixty-year-old woman from Lea Hall was pulled out of the canal at Salford Bridge, struggling to swim, and was taken to hospital. When the police called at her home to tell her family they found that her husband was blind and her daughter was deaf, tubercular, and mentally ill. The daughter had had recent spells in a mental ward and at the Yardley Sanatorium, but since she returned had worn down her mother with worry because she could not sleep at nights, and had begged her mother, "Don't let me go there again, Mum." That morning the mother had gone upstairs and told her daughter, "You're not going to any more hospitals." She then tried to strangle her in her bed. The daughter broke away, but her mother caught her on the landing and again tried to kill her. Again the daughter freed herself and locked herself in the bathroom. The mother went outside and tried to get in through the window, and when that failed came back and broke the door down. The daughter begged for mercy, crying, "Don't do it, Mum. I'll get better." The mother then broke down and said, "I'm going to drown myself," and ran downstairs. This time the daughter followed her and struggled to prevent her mother leaving, but found that the mother made one more determined attempt to strangle her, so she tore herself free and ran to a neighbour's. The old mother ran away, and was seen to collapse in the street outside Long Acre post-office. She was taken into the post-office by passers-by and given amateur treatment. Then, left to herself, she wandered away again, and half an hour later was seen in the canal. The police found a letter at her home addressed to them, saying, "I intend to kill Connie rather than she shall go back to the mental ward again. She can't sleep at night, so I am going to put her out of her misery. May God have mercy on my soul for the wicked thing I am going to do."

That such a tumult, in such pitiful conditions, should end with the appearance of a grey woman in a drab dock on charges of attempted murder and attempted suicide which it was his duty to prosecute did not seem incongruous to Pugh in its departmental classification of the effects of human misery.

In other cases of more tenuous psychotic origin he did not hesitate to condemn, for he had the prosecuting lawman's customary cynicism towards pleadings of psychological inadequacy. "This story is so dreadful that it is quite impossible to comment on it. The man did a most dreadful and callous thing," he said, prosecuting a father for exposing his daughter, only nine hours old, in a manner likely to cause her unnecessary suffering and injury to health. He said that the girl, the man's fourth child, had been born at 2.50 P.M., and that that night the man had got into bed with his wife, and, in a temper, said "I don't want this child because there is German blood in you and in the child."

Pugh continued, "He told his wife to clear out of the house, although she had only given birth to the child a few hours before. She realized he meant what he said, and there would be trouble if she did not go, so she got up and went to her mother's taking all her children with her. At 12.10 A.M. she was seen by a taxi-driver with her children, carrying her nine-hour-old baby in her arms. She was obviously in a state of great exhaustion, and on the point of collapse. The taxi-driver picked her and her children up and took them to her mother. He did not charge her anything, but gave her £1. Just after 2 A.M. the father called at the house, and at 2.55 A.M. looked at the clock and said to his wife, 'I will give you five minutes, and if you don't come with me I shall take the baby.' When the five minutes had elapsed he jumped up, snatched up this little child, and went out into the night air with it. He walked two miles home with the child wrapped in his overcoat, put it in a basket by the side of his bed, fed it with cow's milk and sugar from a teaspoon, and went to sleep. Later that day the wife returned home with her children. A doctor called and considered both mother and child should go to hospital because of the exposure they had undergone. The father refused to let them go. He turned the doctor out of the house and bolted all doors and windows. Later the police persuaded him to allow both to go to Dudley Road hospital.

"It is difficult," said Pugh, "for anyone to appreciate how a father could have acted in such a way as this man admits he has done." The magistrate sentenced him to four months' hard labour. The wife wept bitterly as he went down to the cells. "The sentence is very harsh," she said. "I love him very much. Prison will do him more harm than good. He was discharged from the Army with psycho-neurosis."

Blackmail in Birmingham, as the cases ran in Pugh's files, was with few exceptions on a cheap and sordid scale. A woman ran away with another man, spent what money she had on him, and finally returned to her husband. Her ex-lover used his own wife to demand £60 under the threat of exposing her conduct. A vacuum-cleaner salesman called on a housewife and began an affair with her. The salesman's wife found letters from the woman in her husband's pocket and blackmailed her for £200. A factory commissionaire rummaged through a typist's desk after working hours, and found a diary showing that she had been photographed several times in the nude by her young man. He took the diary and left a note saying she must leave £10 in the drawer, when she would have the diary returned: otherwise it would be sent to her father. At the hearing before the Stipendiary Pugh took the unusual course of asking the twenty-year-old girl to read aloud the extracts from her diary revealing that "Geoff took two more nude photos of me. I don't feel embarrassed at all now. He made love to me just as he used to do. I do love him so." At the end of the evidence Pugh told the Stipendiary. "I want to make it quite clear that there is no suggestion that the photographs have been taken in indecent poses. The police have fully investigated, and the photos, although taken in the nude, are quite decent. They are merely poses. I thought this should be mentioned, as people might form entirely false impressions of what she has done."

Indecent photographs and publications were a continuing preoccupation of Pugh and the police, for Birmingham seemed to qualify as a centre of the trade. Though profit was plentifully earned by it, this was not always the objective of the publications. Prosecuting a Handsworth man for photographing his wife in indecent and abandoned poses with other men, the prints being sent to an international pornography club with headquarters in Milan, Pugh said, "There is no money-making motive involved in the club. It seems to have been the sexual side of it which has been their main interest." Though Pugh used his customary strong phrases condemning the "sink of iniquity" which produced such filth, it was not unusual for him to allow favoured journalists the privilege of coming up to his office to view the evidence. The prosecution of booksellers for offering doubtful publications increased enormously as the Department of Public Prosecutions took over the drive against this offence on a consistent, national level, and Pugh's responsibility in Birmingham became heavier. Often police raids on bookshops ended in books being confiscated by the thousand. On one day the Stipendiary, Mr Milward, was handed a hundred different titles to pronounce on. He adjourned the hearing for ten weeks in order to read the books. "I don't say I read every word in these books," he explained. "I have my own system."

The sordid, the piteous, the perverted, and the plainly risible cases jostled each other in the files. Dress-slashers, hair-snippers, and rings of male prostitutes followed one another into the dock. Occasionally Pugh would use a sexual charge to clinch an indictment for larceny: when a married man from Weoley Castle had made violent love to a spinster of thirty-seven, tricked her out of her money, and extracted an emerald ring from her as a keepsake, Pugh prosecuted him not only for false pretences but for procuring the woman, and he was committed to the Assizes on that charge. A six-foot fifteen-year-old Kingstanding schoolboy fell in love with a married woman aged twenty-two, and spent five nights with her: Pugh prosecuted the woman for indecent assault on the boy. A charge of bigamy was sometimes reinforced by another for procuring. But there were occasions when the Prosecuting Solicitor's department had to concede sheer admiration, at least of technique, when a "Captain's Paradise" case occurred; as when a man was revealed to have shared his life for five years with his bigamous wife on weekdays and his legal wife and seven children at weekends, sharing his wages between them and keeping his secret from each.

Sexual passion was not always physical. Pugh had to proceed under the Public Order Act against a wealthy forty-seven-year-old woman writer who had an obsession for Rudolf Schwarz, conductor of the City of Birmingham Symphony Orchestra; her behaviour caused her to be barred from its concerts, whereupon she became violent in the Town Hall foyer, shouting, "I know he adores me. I will kill Mrs Schwarz. She has done this to me." Nor could it be said that sexual perversion was always a bed of roses: when a foreman at the Botanical Gardens saw a young man and a girl run in panic from some bushes during a British Legion fête he investigated and found a naked man in a statuesque position. The man, an Irishman with a Ladywood address, claimed, after his arrest for committing an indecent act, that he had been sunbathing. "Where he was found," Pugh commented to the magistrate, "there were a large number of holly-bushes. All around on the ground were holly-leaves, which would not make it particularly comfortable if he wanted to recline for the purpose of sunbathing."

A man taking his dog for its evening walk was startled when the dog sniffed at something in the road which was incontrovertibly a human ear. The police traced the owner of the ear who, heavily bandaged, admitted that it had been bitten off in a fight with a fellow-Irishman, and mislaid at the time. Pugh charged the biter with unlawfully and maliciously wounding with intent to maim, disfigure, or disable, but later reduced the charge to inflicting grievous bodily harm, on the ground that the accused was too drunk at the time to have any intent at all. The magistrate gave him four months to taste justice.

A man of sixty-three wrapped two bricks in a bag and took a train from Liverpool to Birmingham. Then, at eight o'clock on an August evening, he threw the bricks through the window of Lewis's Stores, breaking plate glass worth £26. He explained to the police that thirty years previously he had bought a pair of trousers from Lewis's. "They split and gave me bronchitis. As a result I have been ill ever since." Charged with causing malicious damage, the man asked for his case to be dealt with summarily, since the damage was only £26. Pugh obtained a remand in custody, saying that he intended to ask for committal. At Quarter Sessions the man was proved to have had a number of sentences, including four years' penal servitude, for malicious damage to Lewis's windows, and was given a further two years' imprisonment.

While Pugh held office the gaming laws (about which he held strong reservations, particularly concerning off-the-course betting) were more arbitrary than as later amended. In 1952, a year after the reopening of the Birmingham Jewish Club following its wartime bombing, the police decided as a result of information received (primarily from members' wives) that cards were being played there for too high stakes. They raided the club, confiscated poker chips and £2500 stake money, booked forty-two members, and applied for the club to be struck off the register. Pugh, admitting that bridge as well as poker was then unlawful, did not press for the extinction of the club, and was content for the forty-two members to be bound over for a year on condition that they did not frequent gaming-houses. But he indulged in a certain astringency in his light-hearted account of the raid: "One woman member exclaimed, 'Oh, dear, I thought it was gangsters.' A man cried, 'I don't know, everything happens to me.' One man ran into an adjoining room shouting, 'Oi, Oi!' Another said, 'Someone has squealed.' He was quite right. Someone had squealed—it was the wives of certain of the members."

The gaming laws were changed, through no particular effort from Pugh. But he did make case-law through some of his prosecutions. After a doctor's car had been stolen from a cinema car-park, and recovered with narcotic drugs intact inside an unlocked leather case, he prosecuted the doctor under the amended Dangerous Drugs Act for failing to keep drugs in a locked receptacle to which only he had the key. It was the first prosecution of its kind, and was keenly fought by the Medical Protection Society. Pugh successfully maintained that a car with a mass-produced lock could not be called a receptacle that only the owner or another qualified person could open. Previously he had established that a person loitering might be arrested as a suspected person even if the police officer had no knowledge of a previous criminal record. He was prosecuting a man with no criminal record for loitering with intent to commit a felony, being a suspected person, after the man had been seen to open the doors of several cars and examine the contents. "It has been held by a recent court ruling," he claimed, "that a person so arrested must belong to the class of suspected persons, by reason of previous conduct. There has to be antecedent suspicion. But as there has to be antecedent suspicion, I cannot see why it should not as well be ten minutes or twelve months. What is the position going to be if you hold the accused is not a suspected person? The position is going to be this: that in Birmingham or any other large city a man can go out and say, 'I am going to steal. I am going to the first motor-car I see, and, what's more, Mr Policeman, if you see me you can't do anything. I have never been in trouble before; as far as the law knows I am a perfectly upright and law-abiding person."

Pugh also made, as a personal speciality of the prosecutor, extensive use of an old law passed in the reign of Edward III, the Justices of the Peace Act, 1361. He seemed to annex this as a perquisite of the lawman, and invoked it as a method of 'reading the Riot Act' to solitary public nuisances. He prosecuted such a person for being a "blemisher of the peace" or "a disturber of the peace likely to persevere in such unlawful conduct". Pugh always championed the Act, which gives magistrates power to bind people over. "Some people occasionally ask why such an old Act should be bothered with," he said in court. "The better legal opinion is that an Act of Parliament which proves so useful that it remains on the Statute Book since 1361 must have very considerable merits, and is especially fitted to deal with the very unpleasant matter I have to place before you." That particular matter was the nuisance contained in repeated letters to civic and medical authorities written by a man whose son had died in the Birmingham General Hospital, whose efforts he described as "the finest piece of butchery I have ever seen", with other sadly crazed comments. But Pugh used the Act also against exhibitionists with scarcely repressible urges to decorate church-spires with sanitary ware, persistent hospital malingerers, unwanted lovers who would not leave their girls alone, offensive religious bigots, peeping Toms, and transvestites. "Proceedings of this nature are unique," he said. "The accused cannot appeal against the court's decision, neither can he be fined or sent to prison. As a means whereby magistrates can stop people making nuisances of themselves it can best be described as 'preventive justice.'"

Preventive justice was a cause always near Pugh's heart. Guy Sanders, a former C.I.D. chief superintendent, formed with his friend Donald Young the Industrial Police and Security Association. They consulted Pugh, who enthusiastically helped prepare the rules and draw up the constitution. This association is now a national concern, though most of the original members were former City of Birmingham policemen. Pugh became its honorary solicitor. The post involved little work, "but it's nice to be asked," he told his wife.

As he approached the late 1950's Pugh was becoming aware that he was nearing the end of his time in office, and did not wholeheartedly regret it. His temper was a little shorter, his bell-drill orders to his subordinates a little fiercer (particularly when he had embarked on one of the stringent diets he set himself). In court, though he mainly kept his control when opposite prisoners and witnesses—"Lose your temper, lose your case" was a maxim he vigorously urged—he was a little more crabbed and inconsiderate of colleagues in his single-minded quest for speedy justice. But even when he snarled there could be a grain of humour: depositions were still taken in longhand, instead of on a typewriter; one afternoon when Frank Howarth, then Deputy Clerk (now Clerk) to the City Magistrates, had scrawled ceaselessly all day keeping up with Pugh's tireless examinations, he turned one more page and appealed to Pugh, *sotto voce*, to ease his speed. "I've reached 100," he said. "It's my hundredth page today." A century did not impress Pugh outside the cricket field. "What do you expect me to do?" he growled. "Stand up and bloody clap, or take round the hat?" And he continued to pile up the pages at his old speed. Yet when Howarth's senior retired Pugh made no bones about enthusiastically canvassing the claims of the Deputy. "You don't have to look any farther than Howarth," he urged in the appropriate quarters, and when Howarth was appointed, taking his seat for the first time on Easter Bank Holiday, Pugh made a special journey to court to pay a public tribute to him.

He was prosecuting a West Indian charged with playing pitch-and-toss in the street. Harry Faber was defending, and had great difficulty in extracting the fee from the accused in the court lobby before the hearing. Twice Faber sent the man back to take a collection among his many coloured supporters in the public gallery before the contribution approached Faber's mark. Pugh, sympathetically aware of the difficulty, put the case back through the morning list until Faber was ready. Then he cross-examined the accused strongly, following the theme that the man had been taken with loose coins and notes in each of his side jacket-pockets, and arguing that this was a well-known gambler's ploy, the man starting with his reserves in one pocket and putting all his winnings in the other so that he constantly had a fair idea how he stood. The accused wilted under Pugh's choleric attack. "No, sir, it's not a sign that I was gambling," he protested desperately. "I always keep my money in my side pockets." "Where do you keep your money now?" roared Pugh. Almost instinctively the man's hand went to his rear trouser pocket. Then he saw Pugh's eyes on him and shifted quickly to his jacket pocket. "Put your hand in your back pocket!" ordered Pugh, and as the man faltered helplessly he repeated, "Put it in, and take out what is in it." Almost hypnotized, the West Indian put his hand in his trousers pocket and pulled out a great bundle of notes—far greater than the solicitor's fee which he had said he was unable to produce. Pugh's eyes twinkled in triumph. "Does Mr Faber know about that?" he asked drily.

In a motoring case a man made an application for the restoration of his driving licence. He had a fairly good case, but he was very long-winded, and Pugh sighed with impatience as the plea went on. Finally the man finished, and the magistrate, Mr

Milward, asked the dock officer if there were any previous convictions. The officer replied that there were none that mattered. But Pugh, glancing at his brief, interposed, "I think there is one that is relevant. He was convicted for gases not passing through the silencer."

Once his day's work was over, Pugh did not want to meet anyone in the courts, or be trapped for consultations in the corridors. When Kay Fitzmaurice, his son's fiancée, called for him to go home, he would urge, "Let's take the back doubles, Fitzy," and peer round every corner in the court lobbies to see that there was no-one there who might buttonhole him. Once home, his spirits revived. "I propose we do this . . ." he would yell, fixing a social outing. "Those in favour say Aye," and, lifting everyone's hand in the room, he would bustle out to prepare for the treat.

He still had time for the young. In a raid on a club the police booked a number of non-members for drinking there, including a young solicitor whose reputation might have suffered unduly from so early a technical offence. Pugh glanced through the file, and among the people he did not prosecute was the young solicitor. But during the hearing Pugh noticed that the young man had come into the court. He stepped up the condemnation somewhat. The "diabolicals" and the "disgustings" rolled off his tongue. "And there are some," he declaimed, "who have not been prosecuted on this occasion. Let them not depend on further leniency. Let them not think they can get away with it. Let them watch it!" And his eye fell blandly on the offender.

On the 31st of October, 1958, M. P. Pugh retired as Prosecuting Solicitor to the City of Birmingham. In his time there had been over 110,000 cases through his files, of which he had personally prosecuted in well over 10,000 instances, including all the hundred murders. In the year of his retirement the Birmingham Police recorded 17,133 indictable offences—just ten times the number registered when Pugh arrived in 1924. Yet Pugh was conducting his department at the remarkable net cost to the city of under £9000. Pugh did not fade with a whimper, but retained his feeling for the dramatic in advocacy to the last. "How long is a minute?" he tested a hostile witness. "Tell me, starting from now." The silence imposed in court was broken as the witness said,

"A minute." "Twelve seconds," said Pugh contemptuously. In almost his last case he was prosecuting a youth, who had been engaged in a Teddy-boy brawl, for carrying without lawful excuse an offensive weapon—namely, a studded leather belt. The defence maintained that it was not a weapon. Pugh suddenly slipped his hand under his coat and brought the belt down with a metallic crash on his desk. He had been wearing the belt for the occasion. "I don't know whether you noticed that I had it there," he told Mr Milward, "but you see how easily it could be brought out."

The action caught the headlines again, and in Pugh's view the very publication was a deterrent. He sincerely supported crime reporting, for more than its star-making quality. The *News of the World* is the best *news*paper," he repeatedly claimed in lectures he was asked to give to public schools and other institutions. "It gives positive and progressive news, not one man's opinion; and how many times does it have to print an apology?" During his last weeks in office the Tucker Report was published recommending the banning of Press reports on some court proceedings. Pugh, who had given evidence to the investigating committee, stoutly opposed the recommendation and repeatedly put his points to the public: "What matters is that justice should be done and be seen to be done, and this will not be served by secret or semi-secret courts. A public hearing is a check on perjury. If an influential or prominent person is brought before the magistrates in a closed court and discharged on the grounds that there is no *prima facie* case against him, this can easily give rise to the rumour that proceedings were discontinued on account of the prisoner's social standing in the community. The courts and all those who assist in the administration of justice are on trial themselves, provided that the proceedings are held in public. This is a most important safeguard."

Pugh finished his term. On the day after he cleared his office desk he gave a great dinner in the Grand Jury Room of the Victoria Courts for sixty people who had borne the burden of thirty-four years with him: police officers, advocates, and his laboured staff. With his after-dinner wit mellowed by affection, he spoke kindly and memorably of everyone. It was one of the rare occasions when Pugh was not reported, for the Press had laid on their private party for him. But at the official farewell in Number One Court to "the veteran", as Mr Milward described him, "the old warhorse of this court who has prosecuted fearlessly but never sought to press a weak case", Pugh devoted his last words in office to a defence of the right of Press and public to be admitted to all court hearings. "Keep the principle that the courts shall be open," he said. "If there is any case for a closed court, magistrates have ample powers at the moment. I hope that the public will see that they do not get another liberty taken away. If the Press are excluded, although the courts may be open to the few people who can attend, things can go on there about which the great majority of the public will not have any first-hand information. The administration of justice can never be carried out properly without the Press, who are the representatives of the public."

CHAPTER

9

The Lion draws Blood

"LISTEN, boy!"

It was over thirty years since Mervyn Pugh, in his sharp Berkshire accent, had told his brother of his self-imposed mission: "I've got one job in life. That is to protect the police. They can't get up and answer back." Perhaps over the years, though the sentiment had never faltered, its application had faded, for the job was more rarely exercised. There would always be protests at police handling of defendants on and before arrest. Some were justified, but most were optimistic diversions; they were dealt with according to their merits. But what, in 'his' Birmingham Police Force, had largely disappeared were the humiliating cases where defence advocates had secured an acquittal solely because of unsatisfactory police preparation of the prosecution. Pugh had widely taught the police to protect themselves. Now he had severed official connection with the police. His affection for them remained, but his authority had gone. He could no longer check them early in an error by his searing deflationary wit. And an occasion arose when the old lion, unheeded after warning growls, cuffed among the pride with open claw so savagely that the bloodied police fell about, declaring that they had been betrayed, rather than corrected. It occurred when Pugh's old mission, "Protect the police", crossed with his puritan conception of the prosecutor's rôle, with its corollary, "Protect the citizen". For the prosecutor, as an Officer of the Court, had one final duty—to present *all* the facts—and one ultimate loyalty—to Justice rather than to Authority. It was a public conflict that could only happen when Pugh, for thirty-six years The Prosecutor, found himself agreeing increasingly often to act for the defence.

In the beginning of his so-called retirement Pugh kept himself too busy to need or heed any nostalgic magnetism activated by the Steelhouse Lane-Corporation Street block, where Number One Court was no longer "Pugh's Court" but had reverted to being "The Stipe's". M. P. P. never went back there in idleness, but occasionally stood at his old desk before the Stipendiary to prosecute in a routine Ministry of Tranport case against a haulage contractor; the magistrate was once amused to see Pugh's tall son John, now a young solicitor with his own practice and retained by the defence, sitting opposite the prosecutor in the bench where the great guerrillas, Willison and Ladds, and latterly the alert Harry Faber, had itched to spring up in protest and not always restrained the impulse. Young Pugh quietly pleaded Guilty, composedly waited for the wave of his father's censure to break over the defendant's head, then rose and stoutly claimed, "Despite all that my learned friend has seen fit to say, I still have some mitigation left. . . ."

Mervyn Pugh held a steadily remunerative retainer as prosecutor in transport offences for the West Midlands Licensing Authority. To twenty outlying courts in Worcestershire and Herefordshire he journeyed, often chauffeured by his wife—for his erratic driving was further shattered by something of an actor's nervousness before a court appearance—to impart an echo of the majesty of the law. As spruce as ever in his black coat and striped trousers, he was often a cold contrast in habit and style to the local solicitors in their country suits. Pugh was at first appalled by slack court procedure and the lack of finesse in advocacy. Local men from their side saw him as a city automaton, with his level high-pressure opening statements merging into the predictable overtones of scarifying quasi-judicial condemnation of the enormity of using a goods vehicle without a carrier's licence, or failing to keep proper records of drivers' working hours. Pugh was undisturbed by antipathy, and did not alter his ways. To a milder degree the effect was the same as when he had first taken over at Birmingham. Defending solicitors were finding that it was much more difficult to secure magistrates began to respect him, at first only for the economy an acquittal. The Traffic Examiners cherished him. The and efficiency with which he conducted his business. Then the country solicitors perceived beneath his immense authority an undisputed fairness and a rejection of the slick opportunist advocacy which is sometimes adopted by small-time prosecutors. Outside the court the man was undoubtedly a charmer. Within a few months—and his brethren watching from Birmingham were not really amazed—Pugh was an elder statesman in the country courts with a presence that made him a professional attraction on the variety bill of the day's proceedings. Lay magistrates showed exhilaration when their clerk announced, before they took the bench, "Mr Pugh's in court," "We knew," said one, "that he would never waste time; he would certainly be entertaining; and he would make a point, look at the Bench, and give us credit for our intelligence—which many professional advocates are very loath to do."

Retirement gave Pugh the opportunity for extending his favourite relaxations—meeting people and watching sport. The race meetings he had never had time to go to were now open to him, and he and Dr Vera used to drive to Stratford and Worcester and Cheltenham, and all the point-to-points. On bad days he would place shrewd bets from opposite his television screen. There was the true country-town weekend pleasure of gossip with shopkeepers and morning assignments with friends at the pub. At Saturday noon he could be found in the Golden Cross at Bromsgrove, exchanging yarns with 'Prof' Webster or arguing with him, sometimes wearing the Professor's monocle (still attached to the Scotsman's neck). Later he began to build a new home at Droitwich. The architect, Reginald Stone, literally centred the building on a dressing-room planned to hold an enormous fitted cabinet for all Pugh's clothes. Then M. P. P. transferred his levée to the Raven at Droitwich. The move from Fockbury put an end to the Sunday walks with Dr Vera through the fields to church, his cat discreetly following him. But, wherever he had his base, in summer there was always the cricket.

Mervyn's boyish fanaticism for Worcestershire County Cricket Club, maintained through so many arguments in the Mess at the Victoria Courts where barristers and senior policemen seemed but Warwickshire boys, had been crowned by his election to the club's committee in the year of his retirement, on the proposal of a brother solicitor in Bromsgrove, Mr John Sellars. Now it was open to him to watch the play from the wide windows of the pavilion committee room, with a cool glass in his hand and friends responding to his wit. But Pugh found it difficult to abandon the vantage-point of half a lifetime, the group of deck-chairs near the scoreboard and almost behind the wicket. There had always been too few deck-chairs, and one had to get there early—or send one's son—to bag three for the family and fight to keep them until the Pugh contingent was complete. Sometimes, in the struggle to secure seats, good manners froze. Young John once took a seat beside his father by removing the mackintosh reserving it and dropping it to the ground; the rightful owner, observing the ploy, came back, ejected John, elaborately redraped the mackintosh on the chair with the acid observation, "I prefer it that way", and walked away. "I prefer it that way" became a family catchword. Alongside, someone else had ditched another raincoat reserving a deck-chair, and stolidly sat in it. The owner of the mack came up to argue. "I kept it with my mack," he protested. The usurper laid down his ruling. "Bums keep seats, not macks," he pronounced in ripe Worcestershire, and turned his attention to the game. Pugh repeated with gusto this earthy reminder that possession is the strongest tenure of the law. From the cockpit of the deck-chair enclosure Mervyn had taken a rejuvenated view of life, and occasionally stepped in to ease some of its injustices. Jenkins, the Worcestershire player, was once fielding on the boundary very near the deck-chairs. A batsman hit a half-volley for what seemed a certain six, but Jenkins calmly positioned himself with the finest precision so that he had time to stand nonchalantly on the boundary waiting to catch the ball, which he did effortlessly. The deck-chairs holla-ed their applause. The batsman's successor came in, fell for the same trap, and belted another skyward to the motionless fieldsman's hands. Jenkins permitted himself a little complacency. "Like picking effing plums," he observed to the deck-chairs. A scandalized lady rose in her shock and went straight off to the committee to report the obscenity. And Pugh, ex-prosecutor, immediately canvassed the survivors, got them to agree that no-one else had been offended by the witticism, and persuaded the committee not to penalize the player.

The new home in Droitwich was completed, with the great shop-fitment of a wardrobe in the dressing-room as the pearl of the oyster. Pugh took exaggerated umbrage at the Council's rating assessment. At the Valuation Court he propelled a running fire of objections at the rating officer, ranging from the nuisance of a projected motorway near by to "a most delightful view of the washing hanging out in Tagwell Road". Observing the officer staggering, he suggested quickly, "You are a little shaky about the valuation you wish to impose?" With fatal pertness, the officer responded, "Valuations are a matter of opinion. I am no more shaky now than on any other occasion." Poising himself for the coup de grâce, Pugh asked, "Can you tell of any other bungalow in Droitwich with the same or smaller accommodation which is rated more highly?" The officer stammered and said, "No." "Middle stump," observed the appellant. The gross assessment was reduced, by £5. Mervyn Pugh, who had given up a day's court work for the gain, was hugely delighted. He felt on top of his form. Life was actively sweet. His son's wife was pregnant, and would doubtless give him a grandson. And he himself was undertaking a few adventures in advocacy.

He was not giving up his transport prosecutions. But, long years after his début at Marlborough Street, and the magistrate's dry barb, "Despite your efforts, Mr Pugh, I find the prisoner Not Guilty," Mr Pugh was again taking up defence work. It did not come particularly easily to him. Though he was a magnificent impromptu speaker on social occasions, he had, to some extent, to relearn this fluidity in the courts. Thirty-seven years' reliance on hammered and tested details in a prepared brief had had their effect. Any defence he undertook was likely to be painstakingly thorough, but had he the buoyancy to switch tactics as sharply as might be necessary? In his first outstanding case the test was not critical, for he promptly pleaded Guilty and reserved his strength for a powerful speech in mitigation.

It was a silly case, a trivial occurrence overtly not worth three lines in a newspaper: but so are many family farces, and family tragedies even, and much memorable pleading is devoted to them at the time. Some contrast between the triviality of the offence and the might of the law which was dealing with it caught Pugh's imagination, and he sailed into the defence, not with all guns firing, but using the bland, persuasive argument of a father who can remember and forgive the thoughtless excesses of youth: and perhaps, as his time came, it was of his own follies that he was thinking.

A silly case. On a Saturday night after a local-derby Rugby match the team finished the day at a dance and one member tossed an Army thunderflash at another. When it exploded two people were slightly cut, and there was a hint of panic. Dangerous hooliganism, or high jinks, depending on which side of the flash one stood; a similar decision has to be reached after family horseplay in any sitting-room.

The police evidence was given, and Pugh rose to his feet. There was no flame in him, but he was all warmth.

"My first words," he said, "must be to express Mr Evans's[1] sincere apologies for the remarkably foolish thing he did. If later I say anything which may seem to minimize matters I do not want anyone to think that this is treated otherwise than seriously by the defendant.

"Mr Evans stands there, having to plead Guilty to a serious charge in a district where he is well known, and to experience the sense of shame which that brings. He is not a man of the type who goes about doing silly things as a general rule." And Pugh detailed the defendant's fourteen years' service in the Army. The account seemed to revive his own military memories.

"Those of us who had the privilege of serving in the Forces," he went on (the Chairman of the Bench was a lieutenant-colonel), "know that the course of conduct there is a little more robust than it often is in everyday life. I do not suppose there is any of you who has been a soldier who, on looking back to Service days —and I should be the last man to claim this myself—who can look back to Service days and not name something that happened then which he would rather other people did not know about. Evans realizes that he has been foolish, and as a result has been brought into court. News of it will get about among his friends in due course. What greater humiliation can a good and honoured soldier have to face?"

Pugh might already have been accused of pitching it strong, but he increased the tension. "In times of emergency," he declared, "the country is always pleased to have young men of spirit who are prepared to charge across at the enemy carrying grenades.

"I remember serving with a man who won the V.C., and all his friends said that man was a lunatic. But in times of emergency such people are the salt of the earth."

[1] A pseudonym adopted here for narrative purposes.

Perhaps before the Bench successfully sorted out the connection between thunderflashes, grenades, and the Victoria Cross, the advocate was off on another tack. "There is another factor," he revealed. "Evans is a Rugby player. The Bench will know that after matches players enjoy relaxation together."

He was now speaking with reminiscent approval. "It is one of the things that happened when I was a boy," he mused, "and if I am ever blessed with a grandson I hope that sort of thing will still be happening."

But Pugh did not shrink from the grim outcome. "After the match the team had a drink or two and were merry together at the dance. Evans saw a friend dancing and had a stupid impulse to throw the thunderflash to make his friend jump. It was only the twist of fate that, of all the thousands of thunderflashes he had let off in his time, this one did any damage. He bitterly regrets this ill-timed joke. Does the Bench feel that any more punishment than the humiliation Evans now suffers is necessary?"

It was time to end the pathos and introduce a little light relief at the defendant's expense. "Finally I bring to the notice of the Bench," said Mr Pugh, "the exemplary character of this man. His late commanding officer speaks of him as 'able, intelligent, and full of ideas . . .' "

Pugh paused. " 'Although, like many Welshmen,' " he continued quoting, in a court not too far from the border, " 'he is apt to be carried away by his own enthusiasm'."

A fine of £20 was imposed. Considering that the charge was malicious wounding, it was not unsatisfactory. Mervyn Pugh went away to prepare for South Africa's opening match against Worcestershire and the birth of his putative grandson. When the baby was born she was a girl,[1] whom he took into his arms and his heart with quiet tears. The baby, Sally, became a new focus in his life. He declared that he could not wait until she was able to talk—and argue. In the meantime he was constantly singing to her. Her favourite song was *Seventy-six Trombones.*

Pugh found himself undertaking defence cases of an increasingly significant nature. The Worcestershire police were occasionally retaining him to prosecute in difficult cases. He privately thought, considering the overall results, that the police as well as he himself might gain if he were given the smooth as

[1] His grandsons Jonathan Mervyn and Edward Mervyn were born in 1962 and 1965.

well as the rough; but he said nothing to them. Now he was being approached by solicitors to take on more defences. It had been one of the jokes of his retirement to listen to clients who wanted him to defend them, and then to say, "You don't want a lawyer, you need a magician." But he began to feel that, in certain near localities, a shock from a magician's wand might occasionally re-energize the flagging presentation of the law.

Inefficiency in a prosecution had always riled him. He was encountering more inefficiency than pleased him in the conduct of processes by the police of country towns. A case ought to be prepared. Evidence ought to be assessed and weighed. If a prosecution could not be satisfactorily substantiated it should never be brought. He had made this almost a police axiom in Birmingham. But in the outer towns some police officers were either reprehensibly ignorant or else taking a cynical chance of a flash success. If in his professional capacity he crossed with this inefficiency—which directly bred injustice—he felt he must expose it, even at the cost of a weakening in the police prestige which he had striven to build up throughout his career. It happened that the cumulative instances of Pugh's entanglements with inefficient prosecutions occurred in the town of Stourbridge.

In Stourbridge a lad of nineteen was brought before the magistrates on a charge of unlawful wounding. On a summer night two girls had been walking along one side of a hedge, and three lads along the other. The parties knew each other, and there was the slight tension of jealousy over boy-friends between them. They began tossing stones at each other across the hedge, not altogether in fun. One stone—which could have come from a catapult—hit a girl in the eye. When she got home her father complained to the police. The lads were interviewed, and two of them blamed the injured eye on the third boy. He was brought to court. Pugh defended. After the witnesses for the prosecution had given their evidence, and been vigorously cross-examined—Pugh was asked by the presiding magistrate not to 'browbeat' an eye surgeon—M. P. P. confidently submitted that there was no case to answer. He said that there was no evidence against his client, and any one of the three youths could have propelled the stone. The magistrates agreed with him and dismissed the case.

It was not important. A slack prosecution had been neither tightened nor abandoned before the file was put into the process machine. But a busy police-officer in charge of a case can make an occasional mistake. Pugh would have thought little of it if there had not been a sequel.

A few weeks later the same lad found himself again in Stourbridge Court to answer four charges. The first two were alternatives. They concerned a Muscovy duckling in the local park, and a dead duck at that. There was no doubt that the boy had climbed a fence by a pond in the park and picked up a duckling which a bigger duck had been pecking. The bird was dead. He put the duckling in his pocket to climb back over the fence, and was apprehended by the park attendant. The police charges were: "That he unlawfully stole, took and carried away one bird, an ornamental duckling valued at 7*s.* 6*d.*, ordinarily kept in a state of confinement, contrary to Section 21 of the Larceny Act, 1861" and (the alternative charge) "that he did steal the duckling, property of the Stourbridge Council, contrary to the Common Law".

The second charge, a belated addition, was a useful blanket accusation. It omitted any reference to the prickly phrases of the first charge which could, and did, provoke endless legal argument: was the duck domesticated or wild (for an ordinary citizen had wider rights to take a wild duck than a tame one); could it be held to be in a state of confinement when a witness was prepared to swear that there were holes in the wire netting round the lake; was a Muscovy duck edible, and if not, could this dead duck have any value?

As soon as the second charge was read out Pugh, appearing for the defence, interrupted, taking strong exception to the alternative. "It is an abuse of the process of the courts," he said, "to come here at the last moment and prefer another charge like this.

"I have been prosecuting for many years, and I have never in my experience known an alternative charge brought like this at the last minute of the last day." He asked for the cases to be heard separately.

The Bench, however, ruled that both charges should be proceeded with. The witnesses were duly heard and cross-examined. Again there was evidence of a nebulous second, stone-throwing, youth in the case, but he was not called; it was agreed that the defendant had picked up the dead duck. Again Pugh refused to question his client. "There is no case to answer," he declared. "This case was brought against this youth without the slightest investigation, which would have shown that there is no evidence at all.

"He is being hounded by an abuse of the law. On no account will I let him be called on to give evidence. If there is a case to answer he will go before the Chairman of Quarter Sessions."

After a short retirement the magistrates dismissed both charges without calling on the defence.

Pugh was immediately on his feet to cast laurels towards the Bench. "This decision demonstrates," he affirmed, "that the rights of the citizen are going to be protected in this court." But he went on to refer to "this most vindictive prosecution", and, in asking for costs, made a very valid general point about the importance of undertaking the expense of instructing a solicitor. "This youth was brought here some time ago," he said, "and again there was no evidence against him. His parents have been put to expense in order to make an investigation into this, and if he had not been represented here today perhaps some of the facts might not have been brought to your attention. In those circumstances I respectfully ask you to grant something towards the costs."

This application was briskly refused, and the court went on to consider the remaining charges against the boy. The third charge was of climbing the fence, contrary to the Council's by-laws. The prosecution, outlining the case, stated that there were two witnesses of this offence, but did not call them later to give evidence. Pugh called attention to this. He declared, "Evidence is being suppressed by the prosecution, which is bent on harassing and bullying this boy."

The handling of the prosecution was manifestly inept, but to many in the court—perhaps more used to small-town Bumbledom—it did not seem so wilfully unjust as to deserve the strictures which Pugh was pouring on it. But to Pugh the castigation was no theatrical excess. The man who had gone red with passion and screamed "Diabolical!" when he had seen a minor criminal acquitted in Birmingham against the stream of the evidence was not the character to shrug his shoulders when he thought he saw Justice—part his goddess, part his protégée—spurned, even over a council by-law.

"I will not mince words," said Pugh. "I am really beginning to wonder what is happening in this town, where it is said that there were two witnesses to an offence and yet neither is brought here. It makes it absolutely contrary to justice to say that there is a case to answer. My client is suffering from an imposition which should not be tolerated under any circumstances."

Then Pugh affirmed his credo as a prosecutor, the principle he had tried to follow whether in a charge of murder or of climbing a park fence:

"The prosecution's job is to present the facts truly, squarely and fairly, and to bring all relative evidence before the court, whether it is for or against the defendant."

He came back to the petty case before him. "To put a man on trial for an offence of this kind when evidence has been suppressed is, in my submission, a charge of the flimsiest nature which you will have to scrutinize before you come to your decision. If it is an offence to climb over the fence to protect an immature bird, then it is a sorry day for the by-laws if they are so strictly enforced. Suppression by the prosecution is one of the most lamentable things that could ever come before a court, and I trust that when you have heard the evidence you will treat these proceedings with the contempt they deserve."

The magistrates, however, found the youth Guilty of climbing the fence and of the further misdemeanour of riding a bicycle in the park, and fined him £3 in all.

To Pugh it was another instance of apparent incompetence at Stourbridge. "I am really beginning to wonder what is happening in this town" was a judgment not lightly voiced. Incompetence opened the easy descent to injustice. Whether through vanity, or purity of principle, or the idealist's admixture of both, Pugh, in order to combat injustice, would freely jettison any professional approval he had so far acquired inside the country courts.

The occasion came. Out of nowhere, out of the humdrum clash of pressures and weaknesses from which most errors and crimes emerge, rose the case which was to cloud Pugh's 'Establishment' reputation—though never his conscience—as no other case which he fought ever did.

It concerned the action of the police, in the town of Stourbridge.

Pugh's concern began when he was told a commonplace enough story, the truth of which he had to assess:

On the night of Tuesday the 1st of November, 1960, a young man, Abel Abbatt,[1] kissed his wife goodbye and went out to

[1] A pseudonym adopted here for narrative purposes.

work on the nightshift. Abbatt was twenty-seven years old, had been happily married for five years, and held a responsible job in local industry. His blonde wife Alice, a year younger, with no children to listen for, tidied the kitchen and prepared to take the dog for a walk.

Abel Abbatt was due at work at ten, and he walked to the bus-stop on the Broadway to catch his usual nine-thirty bus. At the bus-stop two women passed him from behind. If there was an air of fearful excitement about them it hardly conveyed itself to Abbatt. One woman, wearing glasses, was in fact trembling so violently that she had to support herself on her friend's arm as they passed. Abbatt lit a cigarette, and was vaguely aware that, when a dozen yards beyond him, both women turned and looked intently at him. But at that distance their faces were no plainer than, presumably, his own. The bus came along, he went upstairs, and thought no more about it.

The following account of what happened in the presence of Abbatt, his wife, and his father-in-law during the subsequent thirty-six hours is what they later told M. P. Pugh.

On the next night, Wednesday, Abbatt again left home to catch the nine-thirty bus for work. He allowed some acquaintances to get on first, then mounted the bus and sat in a back seat on top. A man and a woman followed him upstairs and sat three seats in front of him. The woman, who wore glasses, turned round to look at him, and said something to her companion. At the next stop the man and the woman went downstairs, presumably to get off the bus. Abel Abbatt travelled to his fare stage, and went downstairs. As he swung off the bus a man got off behind him, caught his work-bag, and with his other hand took Abbatt's arm. The man said, "I am a police officer. Did you know that?" Abbatt looked at him, recognized him as the man who had been in the bus, and also realized that he lived in one of the police houses on the Broadway. Inconsequentially, Abbatt said, "I believe you know my father-in-law." The man said, "What is your name?" As the bus roared off, and people looked round curiously, Abbatt replied with his full name, and his address. The man continued, "I am Detective Constable Barr[1] of Stourbridge C.I.D. You answer to the description of a man who broke into and entered the Mere Children's Homes and committed an assault there on Saturday night, the 22nd of October, at 11.45 P.M.

[1] A pseudonym.

I am arresting you and taking you to Stourbridge Police Station." "This is a joke," said Abbatt. "Are you pulling my leg?" "No," said the man, "we don't go around joking with people. You are not obliged to say anything unless you wish to do so, but whatever you say will be taken down in writing and may be given in evidence. Now I am going to take you to the police station." "You can," said Abbatt, who had been listening with increasing consternation to an unfamiliar jargon that had been going on for half a minute. "You can, but it wasn't me." They turned, and Abbatt, held by the arm all the way, walked with his accuser to the police station. Halfway there, vaguely remembering the television formula for protection, Abbatt said, "I should like to get in touch with my solicitor." The remark was ignored. Abbatt did not in fact, 'have' a solicitor, and would have been hard pushed to name one. He had never needed one before.

Abbatt was guided into the police station, up some stairs, and into an office, where he was told to sit down. Two more men in plain clothes came in. "This is him, Sarge," said the man who had made the arrest. The sergeant looked at Abbatt keenly. "What made you do it?"[1] he asked. "Do what?" said Abbatt desperately. "You know what," replied the sergeant, very knowledgeable.

As Abbatt recounted his experiences later, the situation increasingly took on the quality of a nightmare. One of the policemen took his station behind Abbatt's chair, and remained there through the long interrogation which followed. The plainclothes sergeant and the detective who had arrested him were in front of him. At first the detective questioned him about his actions on Saturday the 22nd of October. It required some effort to think his way back to that day, though it was less than a fortnight ago. He mentally placed himself within the shift system he was working, and recalled that he had left work at noon, spent the afternoon tidying his garden for the winter, and watched television practically all the evening. At eleven o'clock he had taken his dog for a walk. Here he saw that the detectives were becoming more alert. He said that he had been out with the dog only for some ten minutes, was back by 11.15, and in bed by 11.30. Abbatt answered many questions from the detective, and realized that he had been taken through the series of events a number of times.

Then the sergeant took over. His questions seemed more

[1] Remark deniedby the detective constable; see page 218.

pointedly personal. After questions about work he asked, "What pubs did you go into on the night of the 22nd of October? How much did you have to drink?" Abbatt said that he did not drink. "Have you been in the Army? Do you have any children? Do you sleep with your wife? Do you ever get out of bed in the night? Does your mind ever go blank for a space of time?"

Abbatt's answers became somewhat more protesting.

"So what about this assault?" asked the sergeant.

"Where?"

"At the Mere Children's Home."

"I don't know anything about an assault. Who has been assaulted?"

There was a silence.

"Was it a girl?" asked Abbatt.

"You ought to know," said the sergeant.

A wilder fear than anything he had yet experienced began to rise in Abbatt's mind.

"Come on, own up to it," said the man behind him.

"Where is your wife now?" asked the detective.

"At home."

The sergeant and the detective looked towards one another and nodded.

"Are you going to see her?" asked Abbatt.

"It wouldn't be a bad idea."

The men went towards the door.

"Are you going anywhere?" asked Abbatt.

The sergeant tilted his head non-committally.

"Look, if you're going up to my home, please go and see my father-in-law first. You know him. My wife is in by herself. It's late, and I'd be glad if you would see my father-in-law first."

Without response the detectives left the room, and only the man behind Abbatt remained. The door opened and another man came in. Abbatt recognized him as the superintendent newly in charge of the station. The superintendent nodded to the escort, and the other man left the room. There was a silence. As he looked round the room Abbatt saw that there was a truncheon lying on a table in the corner.

"You may as well own up to it," said the superintendent. "Your wife and your mother-in-law and your father-in-law need never know about this."[1]

[1] Remark later denied by the superintendent.

Abbatt wondered what sort of world they supposed he was living in. He made no reply, and there was a long silence.

"You may as well admit it," repeated the superintendent. "Otherwise I have no alternative but to lock you up in the cells and bring you before a magistrate in the morning."[1]

"Then I am afraid you will have to lock me up," replied Abbatt. "I will not admit to something I have not done."

Again there was silence. Then the superintendent left the room. Abbatt was alone. After five minutes the escort came back.

"You must have a double somewhere," he said.

The detective who had arrested him came in. "We have seen your wife," he told Abbatt. "We didn't tell her you were at the police station."

"Thank you very much," said Abbatt sincerely. "I don't want her worried. I would like to tell her myself."

The detective jerked his head to beckon the escort outside. They talked in the corridor for some minutes. Then they came back into the room.

"I want to take a statement," said the detective, scribbling with a pen. "You are not obliged to say anything unless you wish to do so, but whatever you say will be taken down in writing and may be given in evidence."

"I'll make a statement," said Abbatt.

"Just sign here," said the detective, jerking a paper across the table.

Surprised at the speed, Abbatt read the paper. It said: "I have been told by D. C. Barr that I am not obliged to say anything unless I wish to do so but whatever I say will be taken down in writing and may be given in evidence."

Abbatt signed.

"Now," said the detective, "on the 22nd of October when did you leave work?"

After a few confirmatory questions the statement was completed.

"Just sign here," said the detective.

"Can I read it?"

"Why not?"

Abbatt read: "I live with my wife Alice Abbatt at . . . Stourbridge. I was working at the . . . on Saturday, 22nd October, 1960, until 12 mid-day. I left work there and went straight to my

[1] Remark denied by the superintendent; see page 219.

home. I spent the afternoon working in my garden and in the evening I watched the television with my wife.

"I didn't go out that day until I took my dog for a walk up the . . . Lane at about 11.00 P.M. I was only out with the dog for about 10 minutes and returned to my house at about 11.15 P.M. I then went to bed with my wife at about 11.30 P.M. I did not leave the house again that night.

"I wasn't nowhere near the Mere on that particular day.

"This statement has been read over to me. I understand it and it is true."

Abbatt signed.

"We are letting you go now," said the other man.

"Thank you," said Abbatt.

"I've got a car outside," said the detective in a friendly fashion. "Would you like me to take you to work or can I run you home?"

Abbatt looked at the time. It was twenty minutes to midnight. "I'll go home, please," he said.

The detective took him home. Abbatt opened the front door and called to his wife. There was no answer. "She's not here!" he told the detective in surprise.

At that moment Mrs Abbatt, frantic with worry, was searching vainly for her husband. After he had gone to work she had tidied the kitchen and taken the dog for a walk, then locked up and prepared for bed. She was undressed when there was a knock at the front door. The dog barked excitedly as she hurriedly dressed and went to open the door. Two men were standing outside. "Are you Mrs Abbatt?" one of them asked. "We are police officers," the man went on, "and we want to ask you some questions about your husband."

"Oh, my God!" thought Mrs Abbatt. "There has been an accident at work." "What is it?" she asked the men. "We just want to ask you a few questions," was the reply. "What is it all about?" she insisted. "We are not prepared to discuss it at this point," she was told. "He will tell you himself if he wishes you to know."

"I think we should come in," said one of the men. Mrs Abbatt did not retreat from the porch. "If there is anything you want to ask me you can do it here," she said. "Don't you believe we are policemen?" came the question, and the two men showed her their identification. "I've known your father for eleven years," said one. Mrs Abbatt allowed them to come in.

"Where was your husband on the night of Saturday the 22nd

of October?" asked the man who was doing most of the talking. Mrs Abbatt took time to think.

"He was here with me all night."

"Did he go out at all?"

"We never go out on a Saturday night."

"Did he go to the pub?"

"He never goes out drinking, and we never go out without each other."

"Are you sure?"

"Yes."

"But what did you do that Saturday night?"

"Watched television like we always do."

"What time did you go to bed?"

"The usual time. About eleven or quarter past."

"But you go to bed later on a Saturday."

"Well, maybe a few minutes later. We were in bed by half-past eleven."

"Are you sure?"

"Yes."

"Did he not leave the house at all that night?"

Mrs Abbatt thought carefully for a moment. "Yes," she said. "He took the dog for a walk as usual."

"What time was that?"

"Somewhere between ten-thirty and eleven."

"How long was he away?"

"Five or ten minutes at the most."

"Where did he take the dog for a walk?"

"Where he always does. Round the corner into . . . Lane and back."

"Are you sure he was only away ten minutes?"

"Quite sure. I was waiting for him on the porch when he came back. What is he supposed to have done?" asked Mrs Abbatt, breaking the chain of interrogation.

"I'm sorry, we are not prepared to discuss it."

"What time is he supposed to have done it?"

"11.45."

"Well, he definitely didn't do it. We were in bed with the lights out by eleven-thirty."

"Are you sure?"

"Of course I'm sure."

"How can you be sure? What was on television that night?"

Mrs Abbatt tried to reconstruct the programme. "It was still on ITV when we went to bed. It was a play. I switched it off. I looked at the clock at the time. It was nearly half-past eleven."

One of the men began writing on a piece of official foolscap. "There's a statement," he said as he finished. "Would you sign it?"

"Should I?"

"You are telling the truth," the man said. Mrs Abbatt signed it. "Where is my husband now?" she asked.

They gave no answer. "You had better go to bed," said one. And they left.

Mrs Abbatt sat in frightened reflection for a few minutes. Then she put on a coat, ran to a friend who owned a motor-car, and asked to be taken to the works to see her husband and find out what it was all about. At the works she was told that her husband had not clocked in. In still greater fear she made the journey home, and came back into the house to find her husband sitting down with the detective who had asked her the questions.

"What's all this about?" she demanded of the policeman.

"Abel will tell you," said the detective.

Abbatt told her of his arrest. "Let's have a cup of tea," he asked.

Mrs Abbatt rounded on the detective. "But why did you arrest *him*?"

"Because someone identified him," said the detective. Then he added, "It wasn't Abel. He must have a double. Look, Mrs Abbatt, if someone did something and looked like you and dressed like you, *you* might be mistaken for that person."

"I'll make the tea," said Mrs Abbatt.

They talked together for an hour as the tension ran down. From crime the detective drifted on to the subject of gardening. It was one o'clock in the morning before he said he must go. As he said goodnight the detective remarked, "There must be someone in the district very like you, Abel. If we do find the chap I promise you can come to the station and have a look at him."

The Abbatts went to bed. It had been an unforgettably distressing night. But, apart from the loss of eight hours' work, it had all seemed to have ended fairly satisfactorily.

Next morning, however, Mr and Mrs Abbatt found that they could not dismiss the ordeal so airily. The arrest still hung over them. Mrs Abbatt in particular was beginning to go to pieces with delayed shock. Soon after ten o'clock they went to see Mrs Abbatt's father, Mr Charles Catesby,[1] a local business-man of some standing. Mr Catesby's immediate reaction was to telephone heatedly to the superintendent of police and to counsel his son-in-law to seek legal advice. Mr and Mrs Abbatt now knew which solicitor they wanted to consult, and they went into Stourbridge to see him.

"On the face of it, you were illegally arrested and detained," Abbatt was told by his solicitor. "It was an *arrest* by the detective constable: he did not ask you to accompany him to the police station to help in inquiries, but arrested you and took you there under restraint. Once at the police station you could either have been kept in custody, or charged and released on bail, and in either event prosecuted before the magistrates today. Instead, after you and your wife had been questioned over two hours, you were released without being charged. This suggests that the police have very serious doubts as to your guilt, and I will try and resolve those doubts. I will ask the police for an immediate explanation, and get in touch with you."

Greatly heartened by this vigorous reaction, Mr and Mrs Abbatt returned to Mr Catesby. Mrs Abbatt was now obviously unwell. Her father's protest to the police superintendent had been received with an assurance that the officer would do all in his power to clear up the matter. Within an hour two detectives called to see Mr Catesby. Abel Abbatt, just back from his solicitor, opened the door to them. By now he knew them very well.

The policemen were most courteous. They assured Mr Catesby at great length that nothing had happened the night before that was not in accordance with the law. "But what is it all about?" asked Mr Catesby. He was told: "The Mere was broken into some time ago and someone molested a child. A woman has identified your son-in-law as being the man."

"But that is just fantastic," said Mr Catesby.

"We know it is not Abel," said one of the detectives. "But we must satisfy ourselves and get the man who is responsible for this, because the next time it may be more serious."

"Even though it were my own son," burst out Mr Catesby, stilted in his emotion, "my sense of justice is such that I would not hesitate for one moment until he was brought to justice.

[1] A pseudonym.

But I am shocked and horrified that any suggestion of this nature can be levelled against Abel."

"We know that Abel had nothing to do with this, Mr Catesby," he was assured. "But we must continue the investigations to satisfy this woman that she has made a mistake. She is quite certain, but we are not. Listen. The man who broke into the Mere spoke to the woman who made the identification. We'll get Abel to come to the station and ask the woman to identify his voice. We are sure Abel did not commit the offence. We know it's not Abel. You must have a double, Abel."

"I certainly must have," said Abel Abbatt, who was reacting to the detectives a little more truculently than on the night before. "But the matter is now in the hands of my solicitors. And I will get to the bottom of it."

"We must go," said the detectives. "Perhaps some time, Mr Catesby, you would let us have a look around your works."

The detectives returned to the police station to find their seniors mildly uneasy. Already a letter had been received, delivered by hand from Abbatt's solicitors, asking for an explanation of the police conduct. In the afternoon a further letter came in saying that a doctor had had to be called to Mrs Abbatt, upset as a result of the "false accusations". It demanded that the matter be settled forthwith, and spoke of "serious repercussions". For six days the police betrayed no reaction. On the 9th of November the constable on desk duty at Stourbridge Police Station signed, on request, an unusual chit which acknowledged that he had received a letter addressed to the Superintendent of Police and marked "Urgent. For immediate attention", and further acknowledged that the constable undertook to deliver it within three minutes of receipt to the senior officer present at the station. Such a peremptory missive had never been received before by the Stourbridge Police. It declared that Abbatt had been illegally arrested and detained, and the matter must be settled to his complete satisfaction or proceedings would be instituted. This time the reaction was immediate. Abbatt was informed through his solicitors that he was to be prosecuted for burglary and unlawful wounding, and he was to attend at the police station to be formally charged.

Abel Abbatt gladly agreed that he should be represented at the court hearing by Mr Mervyn Pugh. Before the client and his advocate met, Abbatt was cheered by the extreme vigour which the defence demonstrated even at the formal charging. Abbatt was met in the charge room at Stourbridge Police Station by his solicitor and a young woman with a notebook. He turned to Detective Constable Barr and found his attitude understandably different from the "We know it's not Abel" mood of their last meeting.

"Well, Mr Abbatt," said the detective, "do you know why you have been brought to the police?"

"Yes," said Abbatt.

"You have been arrested for that on the night of the 22nd of October 1960 you broke into the Mere Children's Home, Norton, Stourbridge, and I want you to listen very carefully to what I will tell you. Listen very carefully, Mr Abbatt. Now you are charged that on the night of the 22nd of October 1960 at Stourbridge in the county of Worcester you did break and enter the dwelling-house of Daphne Daniels[1] at The Mere Children's Home at Norton with intent to commit a felony therein, namely to cause grievous bodily harm to some person, and did cause grievous bodily harm to Eileen Ellison,[2] and that was contrary to Section 25, Sub-section (i), of the Larceny Act 1916. Do you wish to say anything in answer to the charge?"

"Not Guilty," said Abbatt.

"You are not obliged to say anything," continued the detective inexorably, "unless you wish to do so, but whatever you say will be taken down in writing and may be given in evidence."

"Mr Barr," said Abbatt's solicitor, "are you going to take the matter before a magistrate?"

"Not today," hurriedly snapped Barr, who was caught in the middle of his charge. "There is a further charge," he told Abbatt. "Listen very carefully. That on the night of the 22nd of October, 1960, at Stourbridge in the county of Worcester you maliciously wounded Eileen Ellison, which is contrary to Section 20 of the Offences Against the Person Act of 1861. Do you wish to say anything in answer to the charge? You are not obliged to say anything unless you wish to do so . . ."

"Not Guilty," said Abbatt, as soon as he could get it in.

". . . but whatever you say will be taken down in writing and may be given in evidence." The detective looked up, conscious of his duty done.

"Mr Barr," said the solicitor, "there are two things I want to

[1, 2] A pseudonym.

ask you. First, could you tell me, please, what time on the 22nd of October it is alleged to have happened?"

"Between 11.45 P.M. and 12.15 A.M."

"That is 11.45 P.M. on the 22nd of October and 12.15 A.M. on the 23rd of October?"

"That is correct."

The detective sergeant who was also at the desk grew restive. "Actually, you know, I don't think that questions of that sort should be asked here," he said. "You will have the opportunity of asking them in court when your client is being tried, and at the moment we decline to answer that one."

"You decline to answer it," noted the solicitor, having already jotted down the answer.

"We are having no questions," said the sergeant. "We are not going to be the subject of cross-examination. Look, you have got a shorthand writer here."

And, indeed, the solicitor's young woman was writing down every word.

"You are entitled to have one here if you want to," said the solicitor. "Why are you criticizing me for having her here?"

"Let's get on with the job," said the sergeant.

The detective gave Abbatt and his solicitor copies of the charges.

The solicitor addressed the sergeant.

"I trust," he said, "that you will make yourself available to be in attendance on the 2nd of December at the Stourbridge Magistrates' Court."

"If I am required to do so, I will," said the sergeant.

"I have told you that you will be required," said the solicitor.

"I act on the instructions of the superintendent," said the sergeant, and tried to get back to the formalities. "He is bailed for the 2nd of December."

"You are Detective Sergeant?" asked the solicitor.

"I am at the moment."

"Based at Stourbridge?"

"That is correct."

"Temporary or permanent?"

"The detective sergeant is away, and I am doing it for three months," said the sergeant, and again indicated Abbatt. "£20, on his own surety."

The solicitor turned to the detective constable.

"How old is Eileen Ellison?"

"Twelve, sir," said the detective.

"Thank you," said the solicitor, and, after seeing that Abbatt signed his surety, he ushered his party out of the station.

Abel Abbatt emerged encouraged by the thought that it was possible to stand up to the police and wield a useful sabre. But a few days later he was surprised to find that the same sort of steel could be turned against himself.

On the weekend before the court hearing M. P. Pugh called a conference of the principals concerned in the defence at the sunny orchard bungalow which he and Dr Vera had built for their retirement. There, in an incongruous setting of flowered cretonne lit by yellow November sunshine, Abbatt endured a confrontation of remorseless, sapping pressures which he could hardly have expected.

He had arrived, in a mood of fair confidence, with his wife and her parents, whose agitation was far more patent than their son-in-law's. They were met by their solicitor, who introduced them to M. P. Pugh. Dr Vera brought in a tray of coffee and left the room. Abel Abbatt had a few minutes in which to try to study this effortlessly competent, grey, rather rock-like man to whom he was entrusting his reputation. Then the conference began with a review of the statements already made by Mrs Abbatt and Mr Catesby.

Mervyn Pugh then studied his copy of the short statement which Abbatt had made to the police in the Stourbridge station on the night of his arrest. Pugh began by going through the simple list of Abbatt's movements, item by item, checking each sentence and occasionally making a note in the margin with his red ball-point. Then, ranging beyond the typed statement, he checked carefully the actual words with which, according to Abbatt, the superintendent and the detective sergeant had encouraged him to confess, and made a note of them. "Were you actually threatened?" he asked. Abbatt replied, "No."

"Now, Mr Abbatt," said M. P. P. "You must realize that the solicitor for the prosecution will be a much cleverer man than you are. The whole object of his questions will be to obtain an admission from you. It is therefore essential that you answer with the utmost care any question that he puts to you.

"With the utmost care," Pugh repeated gravely. Abbatt tried to speak, cleared his throat, and nodded.

Suddenly, it seemed to Abbatt, 'his' defending solicitor had turned into an enemy. There seemed no warmth in those remarkably clear blue eyes. The man was gazing at him with unremitting sternness over the top rims of his half-glasses. "I want nothing but the truth," he was saying harshly. "I will not be associated in any way with any lies or any half-truths. You must realize that it is only on that basis that I will appear for you."

"I promise you I did not do it," said Abbatt. "What I tell you is the truth."

"Very well," said Pugh. "But you must understand that I have to ask you the sort of questions that the prosecution are likely to put to you. I have to satisfy myself as to the facts."

"I am ready," said Abbatt.

"Right, Mr Abbatt. Now on the night in question, the night of the 22nd of October, you went out to take the dog for a walk."

"Yes."

"At what time?"

"At eleven o'clock."

"How did you know it was eleven o'clock?"

"By the television. It was on, but I wasn't very interested. Candid Camera had finished, and I thought it was about time I took the dog for a walk."

"What programme was showing on the television?"

"I think it was some sort of play."

"You think it was?"

"Yes. Some sort of play. Something about an astrologer, I think."

"How long were you out with the dog?"

"For about ten minutes."

"Back just in time to see the News?"

"Oh, no, sir. The News wasn't on until 11.40. We had switched off and gone to bed by half-past eleven."

"How do you know?"

"Pardon, sir?"

"How do you know the News was not on until 11.40?"

There was a pause, first of surprise and then of embarrassment. Finally Abbatt said, in a tone of uncertain justification, "I've looked it up."

"You've looked it up?" Pugh repeated acidly.

"Yes."

"You've looked it up since?"

"Yes."

"In the printed programme in the *TV Times*?"

"Yes."

"So you must also have looked up the Candid Camera programme, and what you have described as 'some sort of play'."

"I checked on them, yes."

"You don't 'think' it was some sort of play. You know it was a play. A play called *The Dragon's Tail.*"

"Yes."

"You don't 'think' it was something about an astrologer. You know it was about an astrologer. Because there is a full description of the plot of the play on page 9 of the *TV Times* dated October the 14th, 1960."

"Yes."

"So it is really a deception, this suggestion of vagueness about the television programme."

"I was putting myself in the mood I was in at the time, sir."

"What mood were you in on the night of Saturday the 22nd of October?"

"No particular mood, sir."

"No particular mood of vagueness?"

"Only about the last television programme."

"You aren't vague about where you went on that Saturday night?"

"No, sir."

"Not vague about going to the Mere?"

"I didn't go to the Mere. I was nowhere near it."

"You know what goes on at the Mere?"

"What do you mean, what goes on?"

"You know what the place is at the Mere?"

"It's a children's home. It always has been."

"You know your way around it?"

"I've been in the grounds, yes."

"You know which are the boys' bedrooms and which are the girls' bedrooms?"

"No. Why should I?"

"You haven't marked down, when you've 'been in the grounds', you haven't made a note of which are the girls' bedrooms?"

Mrs Abbatt suddenly realized the implications of the line of questioning. She sat tense and gaping as if she had been struck in the face. Mr Catesby stiffened, staring and fearful.

Abel Abbatt made a throaty sound, and then cleared his throat and yelled "No!" savagely. Pugh had not waited for the denial, and his next question was already half uttered.

"You are not interested in the girls' bedrooms?"

"No."

"You haven't been hanging around, when it was time for the girls to go to bed, on the chance that you might have a glimpse of them undressing?"

"No."

"You're not interested in watching girls undress?"

"No."

"You haven't followed this up, on those convenient midnight walks with the dog, by slipping into the Mere grounds, making an entry into the house, and prowling round the bedrooms of the girls?"

"No."

"Nor finally responded to some dark passion by physically beating one of the sleeping girls as she lay in her bed?"

"No."

"Then why were you positively identified by the foster-mother at the home as the man she had seen, challenged, and even talked to, in a bedroom at the Mere children's home, at midnight on Saturday the 22nd of October, while a girl screamed after being beaten up in her bed, and her blood flowed over the sheets?"

The battering had had its effect. Abel Abbatt was reacting now with fading truculence, as if stabbed in the back by the piercing injustice of disbelief in his story. He said slowly, with bitter conviction:

"It is a false identification. I had nothing to do with it. I was nowhere near the Mere that night."

Mervyn Pugh snatched off his half-moon glasses and swept them wide to his left in an actor's gesture of finality. With the speedy walk which was often so unexpected from his large frame, he strode over to Abbatt with his right hand out. He took Abbatt's hand and shook it warmly.

"You will be all right, lad," he said.

The conference was over.

The trial opened on the morning of Friday the 2nd of December, 1960, in the large, light, well-timbered Magistrates' Court at Stourbridge dominated by a huge painted coat of arms, emblazoned DIEU ET MON DROIT and HONI SOIT QUI MAL Y PENSE, behind the Bench.

Abel Abbatt had stood amid his family looking curiously for the woman who had identified him, and who was his only accuser. Then he was placed in the dock. Pugh had also had his eye on the prosecution witnesses. "Is Eileen Ellison here?" he asked, seeking the girl whom Abbatt was alleged to have assaulted. "No," he was told. "I want her," ordered Pugh. This was the culmination of a strong exchange of letters between the solicitors for the prosecution and the defence before the case was heard. The prosecution had said that the girl would not be called to give evidence, or, indeed, be present at the court hearing; she could give no account of what occurred on the night of October 22nd. She was upset, and the prosecution did not wish to add to her disturbance by bringing her to court. The defence insisted that it was the duty of the prosecution to tender her as a witness since the maximum penalty for the offence which Abbatt was alleged to have committed was imprisonment for life. The prosecution replied that the girl's only physical injury had been a cut mouth, but that the psychological injury could not be assessed. The girl was not, in fact, brought to court. But, when Pugh insisted, a policewoman was sent to fetch the twelve-year-old victim of the attack that had started the whole affair.

The trial began without her. M. P. Pugh rattled characteristically into action as soon as the charges were read. They were of breaking and entry with intent to cause a felony, namely grievous bodily harm, of causing grievous bodily harm, and alternatively of malicious wounding.

"I object to the wording of the charge," he said. "Anyone coming before the court is entitled to know what he is charged with. As it stands the indictment contains the elements of three separate charges. This case, if sent to the Assizes, may eventually be probed by the highest court in the land. I take a most serious view of it. This charge alleging the felony is a fictitious one brought to cover up an illegal arrest."

He was disclosing his fire-power from the start. The defence were contending that the original mistake of Abbatt's peremptory arrest before he could be given an opportunity, either at the bus-stop or the police station, to explain his movements, should immediately have been acknowledged. Instead, the original charge of break-in and assault had been inflated to include the intention and actual committal of a felony on the ground, Pugh contended, that if this charge could be substantiated the summary arrest was justified.

It was always in Pugh's mind—and counsel who gave an opinion on this case at a much later date specifically suggested—that the police had been stung into their decision to prosecute by the early threat of civil proceedings, and that but for this threat the whole matter would have been dropped. If Abbatt were convicted it might well be that he had been brought in peril only through the aggressive pressure—such as the time-bomb letter with the three-minute fuse demanding immediate satisfaction or else promising retaliatory proceedings—of the defendant's solicitors. For this pressure M. P. Pugh was in large part responsible, for he had been consulted from the start, and had advised the tone of the resistance; and possibly he would have taken a milder line if he had not already been exasperated by police incompetence at Stourbridge. But if Pugh, in puritan zeal, was using the case as an opportunity to forcibly feed a bitter draught that would purge local prosecuting procedure, he was still advancing on the police behind the body of an accused man who would be scarred by ill-repute and seared by prison if Pugh failed. The responsibility was therefore heavy.

After consulting the Clerk, Mr G. M. King, and his colleagues the Presiding Magistrate parried Pugh's first thrust. "We accept the charge as it stands," he announced. Witnesses were ordered out of court. Pugh smoothly put his next point. "Since a vital part of this case rests on evidence of identification," he said, "and since no doubt witnesses for the prosecution will be called on to identify my client, may I ask that he be allowed to leave the dock and sit among others on the public benches where he will be less conspicuous?" This request was considered and granted. Abel Abbatt stepped down and went to the back of the court. He chose to sit next to his brother, who was among his family supporting him, and the action seemed to ensure that any matter of identification would be a fair test.

For Pugh the camouflage was an ironic reversal of events. The last time he had done this was to protect the police. He was defending a police officer accused of assault within a police station. He had made the officer sit on a bench in court with a dozen other policemen in uniform alongside him, and when it came to the challenge the officer was never identified.

Mr J. M. C. Higgs, the solicitor prosecuting for the police, began to outline the case. But he had not gone far when the alert Pugh, his eyes ranging round the courtroom, rose to make another objection.

"One of the police officers in this case, Detective Constable Barr," he said, "is watching proceedings through the glass windows of the doors of the courtroom. Since he has access to witnesses not yet called, the purpose of seating my client in the public seats may be defeated."

An officer was immediately sent to clear the approach to the courtroom.

The prosecuting solicitor continued with his opening statement. He said that the Mere was a home for children in the care of the County Council. On the night in question four girls were asleep in the reception centre at the home. Some time after 11 P.M. two of them were woken up by another one shouting that a man was hitting her. They saw a man hitting her on the face. She was crying and there was blood on her pillow. Then the man ran from the room.

"The prosecution do not pretend that either of the girls is able to recognize the man. But he was seen clearly by Miss Daniels,[1] one of the staff, who had been disturbed by the noise."

On November the 1st, continued Mr Higgs, Miss Daniels saw this man again walking in the Broadway, Norton. She told the police, and the next day when she and Detective Constable Barr followed him on to a bus she was able to confirm the identification.

Mr Higgs spoke of the victim of the attack. "She can give no account at all of what happened that night. One of the worst things that can happen to a child is to be woken up by violence, and this must have been a very frightening experience. The girl was moved to another home, but she has been brought back to the Mere for the day so that she can be called if necessary."

The first witness was a girl aged twelve, one of the children who had been sleeping in the room where the attack took place. She described how she had been awoken by a scream. The room was in darkness, but the door was open and a dim light came in from the corridor. She saw a man standing between her bed and Eileen Ellison's bed, and he was hitting Eileen. Eileen shouted, "Someone is hitting me," and the man turned and ran out of the room. In the crying and confusion that followed nobody put the light

[1] A pseudonym.

on, but some time later their matron, Miss Daniels, came in and switched on the light. Then she saw that Eileen Ellison's mouth was bleeding.

Pugh rose to cross-examine. As always with a child witness, he was extremely gentle with the girl.

"This must have upset you a lot?" he asked, using her Christian name. "Yes," she said.—"What time do you think this happened?"—"It was about twelve o'clock."—"And was your room light or dark?"—"It was dark."—"So who do you think it was in the room?"—"It might have been anyone," said the girl.

"It might have been anyone. Could it have been a boy?"—"It might have been a boy."—"It might have been quite a little person?"—"It might have been a little person," said the girl, concentrating seriously, "but not a very little person."—"Could it have been a girl wearing trousers?"—The idea had clearly never occurred to the witness. "It might have been," she said. "All I know is that it was someone." But the careful probing continued. "Are there any men on the premises at the home?" asked Pugh. "Yes," she said, and named some of the staff. "Do you know how many boys there are at the home?"—"No."—"Could it have been one of those?"—"It might have been one of those, for all I know."

Another little girl who had slept in the room was called. She had been woken up by the screaming, but although she saw the man she did not see his face, and although he said something she could not tell what he said. When the light was put on she could not see a cut on Eileen's face, and she thought that what blood there was on Eileen's pillow came from a cold sore she had on her lip. In answer to Pugh's questions she said, "It might have been one of the boys from the school. I thought it was one of the boys from the school. I told Miss Daniels that it might have been one of the boys from the school."

The prosecution then called Miss Daphne Daniels, the foster-mother who was in charge of the reception centre at the Mere Children's Home. Abel Abbatt recognized her as the woman who had followed him on to the bus a month ago. The defence heard for the first time the details of what was alleged to have occurred at the Mere on the night of the 22nd of October. The witness told of being disturbed in her bedroom at 11.45 P.M. by a loud scream. When she came out of her room she did not go immediately to the girls' room next door—from which she later found the scream had come—but to a room the door of which she saw was open. In this room four boys about seven years old were sleeping.

"There were no lights on in that room," said Miss Daniels, "and I did not put the light on when I went in. I saw a man there, at the French window, trying to open it. He turned round and asked what was the matter, twice. I did not say anything. I was standing in the doorway, and he pushed past me. I asked him who he was and what he was doing in the house. He said he was going home, and walked along the corridor. I said, 'Come back here. What are you doing and who are you?' He turned round and said, 'I'm going home. How do I get out of here?' He went to the end of the corridor and turned right into the hall. I said, 'Get out!' and he tried to unbolt the door leading to the outside. That bolt is stiff. He couldn't unbolt the door, and he said to me, 'You come and do this. I can't do it.' I was within four or five feet or a little more of the man when he said this. There was a light on, I think a hundred watt. I just said 'No!' and ran to the flat where one of my assistants was sleeping. I then came back to the hall and found that the door leading outside was open and the man was gone.

"The first thing I did was to find where the man had got in. I found that the window in the corridor opposite the bedroom where the boys were sleeping was open. I sent three elder boys to get Mr Frazer,[1] the superintendent, from his house. I then went with my assistant to the girls' room next to my bedroom. I saw that Eileen Ellison was crying rather hysterically, and that her top and bottom lips were quite badly cut. The police were informed, and Mr Frazer came."

Miss Daniels then went on to describe her identification of Abel Abbatt.

"On Tuesday the 1st of November, 1960, I was with a Mrs Gatsby[2] at the top of the Broadway in the evening. She was walking part of the way home with me. This was at about 9.25 P.M. In the street I saw a man going down the Broadway. He was in front of me when I noticed him, and I overtook him. As I did so I could see him, but not very clearly. When I saw him it struck me that it was the man who was in the reception home."

[1, 2] A pseudonym.

Mr Higgs, having smoothly traced the story so far, asked, "Can you see that man in this room?"

"Yes," said Miss Daniels.

"Will you leave the witness-box and touch that man on the shoulder?"

After a little hesitation about her steps, the witness, a woman of thirty-seven, walked across the court to where a group of men were sitting together. She put her hand on the right shoulder of one of them. It was Abel Abbatt.

She came back to the witness-box and continued her evidence. "We carried on down and turned round and saw that he was waiting at the bus-stop. On the Wednesday I spoke to Detective Constable Barr, and on that evening, the 2nd of November, I was with him in a motor van in the Broadway near to that bus-stop at about 9.20 P.M. I saw the same man coming down the Broadway the same way as he had come the night before. This man went to the bus-stop and waited there. There was a street light on a short distance away from the bus-stop. Detective Constable Barr got out of the van and went over to the bus-stop. We waited there until the bus came. We hung back, and the man got on the bus and went upstairs. Detective Constable Barr and I followed, and we sat three seats in front on the same side. I looked at his face as I went past him to my seat. This man is the accused, whom I had seen in the Mere on that night in October. After I had sat down I turned round once to look at him. I got off the bus at the school at the bottom of the Broadway. Detective Constable Barr went down the stairs in front of me, and as I got off I had another look at him."

Mr Higgs indicated to Mr Pugh that the witness was his.

"This must have been a very harrowing and worrying time for you," began M. P. Pugh. Miss Daniels agreed.

"Mistakes can be made."

"I know that."

"You do not know the accused?"

"No."

"So it is possible that you can make a mistake?"

"It is possible I could make a mistake, but I have not in this case."

"What did you say to Mrs Gatsby when you first saw the accused?"

"I said that I thought that was the man."

"And the next night, what did you say to Detective Barr when you saw the accused?"

"As the man stepped on the bus I told Detective Barr that this was the man."

"You were certain?"

"I was certain that this was the man when I stepped on the bus."

"If the accused was in bed on the 22nd of October at his home, it would be impossible for him to be at the Mere at midnight?"

"Yes."

"But did you not hear that the police were satisfied that Mr Abbatt was not the man, and that he must have a double? Did you not hear that when you saw the police on the 3rd of November?"

"No."

"The police told you that they were impressed with Mr Abbatt's explanation?"

"No."

"You have not made a mistake about that?"

The 'mistake' theme was being made to recur like the tolling of a litany. Pugh switched to another sequence. "When did you speak to Eileen Ellison about the events of this night?" he asked.

"I spoke to her on the night of the incident and the morning after."

"Tell the court about the first occasion."

"Eileen Ellison spoke to me when I went into the room. I asked what the matter was, and Eileen said she had woken up with this man hitting her. She did not say much more that night because she was crying."

"And the next morning?"

"The next morning she said she . . ." The witness hesitated, and Pugh intuitively pressed her.

"Yes."

"She said she thought it was Harry Hart."[1]

There was an immediate objection by the prosecution that hearsay evidence was being introduced. But a name had been mentioned. Pugh had not heard it before, but he would not let it go. "Who is Harry Hart?" he asked.

"He is one of our big boys."

[1] A pseudonym.

"And when Eileen Ellison said she thought it was Harry Hart, what did you say?"

"I said, 'It was not Harry Hart, because I had to wake him to go down to get Mr Frazer.'"

"Did you know that the prosecution were not going to call Eileen Ellison?" Pugh asked quickly.

"No."

"And did Eileen Ellison mention Harry Hart again?"

"She refused to talk with anyone after that."

"Not even to the police? Did the police interview her?"

"Yes. Detective Constable Barr and Police Constable Isaacs[1] interviewed her on the Sunday morning. She did not say anything."

"How do you know?"

"I was present, and she did not say a word to the police."

"But did you tell the police that she had said she thought it was Harry Hart?"

"Yes. She also thought afterwards that it might have been her father. I told this to the police."

"When did you tell the police?"

"On the Sunday."

Pugh referred to a file of correspondence on his desk. "So on the 25th of November the police knew about this?"

"Yes."

Pugh switched the subject again. "Was Eileen Ellison attended by a doctor on the night of the incident?"

"No."

"Who suggested that Eileen should be examined by a doctor?"

"It was the police."

"Why? Did you not think the injury warranted the attention of a doctor?"

"No."

"Grievous bodily harm," said Pugh to no-one in particular. "Did you see the man in the girls' room?"

"No."

"Had you ever seen the accused before?"

"No."

"So when did you first see the accused?"

"The first night I saw him I was with Mrs Gatsby."

"But you said then you only 'thought' that was the man."

[1] A pseudonym.

"I said then that I thought it was the man, but that I was not positive because of the bad light. I was there on the 2nd of November to get a better look."

"You told the police you were not positive?"

"I told the police I was not positive the night before and that I should like to have another look at him."

"Would the accused have recognized you the first time?"

"No."

"Would he have recognized you the second time?"

"He had the same opportunity to identify me as I had of him."

"What were you wearing on the night of the incident at the Mere?" Pugh suddenly asked.

"I had my pyjamas on."

"Were you wearing glasses?"

"No."

"You did not have your glasses on?"

"No."

"Miss Daniels, you are wearing glasses now. What sort of glasses are they? Do you need them for reading?"

"I cannot read without my glasses."

Pugh had been studying the witness's general air as she looked at him. "But we can take it that your sight is good when you are wearing your glasses," he suggested. "Miss Daniels, you see that coat of arms behind the Bench?" And he indicated the large painted Royal Arms on the wall with its motto HONI SOIT QUI MAL Y PENSE.

"Yes."

"What is the writing underneath the arms?"

Miss Daniels gazed at the wall. "I don't know," she said.

"You mean you can't read it?"

"I can't make it out."

"Even with your glasses on?"

"No."

"But normally you wear your glasses all the time?"

"Yes."

"But on that night when you saw the intruder you did not have your glasses on?"

"No."

"Miss Daniels, you haven't made a bad mistake?"

"No."

"You still think you could not possibly have made a mistake?"

"No."

There was only one further question to put to the witness: "Miss Daniels, before you gave your evidence, were you standing outside the glass door of the court with Detective Constable Barr?"

"Yes," said Miss Daniels.

M. P. Pugh sat down.

The next witness was the doctor who had examined Eileen Ellison on the Sunday noon after the incident. He had found that her lower lip was swollen and bruised and there was a small wound where the skin was broken both inside and outside the lip. This might have been caused by a blunt instrument like a fist. In cross-examination Pugh asked him three questions:

"Could any blunt instrument have caused this?"

"Yes."

"What treatment did you give for it?"

"There was no treatment to give. It was a trivial wound."

"Was there any need to send for you?"

"No."

By this time a message had been passed to the advocates on both sides, and Pugh now nodded to the prosecuting solicitor.

"Call Eileen Ellison."

The young girl was brought in and sworn. The prosecutor merely asked her her name and address and handed her over to Pugh.

"Eileen," he said, "you remember the night of the 22nd of October, 1960?"

"Yes, sir."

"And you remember what happened. Did you tell Miss Daniels you thought this person in your room was anyone in particular?"

"I told her I thought it was Harry Hart."

"Did you see Harry Hart that night?"

"Yes."

"When did you see him?"

"When I was having supper."

"But you said you thought it was Harry Hart in the room?"

"It was Janet who said it was Harry Hart."

"Janet?"

"Yes, Janet Jackson said this."

Janet Jackson[1] was the name of the first witness.

[1] A pseudonym.

"But do you *know* who hit you?"

"No. Janet saw the person who hit me, and she said it was Harry Hart."

"Did it hurt very much?" asked Pugh gently.

"No, not very much."

"You had a sore on your lip at the time?"

"Yes."

"Did the blood come from the sore on your lip?"

"It came from there and from inside my lip."

"But you thought it was Harry Hart and you told Miss Daniels this?"

"I thought it was until Miss Daniels said . . ."

"That's all right, Eileen. You don't have to tell us what Miss Daniels said. Miss Daniels said something, eh?"

"Yes, sir."

"And are you frightened to go against what Miss Daniels said?"

The girl made no answer.

"Eileen, are you frightened to go against what Miss Daniels said?

"Are you frightened, Eileen?"

But Eileen Ellison gave no more evidence.

"I want to recall Janet Jackson," said M. P. Pugh.

The first girl was brought back into the witness-box.

"Now, Janet, remember that you have taken the oath, and it is a promise to tell the truth that you still swear to keep," said Pugh. "Did you say that it was Harry Hart in the room?"

"Yes, sir."

"Did you see him?"

"I didn't see him. I just thought it was him."

"Did you tell Miss Daniels who you thought it was?"

"Yes."

"What did she say?"

"She said it couldn't have been one of the big boys because they were all asleep."

"So who do you think it was now?"

"I still think it was Harry Hart in my own heart."

"That is all," said Pugh.

The prosecution called Detective Constable Basil Barr.[1] He told of his investigations at the Home after the incident, of Miss Daniels's identification of Abbatt on the bus, and of the arrest.

[1] A pseudonym.

He described Abbatt's constant denials at the police station and the detectives' interview with Mrs Abbatt.

M. P. Pugh rose to cross-examine. After nearly four hours of question and answer it was now well into the afternoon, and, except for the doctor, this was the first man he had in the box opposite him. His manner had hardened perceptibly.

"Have you inquired into the character of the accused?" he asked.

"I have."

"And you found it good. He bears an excellent character. You will agree that the time of this offence is important?"

"Yes."

"Now you went to see Mrs Abbatt. And she had no idea why you and the other officer had visited her?"

"That is true."

"But she told you that she and her husband went to bed that night at 11.30?"

"Yes."

"She corroborated Abbatt's statement up to the hilt?"

"Yes."

"Did that impress you?"

"Yes, it did impress me."

"Now, as a police-officer you know about your powers of arrest."

"Yes, sir."

"But you arrested the accused at the bus-stop."

"I did."

"Really, this is one of the biggest public scandals I have come across. You agree that if there was no intent to commit a felony there was no power to arrest him?"

"I agree."

"Is that why this fictitious charge of burglary has been prepared, to cover your unlawful arrest of the accused?"

"No, sir."

"You made many inquiries into this matter before you arrested the accused?"

"Yes."

"Including inquiries at licensed premises?"

"Yes, sir."

"At how many?"

"At some eight to ten."

"Why did you make these inquiries?"

"I thought it was possible that the man had been drinking."

"Did you ask Miss Daniels if the man at the Mere smelt of drink?"

"I did ask her, but she said she was not sure."

"Have you heard of people trying to shield others?"

"Yes."

"Did you make inquiries among the males who were resident at the home that night?"

"There was no-one at the home of the description Miss Daniels had given."

"But supposing there was someone at the home whom she was trying to shield?"

"I have never had that idea at all."

"Was no name mentioned during your inquiries at the Home?"

"There was the name of a boy of sixteen or seventeen years of age mentioned. He did not fit the description we had been given."

"But if Miss Daniels had given you the wrong description that would not have been worth anything?"

"No, sir."

"Did you interview Eileen Ellison at the Home?"

"I did, but I could not get a thing out of her."

"She did not mention the name of Harry Hart?"

"Now I come to think of it, she did mention Harry Hart."

"You knew that the man in the bedroom had spoken words?"

"Yes."

"And possibly left fingerprints. Did you find any fingerprints?"

"We found no-one's fingerprints that night."

"Did you look later?"

"Detective Constable Knapp[1] came to take fingerprints. He is a specialist in fingerprints."

"But you found nothing?"

"We found some smudges."

"Now I come to the night of the arrest. You arrested the accused on the 2nd of November?"

"Yes, sir."

"When arrested, did he ask to get his solicitor?"

"Yes. But I did not take any steps to do so."

"Was that because you wanted to brainwash him?"

[1] A pseudonym.

"He was not brainwashed."

"Have you never heard of brainwashing being carried out in the police cells?"

"No, sir."

"How long have you been in the Police Force?"

"Eleven years."

"You have never heard of it during the whole time you have been in the Force?"

"No, sir."

"For over two hours you brainwashed him in order to try to wring a confession out of him, but you were not successful?"

"That is definitely not correct."

"You have no more evidence today than you had on the night of the 2nd of November?"

"No, sir."

"Why did you release him that night without charging him?"

"It is not up to me to charge him. He was released and told further inquiries would be made."

"But if he had made a statement admitting the offence he would have been detained?"

"Yes."

"Why was he not detained?"

"It appears that those in authority were not satisfied that he was guilty of the offence."

"You took him home, and you went in and had a cup of tea?"

"Yes."

"It was then that his wife first heard about this offence?"

"Yes."

"Did you say, 'It wasn't Abel. He must have a double'?"

"I called him Mr Abbatt."

"Did you say 'It wasn't him. He must have a double'?"

"I think I said, '*If* it wasn't him, he must have a double.' "

"You are in very grave peril over this matter, aren't you, officer? Has it struck you that unless you could prove intent to commit a felony it was an unlawful arrest, for which you might be taken before a civil court for damages?"

"Yes, sir."

"Is that why this fictitious charge of burglary has been brought —to cover your mistake?"

"No, sir."

"You called at his house again on the 3rd of November?"

"No. I went to his father-in-law's house."

"Why did you go there?"

"I went there because his father-in-law rang the police station and appeared to be acting as his legal adviser. I went with Sergeant Lanigan."[1]

"And you told his father-in-law that you were satisfied that the accused was not responsible?"

"No, sir. Sergeant Lanigan told Mr Catesby that we were not entirely satisfied that it wasn't his son-in-law."

"But the accused was rather convincing?"

"Yes."

"And Eileen Ellison had told you she thought it was Harry Hart?"

"No, sir. Eileen Ellison did not tell me she thought it was Harry Hart. One of the girls told me she thought it was Harry Hart. I do not know which one."

Pugh confirmed this correction of evidence. Then he asked: "How long did you detain the accused?"

"He was detained for about two hours."

"And he denied it right through?"

"Yes, sir."

"Where was the accused when you first spoke to his wife?"

"He was kept in the police station while I went and checked with his wife."

"This man asked for a solicitor, but you ignored that, didn't you?"

"He asked on his way to the police station. If he had asked again in the station I should have consulted my superiors, and their answer would probably have been Yes."

Pugh's sharp voice became more strident. "I'll tell you why you never called a solicitor in. You kept him there for hours trying to wring a confession out of him. Didn't the sergeant say to Abbatt, 'What made you do it?' "

"No."

"Didn't the Superintendent of Police come on the scene during the questioning? There is this article in this morning's paper"—Pugh displayed a copy of the *Daily Mail* with an article headed "Under the blue lamps of Britain's police stations BRAINWASHING"—"You detained this man for over two hours and some very funny things went on. In fact, for over two hours you and

[1] A pseudonym.

other police officers brainwashed him. It follows the old pattern set out in this report here. First you, then the sergeant, and then the superintendent himself had a go at this man. Wasn't he told by the superintendent, 'Either you admit doing it and get charged or you will be put in the cells until morning'?"

Barr said, "The superintendent did arrive during the interview, but no such threat was made."

Pugh glanced at his notes. "Not perhaps while you were in the room," he said. "Did you leave the room?"

"Yes, sir."

"Why did you leave the room?"

"I telephoned Miss Daniels at the Mere."

"Why did you telephone her? What did you say?"

"I said, 'Are you quite sure that this is the man?' She said, 'Yes, definitely.'"

"Why did you make this call to Miss Daniels? Because you believed she was wrong?"

"The accused was fairly convincing, and I was not sure."

"You had a doubt in your mind?"

"I had a doubt in my mind when I telephoned Miss Daniels."

"Are you in doubt now as to whether the intruder is the accused?"

"I wouldn't like to say one way or the other if I am in doubt or not about whether it is him."

There was a brief re-examination and a final question from Pugh, but he considered that his main impact had been made. The police superintendent was called, but not questioned by the prosecution. In cross-examination he agreed that mistakes were often made, but denied that this had been an illegal arrest which the police were trying to cover up by a fictitious charge. To Pugh's suggestion that he had told the accused that if he did not admit the offence he would be put in the cells he answered, "Nonsense. That is a complete fabrication."

The hour was late, and Pugh, having vainly asked the prosecution to withdraw the case, rose once more to submit with forceful brevity that there was no case to answer.

"A more fantastic prospect I have never heard," he declared, "than to ask Stourbridge Magistrates to commit a citizen of this borough to take his trial on such slender evidence." He mentioned the identification by one person alone, who was not wearing her glasses when she saw the intruder. He called attention to the absence of any proof of burglary. He ridiculed the charge of causing grievous bodily harm in the light of the doctor's evidence. "You would not send a cat on this lot!" he exclaimed.

"It may well be," he continued, "that they are trying to shield somebody else. I do not know. Maybe Miss Daniels is suffering from delusions. She made a most dreadful mistake, and I think you know it.

"I am amazed that the prosecution has not withdrawn the case. There has been a suppression of evidence that only came to light when I fought for it and dragged it out. Until I got the girls into the box no-one had mentioned that suspicion had fallen on a boy at the home. No jury in the land," he concluded, "would be likely to convict on that evidence."

The magistrates conferred and mainly rejected Pugh's submission; but they struck out the charge of causing grievous bodily harm. Pugh confirmed that his client had elected to make his defence before the magistrates rather than reserve it for the Assizes, and the case was adjourned for eight days. "At the next hearing," Pugh reminded the court and the Press, "Mr Abbatt will give evidence that he was in bed at the time of the incident. His wife has corroborated his story to the police, though she did not then know that there was a complaint against her husband."

It was the best he could do for his client's reputation. Defendants are always at a disadvantage in the interval of an adjourned case when only the prosecution has been heard. But Pugh had fought tenaciously and slightly redressed the balance of publicity. As for his own standing, his allegations of brainwashing had made a national headline, and the ring of professional gossip was already rippling outward: "Pugh has turned on the Police."

The second hearing took place on Saturday the 10th of December. At the beginning Pugh made the surprise announcement that he would be calling as witnesses for the defence both the detective constable and the police superintendent who had been concerned in the arrest and interrogation of Abel Abbatt. Mr Michael Higgs, the prosecuting solicitor, observed that he could not recall a case in which anyone who had given evidence for the prosecution was called as a witness for the defence. "I have known it happen many, many times," said Pugh airily, and the Chairman of the Magistrates, allowing the request, directed the two police officers to leave the court with the other defence witnesses.

Pugh immediately called Abel Abbatt. At the outset the young man declared, "There is no truth in these charges whatsoever. I am ready to face up to any questions anyone may ask me. That is why I am tendering myself as a witness at this hearing."

For well over an hour Abbatt detailed the succession of events on October the 22nd, then on the night of his arrest and on the following day. Under cross-examination he conceded that he did not tell the police who his solicitor was. He affirmed that the superintendent had truly threatened him with confinement if he did not confess. He said that although there was a truncheon on the table at the time there was no mention of using it, and no violence was used throughout. On re-examination he confirmed that a voice identification parade, though suggested, had never been held.

Mrs Abbatt was then called, and recounted the succession of domestic events on the night of October the 22nd, then told of her questioning by the police on the night of the arrest. Under cross-examination she agreed that if she had been told why the police had called, her account of the night of the crime would have lost its value. Her father followed her into the box. He reiterated that the police officers who had visited him had said, "We know it is not Abel."

Pugh then called the two police officers most concerned with the case, and the lawyers in the court at least could see that, whatever valid addition to the present case their evidence would give, it would be eminently quotable in any future action. In very brief examinations the detective constable confirmed that it was he who had arrested the accused, and that he had taken him by the arm, but "I do not think I held it all the way to the police station". The superintendent said, in answer to questions, "From the time I came in I took command of inquiries. I take responsibility from the time that I first saw the accused."

No more witnesses for the defence were called. Pugh began his closing speech, and virtually the closing speech of his career. He declared that the case must be thrown out because his client was innocent, and because the case was bad in law: it had been framed as a felony instead of a misdemeanour in order to cover the fact that Abbatt had been arrested instead of merely summonsed. The break-in charge was fictitious—not the slightest proof of burglary had been attempted; and there was no evidence connecting Abbatt with unlawful wounding.

"Over a great number of years," he said, "I have had most happy relations with police officers. I am second to none in my admiration for the Police as a whole, for I appreciate the responsibility they carry and the difficulty of their job. But it has been my most unpleasant duty in this case to put forward certain criticisms, not of the Force in general, but of part of it. And I have had to make these criticisms. By covering up something that is wrong, a great deal of harm can be done.

"You have a child," he continued; it was clear that he was speaking, and not with empty eloquence, of the corps whom he had nagged and groomed and championed throughout all his civilian career. "You love that child. But the child does wrong. You do not ignore the wrong, gloss over it, pretend that the fault has not occurred. You take pains to put it right. And you do these things, which are sometimes stern, because you love the child.

"Now I must call your attention," he told the Bench, "to some elements which have upset me and caused some concern. The first is the attempt to suppress the evidence of the girl." Pugh then read the correspondence on the subject which had passed between the solicitors for the defence and the prosecution. He laid emphasis on a letter of the 25th of November—the date he had carefully verified with Miss Daniels as the day on which the police knew that Eileen Ellison had said she thought her attacker was Harry Hart. This letter, from the prosecuting to the defending solicitors, said: "As to Eileen Ellison, as at present instructed, she has made no statement to anybody about this matter." The assumption was that the police had not told their legal advisers about Eileen Ellison's alleged remarks. Pugh warmly justified the insistence by the defending solicitors that the girl who was alleged to have been injured should be present at court.

"Thank God that girl came here, or an injustice might have been done to this man. An injustice is being done to him for every moment he is kept here. I stake my reputation that he will be acquitted, but every second he is kept in this dreadful peril is ruining his health and putting a dreadful strain on his little wife. The police have made a ghastly mistake.

"The original intention of the prosecution not to call the girl," Pugh averred, "was with the idea of trying to trap the accused. But it has boomeranged on the prosecution. They know that these charges should have been withdrawn, as I asked earlier on, and

I am amazed they have not done it. Mr Higgs knows what he is doing, and I know what he is doing. And I know what I am doing," Pugh added darkly, and, in the ruthlessness of the moment, made an unfraternal onslaught on the prosecuting solicitor. "I feel that even Mr Higgs will have some relief that he is not to take a case of this nature to the Assizes. I am sure he would not sit very happy in court and hear the observations of the judge.

"As soon as mention was made that the girl thought one of the boys at the home had been in the girls' room, Mr Higgs got up and objected.

"Thank God that your Clerk, who I know is a distinguished lawyer, advised you to admit that evidence. It was the turning-point in this case. I am most grateful for that ruling of the Clerk."

Pugh turned to the evidence of identification. "I do not call Miss Daniels a liar," he conceded, "but just say she made a ghastly mistake. She saw an intruder without putting her glasses on. Then, putting her glasses on, she helped the police to look for a man. She saw Mr Abbatt at a bus-stop and identified him as the intruder, and he was arrested. He protested that on the night of the crime he had only left his house for ten minutes. But Miss Daniels stuck stubbornly to her story. Only later is it revealed in evidence that a boy at the home was suspected of being in the girls' room.

"Three girls think that it was a boy in the room. The prosecution did not want the girl to come to court because she was going to say this boy had done it. But that information was to be kept from you.

"When one of the girls said that a boy might have been in the room and caused the injury, did Mr Higgs ask who was that boy? That is where suppression of evidence comes in. Another girl has said, 'I still think in my heart it was Harry Hart.'"

Now Pugh moved to the moment of arrest. "The reason the police did not issue a summons was because they wanted to get Abbatt to the police station and get him to make a statement admitting the offence. But he refused. When the police received a solicitor's letter they realized there might be an action brought against them, and so they started proceedings against Abbatt to cover themselves.

"The police never took fingerprints or looked for footprints in trying to trace the intruder. They relied entirely on an unhappy woman who was woken up in the middle of the night and, without her spectacles on, saw someone. It is all very fine for Mr Higgs to say you must support Miss Daniels. Mr Higgs may be an important man in the county"—the prosecutor was Chairman of the Worcestershire County Council, a former M.P. for Broomsgrove, and an acquaintance of Pugh's—"but," M. P. Pugh told the magistrates, "you must not be influenced by that. You are here to do justice.

"There is no evidence against Mr Abbatt in this case at all. The charge of burglary was put in, and when one puts in something like that it is often not very good. It is a fictitious charge. The original charge was wrong, and then they fiddled it. When you try deceit, and try to pull the wool over somebody's eyes, it will come out in the long run. This charge should have been for a misdemeanour and not a felony. But in any case it is entirely unsubstantiated. There is not a shred of evidence, and the charge is bad in law."

Mr Michael Higgs rose to make a brief summing up for the prosecution. In a delicate animadversion on Pugh's "robust style of advocacy" he refuted any suggestion that he had suppressed evidence—and, indeed, there had been every indication throughout the trial that the name of Harry Hart had been previously unknown to the advocate. "I do not like to sit here," said Mr Higgs, "listening to him saying things like that, particularly from one whose reputation is such that I expect to get courtesy in court."

Pugh jumped up. "If I have said anything that is unfair to Mr Higgs, I am very sorry," he declared. "I do not attach any unworthy motives to Mr Higgs. If I did not make it clear, I apologize."

The magistrates retired. Within ten minutes they returned and announced that the case was dismissed. Abel Abbatt was discharged.

For the last time Pugh rose to his feet. "I do not make an application for costs," he said. "You will appreciate from my observations that that can be dealt with elsewhere."

A solicitor was at the elbow of the Superintendent of Police. "Mr Superintendent," he said, "it is my duty to serve you with this. This is a copy of a writ which has been issued against you. I have the original in my hand if you care to see it." The Superintendent took the writ, which had been prepared two days earlier, claiming damages for wrongful arrest, assault, and false imprisonment. The solicitor crossed to the detective constable and served on him a similar writ.[1]

M. P. Pugh moved slowly from the courtroom. He could not be elated at the outcome of his pleading. The events of the day had drained him emotionally and physically. Physically, he had in addition become suddenly and alarmedly aware, his lion heart was faltering.

It was a time when he needed all his courage. For in the circles which he had long regarded as his professional sanctum, in the Senior Officers' Mess at the Victoria Courts and through County Police Headquarters in the Midlands, there was a murmur swelling to open criticism, a harsh resentment of his action at Stourbridge. He sought out those who blamed him—the condemnation was not universal. He made no concessions in justifying his attitude, and he convinced some critics of the rightness of his stand. But he had not now the energy to trace all his disparagers. Above all, he had not the time.

[1] On the 17th of November, 1961, it was announced by 'Abbatt's' solicitor and confirmed by the solicitor for the police: "The action against the police superintendent and the detective constable is withdrawn. Payment of costs has been agreed and will be paid by the police to Mr ——. The amount represents the costs which Mr —— might have been awarded if application had been made before the Magistrates at Stourbridge and in consideration of this payment Mr —— is withdrawing his action. The case can now be regarded as closed."

Epilogue

ON the 17th of April, 1961, M. P. Pugh saw a heart specialist, who earnestly advised him to stop working. He ordered his affairs, continued with the preparation of cases he had agreed to take on the following two days, and returned the rest of his files to be allotted to other advocates. On the 19th of April he made his last court appearance, at Worcester City Magistrates' Court, and prepared somewhat impatiently to rest. On the 24th of April, at noon, in a last and characteristic gesture, he sent out for more newspapers, and when his wife returned he was dead. Death had been swift in his arrest, but Mervyn Pugh had fought to the last.

> And you, my father, there on the sad height,
> Curse, bless, me now with your fierce tears, I pray.
> Do not go gentle into that good night.
> Rage, rage against the dying of the light.

If anyone had been in serious doubt about his final place in the hearts of his policemen that uncertainty was dispelled at his passing. The Birmingham Police Force claimed the right to bear him through their own ranks to his burial; and their senior officers, with Chief Constables from Worcestershire and other Midlands forces, followed to form, for the last time, the procession of The Prosecutor.

ACKNOWLEDGMENTS

I am greatly indebted to the Director of Public Prosecutions for help most kindly extended during the making of this book, and to the Law Society for the generous approval expressed on its completion.

During the research for this biography I met and drew on the reminiscences of so many highly placed policemen and advocates that it was difficult not to add a personal 5 m.p.h. to the speed limit on the M1 down which I so frequently travelled. But, with my licence still clean, I sincerely thank:

Mrs Joyce Andrews, my jewel of a research assistant; Mr Fred Baguley, former Assistant Chief Constable of Birmingham; Mr Howard Baker; Mr W. L. Barrows; Mrs Jessie Baylis; Mr Eric Belk, Editor of the *Bromsgrove Messenger*; Mr Harold J. Black, Birmingham's veteran newspaperman; Mr George J. Blackborow, Assistant Chief Constable of Birmingham; Mr Norman Brown, Clerk to the Prosecuting Solicitor of Birmingham; former Chief Inspector E. S. Burgess; former Detective Inspector J. W. Champkin; Mr Arnold Churchill; Mr Edwin Clayton, I.S.O., formerly with the Department of Public Prosecutions; Mr F. N. Clements, Chairman of the Bromsgrove Magistrates; Mrs Pat Clowes; Mr Roger Cobham; Mr Dudley Cooper; Mr Eddie Daniel, one-time court reporter; General Sir Miles Dempsey, G.B.E., K.C.B., D.S.O., M.C., D.L.; the late Sir Edward Dodd, C.B.E., H.M. Chief Inspector of Constabulary; Mr Norman Duffell; Mr Roy M. Dunstan, Deputy Prosecuting Solicitor in Birmingham; Mr J. Percy Eames, O.B.E., former City Treasurer of Birmingham; former Detective Chief Inspector G. A. Edwards; Mr Harry Faber; Mr A. E. Field, former Clerk to the Prosecuting Solicitor of Birmingham; Sir Donald Finnemore; Mr C. R. Fox, former Chief Constable of the City of Oxford; Mr T. R. Gaylor, Assistant Chief Constable of West Mercia; Mr Gilbert Griffiths, Recorder of Dudley; Mr Arthur Hall-Wright; Mr Harry Hatchard, Clerk to the Walsall Magistrates; Mr J. Haughton, Chief Constable of Liverpool; Mr. Harry Hawkes, chief crime reporter of the *Birmingham Evening Mail*; Mr Dennis Heath; Mr Ray Hill of the *Daily Mirror*; Mr T. C. B. Hodgson, Chief Constable of Berkshire; Mr W. J. Horton; Mr Frank Howarth, Clerk to the Birmingham Magistrates; Mr W. Field Hunt; Sir William Johnson, C.M.G., C.B.E., formerly H.M. Chief Inspector of Constabulary; Mr Charles Ladds; former Detective Chief Inspector W. Lowe; former Constable Harry Lowe; Mr John McKay, C.B.E., M.A., H.M. Inspector of Constabulary; Dr S. Orgill Massey; Mr Kenneth Milliken Smith; Mr J. Frederic Milward, Birmingham Stipendiary Magistrate; Mrs Pauline Morrell; Mr Barry Pain, Assistant Chief Constable of Staffordshire and Stoke City; H. J. Parham, C.B.E., formerly with the Department of Public Prosecutions; Mr W. Pratt, former Assistant Clerk to the Birmingham Magistrates; Mr John Pugh; Mrs Kay Pugh; Mr Maurice Pugh; Dr Vera Pugh; Mr K. B. Purnell; former Detective Chief Inspectors Oliver Quinton and F. Renshaw; Mr W. J. Richards, Chief Constable of Manchester; Mr F. Richardson, former Assistant Chief Constable of Birmingham and Mrs Richardson (Miss Selwyn); Mr James Ross, Q.C.; former Constable George Skerratt; Lieutenant-Colonel C. L. Speers, The Duke of Edinburgh's Royal Regiment (Berkshire & Wiltshire); Mr Charles A. Smallwood, Assistant Prosecuting Solicitor in Birmingham; Mr Stanley Shortt; Mr B. J. Webster, Editor of the *Worcester Evening News*; Professor J. M. Webster, C.B.E., F.R.C.S. (E.), M.D., LL.D., M.A., B.Sc.; Mr Philip Williams; Mr F. L. Withers, Chief Librarian of the *Birmingham Evening Mail*; Colonel Sir Arthur Young, C.M.G., C.V.O., Commissioner of Police for the City of London.

The lines quoted at page 226 are from "Do not go gentle into that good night" (from *Collected Poems*, by Dylan Thomas), and are reproduced by permission of J. M. Dent and Sons, Ltd, and of the Trustees for the copyrights of the late Dylan Thomas.

INDEX

ABORTION COMMITTEE, 105
Ager, A. E., 53
Arbuthnot, Captain, Chief Constable, 81, 87–88
Asquith, Mr Justice, 117
Auchonvillers, 37

BAGULEY, F., Superintendent (Assistant Chief Constable), 110, 160
Baker, Howard, 43, 102
Baldwin, Lady, 105
Bancroft, George, 51
Barnett, W. J., Inspector (Chief Constable), 88, 94
Bath, Mrs Helena, 98
Baxter, executioner, 30
Beaumetz-le-Cambrai, 34
Beaumont Hamel, 36
Berkeley, Sir Comyns, 105
Béthune, 32
Birkett, Norman, K.C. (Mr Justice; Lord), 28–29, 66–69, 89, 105, 146
Birmingham: Acocks Green, 116; Aston Hippodrome, 56; Balsall Heath, 164; Barnt Green, 131; Beehive pub, 23, 24; Billesley, 166; Botanical Gardens, 170; Broad Street, 11, 52; Bromsgrove Street, 131, 135; Brookfields, 164; Calthorpe Park, 52; Children's Hospital, 59; Clissold Street, 18; Corporation Street, 13, 51, 131, 147, 179; Dudley Road Hospital, 168; Edgbaston, 58, 132, 149; Erdington, 116, 151; Grand Hotel, 56; Great Barr, 131; Great Charles Street, 148; Great Hampton Street, 21–22; Grey's Café, 130, 134; Hagley Road, 55–56, 58–60; Handsworth, 116, 153, 155, 169; Heath Green Road, 22–23; Himley Park, 11; Hockley, 27; Kenyon Street, 20–24, 43; Kingstanding, 117, 170; Kynochs, 149–150; Ladywood, 170; Lea Hall, 166; Lewis's store, 171; Livery Street, 21, 75; Lodge Road, 18, 19, 21; Long Acre, 167; Midland Hotel, 56, 59; Nechells, 164–165; New Street, 131; Newton Street, 13–14, 129; Oddfellows Club, 75; Plough & Harrow, 56; Pype Hayes, 107; Queen's Hospital, 116; Queen's Hotel, 56; Quinton, 152; Rosebery Street, 18; Shirley, 120, 131, 134; Smallheath, 115; Snow Hill, 13, 19; South Yardley, 165; Station Green, 131; Steelhouse Lane, 13, 14, 59, 123, 179; University, 59, 69, 112; Ward End, 107; Weoley Castle, 170; Western Road, 21; Willows Crescent, 64–67; Winson Green Jail, 27, 30, 150; Winson Green Mental Hospital, 18, 165; Winson Green Road, 18–19; Yardley, 166; York Road, 60
Blackborow, George, Assistant Chief Constable, 160
Bodkin, Sir Archibald, D. P. P., 38, 40
Bourke, J. F., 121, 132, 146–147
Bourlon Wood, 34–35
Bourne End, 77–78, 86
Bousfield, Mr, 28
Bowker, A. E., 29, 66–67
Bray, 78
Bromsgrove, Golden Cross, 180
Broomhead, Charles, 18–22, 24–25
Brown, Norman, 104, 148
Burgess, E. S., Sergeant (Chief Inspector), 107, 109
Burnett, James, Chief Detective Superintendent, 17, 20–23, 27, 41, 43, 48, 52, 60
Burney, Detective Inspector, 155
Bushell, Miss, 57
Butler, R. A., 145

CADBURY, DAME GERALDINE, 108
Cambrai, 35
Cannes, 60, 78
Canning & Co., 21
Cape Hill, 22
Champkin, Detective Constable (Inspector), 46
Cheltenham Training College, 31
Churchill, Arnold, 49
Clayton, Edwin, 38
Colchester, 83

Conway, Philip, 37–38
Cook, Superintendent, 60
Cookham, 78
Coventry, Sir Reginald, K.C., 28–29
Cowley, 81, 86–87
Crawford, Henry 159
Crease, Misses, 55, 57–58
Croom-Johnson, Mr Justice, 150, 151, 153
Crump, James, 53
Cullwick, H. E., 59, 61
Cullwick, Dr Vera—*see* Pugh, Dr Vera

Daniel, Eddie, 54
Daniels, Mr, 13
Darling, Mr Justice, 53–54
Davies, John, Chief Detective Inspector, 121
Davis, Jack, 22–23
Dempsey, General Sir Miles, 33, 35, 37
Devlin, Mr Justice, 165
Dodd, Sir Edward, Chief Constable (H.M. Chief Inspector of Constabulary), 159–160
Dodford, 159
Droitwich, Raven, 180, 181–182
Dunstan, Roy M., 160

Eames, J. Percy, 55–57
Earls Court, 82
East Midlands Forensic Science Laboratory, 111
Edwards, G. A., Detective Sergeant (Chief Inspector), 19–25, 27–28, 30
Elias, Tom, 55
Equancourt, 35

Faber, Harry, 69, 70, 156–157, 174, 179
Field, A. E., 12, 14, 50, 104, 148
Finnemore, Donald (Mr Justice), 67, 103
Fitzmaurice, Kay—*see* Pugh, Mrs John
Flint, A. J., 89
Fockbury, 143, 149, 158–159, 180,
Foreman, Inspector, 155
Foster, John, 89
Fox, C. R., Chief Constable, 81, 86, 88–89, 93–94

Givenchy, 34
Glover, Captain Guy, 153–157
Goodchild, Superintendent (Chief Constable), 88
Gough, Corporal, 154
Gouy, 33
Gray, editor, 53–54
Green, Captain W. J., 33
Gregg, J. Frank, 160
Grevillers, 33
Guedecourt, 36–37
Gwinnell, 65

Haas, Dr Hans, 165
Hall, Sir Edward Marshall, 42, 68
Hall-Wright, Arthur, 42
Harrison, Superintendent, 60
Hawke, Mr Justice, 73
Hawkins, Chief Inspector, 20
Hay-on-Wye, 31
Healy, Maurice, K.C., 67
Henley, 77, 81, 86
Hereford, 31
Hewart, Lord, 64
Hewins, Detective Constable (Inspector), 21–22, 27, 101–102
Higgs, J. M. C., 206, 209, 220, 224
Highcliffe, Hants., 59
Hilbery, Mr Justice, 63
Hill, Ray, 73
Hobbs, Alfred, 81, 85, 90, 92
Holden, Dr, 111
Hooton, Ernest, 148, 160
Housmans, 143, 149, 158–159
Howarth, Frank, 161, 173, 174
Hudson, Superintendent, 77, 81
Humphreys, Travers (Mr Justice), 40, 64, 67, 115
Hunt, Lieutenant-Colonel G.P.S., 36
Hunt, W. Field, 146
Huntercombe, 78, 81

Ilkeston, Lord, 13–15, 26, 49, 73, 114, 122, 124, 126, 130, 154, 156–157, 163
Industrial Police & Security Association, 173
Ipswich, 79

Jenkins, R. O., 181
Johnson, W. C. (later Sir William), Deputy Chief Constable (Assistant Chief Constable; Chief Constable; H.M. Chief Inspector of Constabulary), 104

Kenyon, Don, 158
King, G. M., 205

Ladds, Charles, 71, 179
Lowe, Harry, Constable, 158
Lynskey, Mr Justice, 166

McKay, John, Assistant Chief Constable (Chief Constable; H.M. Inspector of Constabulary), 161
Macnaghten, Mr Justice, 111

Manancourt, 35, 37
Marks, Rev. Frank, 159
Marlborough Street Court, 37, 182
Marshall, A. P. (Mr Justice), 103
Marston, Sidney, 64–67
Massey, Sergeant, 104, 148
Mavity, Corporal John, 153–157
Mere Children's Home, 189–219
Milliken Smith, Kenneth, 55–58
Milward, J. F., 163, 169, 175–176
Moriarty, C. C. H., Chief Constable, 107
Muscroft, Detective Constable, 46

NEUWIED, Moravian School, 32
Norton, the Broadway, 189, 206–209
Nuffield, Lord, 76–100

OLIVER, MR JUSTICE, 116
Oppy Wood, 33
Oxford, Clarendon Hotel, 86–87

PARDHY, K. M., surgeon, 120–147
Paull, Gilbert, K.C. (Mr Justice), 132–133, 135, 137, 140, 142, 146
Pearce, Harold, 38
Pearce, Seward, 38
Penrice, Superintendent, 20, 24
Phippen, George, 31
Pin Mill, 79, 80, 83, 90, 92
Pinkerton, Superintendent, 60
Plummer, Leslie, 53
Potter, Bernard J., 160
Potts, Lieutenant, 155
Power, James Joseph, 22–30
Pugh, Douglas, 31
Pugh, Edward Mervyn, 184
Pugh, Elizabeth, 31
Pugh, Gwynne, 31–32
Pugh, Henry Thomas, 31–32, 59, 61
Pugh, John Mervyn Cullwick, 60, 158, 179, 181
Pugh, Jonathan Mervyn, 184
Pugh, Kay (Mrs John Pugh), 175, 184
Pugh, Maurice, 17, 31–32, 178
Pugh, Mervyn Phippen, *passim*
Pugh, Owen, 31–32
Pugh, Sally, 184
Pugh, Dr Vera (Mrs Mervyn Pugh), 58–60, 62, 158–159, 180, 200
Purchase, W. Bentley, 105

RAMSDEN, MAJOR A. G. F., 77–100
Ratcliffe, F. J., 32
Reading, Berks: Kendrick School, 31; law practice, 32, 37; Nuffield kidnap, 78; province, 15; Reading Collegiate School, 31; Town Council, 32
Richards, W. J., Detective Constable (Inspector; Chief Constable), 45–46, 162
Richardson, F., Detective Constable (Inspector; Assistant Chief Constable), 23, 160
Roberts, G. D. ("Khaki"), K.C., 121, 125–127, 129, 130, 132, 134–135, 137–139, 142
Robinson, Captain N. S., R.A.M.C., 155, 157
Rocquigny, 37
Rooke, James, 19
Ross, James, Q.C., 160
Royal Berkshire Regiment, 32–37

SANDERS, GUY, Detective Chief Superintendent, 173
Schwarz, Rudolf, 170
Scotland Yard, 81–82
Sellars, John, 158, 180
Selwyn, Miss (Mrs Fred Richardson), 14, 62, 101, 104, 109, 148
Sharp, W. H. Cartwright, K.C., 89, 90, 94, 96–99, 111
Shurmer, Percy, 51–52
Singleton, Mr Justice, 103
Smallwood, Charles A., 160
Smethwick, 19, 21
Smith, Miss, 109
Spilsbury, Sir Bernard, 40, 67
Stone, Reginald, 180
Stourbridge, 185–186, 188, 190, 196–199, 203, 205, 219, 225
Strachey, John, 53
Swift, Mr Justice Rigby, 28, 30

TAYLOR, SIR FRANCIS, K.C., 51
Thame, Spread Eagle Hotel, 84, 86, 96
Thay, Emily, 64–68
Thompson, Harry, 64–67
Thorneycroft, Peter, 73
Thornton, John Bruce, 76–100
Tréport, Le, 80
Tucker, Lord, 145
Turner, Second Lieutenant A. B., 33
Turner, Olive, 18–19, 23, 25–26, 29
Turner's Court, 79

WALKER, W. H. S., 26
Ward, Arthur, 89–91, 93, 99
Warwick, 13, 47
Webster, Professor J. M., 103–115, 117–121, 123, 128–129, 133, 137–139, 142–143, 146, 153, 164–165, 166, 180
Welch, Lance-Corporal J., 34
West Midlands Forensic Science Laboratory, 103–104, 108–109

Whitehouse, Superintendent, 67
Williams, Philip, 41
Williams, P. W., 25, 27–28
Willison, Herbert, 13–17, 24, 41, 45–47, 51–52, 66, 69, 73, 75, 111, 124, 179
Windle, F. W., 165
Winning, Norman, 132, 146
Witcomb, A. D., 164–165
Wolverhampton, Royal Hospital, 59
Worcestershire C.C.C., 11, 180
Wrottesley, Mr Justice, 91, 99, 134, 144

YELLOW, MARJORIE, 64–68
Young, Donald, 173